# English Hours

*Westminster Abbey*

HENRY JAMES

# English Hours

*Edited with an Introduction by*
ALMA LOUISE LOWE

WITH ILLUSTRATIONS BY
ANTHONY GROSS

READERS UNION

HEINEMANN

LONDON 1962

Introduction, Notes and Bibliography © ALMO LOUISE LOWE 1960
Illustrations © ANTHONY GROSS 1960

*This RU edition was produced in 1962 for sale to its members
only by Readers Union Ltd at Aldine House, 10–13 Bedford
Street, London W.C.2 and at Letchworth Garden City, Herts.
Full details of membership may be obtained from our London
address. The book is set in 11 point Bembo type leaded and has
been reprinted by The Windmill Press Ltd, Kingswood, Surrey.
It was first published by William Heinemann Ltd.*

# Contents

# Illustrations

For
REBECCA SMITH LEE
who first introduced me to HENRY JAMES
and
MARION DAY MULLINS
so 'finely aware' and 'richly responsible'

# Acknowledgments

The Introduction to this edition grew out of a longer study, 'The Travel Writing of Henry James', a doctoral dissertation completed in 1955 at William Marsh Rice University. Some of the opinions expressed here, however, go back to an earlier master's essay written at Texas Christian University. To the professors who directed these two studies I owe a special debt of gratitude: Dr Alan Dugald McKillop and Dr Carroll Camden of the Rice University; Dr Willard Thorp of Princeton University; and Dr Rebecca Smith Lee, formerly chairman of the English Department at Texas Christian University.

I am also indebted to Mr William James, literary executor of Henry James, for his interest in this new edition of *English Hours* and for his kindness in reading my manuscript. I wish to express my thanks as well to: Dr Robert Charles Le Clair, who published the first study of James as a traveller, for reading the Introduction and giving me the benefit of his wise counsel; Dr Edward Hake Phillips for reading my editorial work with all the care, the accuracy, and the attention to detail of a true historian; Dr Walter F. Starkie for his encouragement and helpful suggestions; Mrs W. St John Garwood for taking time from her own literary efforts to read mine; and Mr Carroll Fitzhugh for sharing with me his wide knowledge of literature as well as his magnificent library.

In the preparation of this edition, I have been especially grateful to Leon Edel and Dan H. Laurence who – carrying on where Le Roy Phillips left off – have made the task of finding and dating James's work a pleasure with *A Bibliography of Henry James* (1957). I have been indebted as well to a whole host of editors who have rescued James's early reviews, stories, essays, and travel sketches from the limbo of dusty magazine files. Particularly helpful have been: John L. Sweeney, *The Painter's Eye*

(1956); Leon Edel, *Selected Letters of Henry James* (1956); Albert Mordell, *Literary Reviews and Essays* (1957); Leon Edel and Ilse Dusoir Lind, *Parisian Sketches* (1957); and Morton Dauwen Zabel, *The Art of Travel* (1958), as well as the excellent studies listed in the Bibliography to this edition. And thanks to Mr Edel and Mr Le Clair those 'Untried Years' of 'Young Henry James' have now been made more explicit.

Especial thanks are due to: Miss June Roethlisberger, assistant librarian at the University of St Thomas; Mrs Charles W. Hamilton, Mrs John Rodell, and Miss Pender Turnbull, librarians at Rice University; Mr John S. Van E. Kohn of New York City for his assistance in securing many out-of-print books for me; Miss Anna Englert, one of my students, for her hours of research in the libraries of New Orleans; and Mr David Machin of William Heinemann Ltd., London, for his unflagging patience and his expert guidance through the tedium of publishing. This edition also owes much to my husband who is, in reality, co-editor.

Thanks to Mrs Kenneth Dale Owen, *English Hours* once again has 'the great advantage' and 'the company and support' of illustration – this time the drawings of Anthony Gross.

# A Note on the Text

In the 'Note' appended to the first edition of *English Hours*, Henry James stated that the essays were being reprinted[1] 'for the great advantage they will be felt to derive from the company and support of Mr Pennell's illustrations'. James had long been aware of the value of illustrations. As a small boy he had pored over illustrations in books and magazines: 'the tall entrancing folios of Nash's lithographed Mansions of England', the *Illustrated London News*, and *Punch*. As an adolescent, he had tried his own hand at illustrating; and later he wrote a series of essays in praise of illustrators.[2] In 1883 he wrote 'sketches on "drawing-paper"' of a little tour in France which were 'to cling for countenance and company' to a series of Pennell's drawings;[3] and again in 1888 James asked Pennell to illustrate the now famous essay 'London'. When Pennell inquired about the type of illustrations James wanted, the reply came back:

> Follow your own fancy. . . . The article from being so general is difficult to illustrate – and the thing, I should say, ought to be freely and fancifully done; *not* with neat, definite, photographic 'views'. . . . But do your own London, and it will be sufficiently mine.[4]

James no doubt was pleased with Pennell's 'London', for ninety-two of his drawings accompanied *English Hours* (1905) and sixty-four of his illustrations (thirty-two in colour) helped to make *Italian Hours* (1909)[5] the most beautiful of all the travel books.

But in spite of his admiration for the art of illustrating, James emphasised that illustration was an independent art which should 'quite stand off and on its own feet . . . as a separate and independent subject of publication'. It should not in any way relieve prose of its own 'plastic possibility'. He cautioned:

Anything that relieves responsible prose of the duty of being, while placed before us, good enough, interesting enough and, if the question be of picture, pictorial enough, above all *in itself*, does it the worst of services, and may well inspire in the lover of literature certain lively questions as to the future of that institution.[6]

Certainly that future is safe in the hands of Anthony Gross, whose drawings for this second edition of *English Hours* have in no way relieved prose of its responsibility nor of its 'pictorial spirit'. Indeed, some of Mr Gross's illustrations are, as James would have wished, 'expressions of no particular thing in the text, but only of the type or idea of this or that thing'.[7]

James had another reason, however, in addition to the value of illustrations, for publishing *English Hours* in 1905. He felt that the 'wonderments and judgments and emotions' set forth in the essays had, perhaps 'something of a curious interest'. One of those 'judgments' has indeed more than 'a curious interest', and it alone should give validity to this new edition of the essays. James saw in the last half of the nineteenth century the need for unity among 'the English-speaking territories of the globe', a need that two world wars and a threat of a third have made more apparent. He proclaimed again and again the importance of maintaining the ideals of the English-speaking democracies, and he insisted that because of 'the threat from the East', we should consider our differences 'idle and pedantic'. Only Sir Winston Churchill has been as eloquent on the subject. Mr Eisenhower, however, has continuously emphasised the necessity for 'the close, though not exclusive, association of the English-speaking peoples in their resolute defence of human liberty'; and the statement he made in England last autumn expressed what James had been 'all the while' saying: 'Indeed the future of the world would be bleak if two countries as closely allied as these could not walk side by side.'[8] Her Majesty Queen Elizabeth II, during a recent visit to the United States, expressed more succinctly than James ever could have what he had been saying for nearly half a century: 'On the maintenance of understanding between us the future of the free world depends.'[9]

The essays in *English Hours* (long out of print except for selections reprinted recently by Mr Zabel)[10] may be 'felicities or mistakes'; but they tell us much about the mind and character of Henry James; and they are still an excellent guide for the modern traveller who is interested in the literary and historical background of England. Delightful and informative, *English Hours* is perhaps best characterised by James's remarks about London: 'Out of its richness and its inexhaustible good humour it belies the next hour any generalisation you may have been so simple as to make about it.'

A. L. L.

# Introduction

'I wanted to do very much what I have done, and success, if I may say so, now stretches back a tender hand to its younger brother, desire.'

Henry James, the American, loved England steadily all his life. He had gone there first in 1843 at the age of six months; and after repeated visits during his youth and young manhood, he decided in 1876 to make London his permanent home. He later moved to Rye and the year before his death in 1916, he became a British subject. In doing so James underlined his American idealism and his faith in the democratic way of life for which his native country stood and which his adopted country was battling to defend. He felt England to be right in standing up to the Germans, and he hoped that his action would show America 'a little something of the way'.[1] He did not wish to be an alien in the land he loved, nor did he wish to be restricted in doing whatever he could for the war effort.[2] Unable to go to war himself – as so many Americans were to do both in World War I and World War II long before their own country entered the fray – he did in effect give his life[3] for a cause which next to his love for his art was his most abiding passion: the preservation of 'the English-American world', a world so united by history and literature that it was in reality 'different chapters of the same general subject'.[4] Again and again he affirmed his faith in the destiny of 'the English-speaking territories of the globe', and he proclaimed 'how great we all are together in the light of heaven and the face of the rest of the world, with the bond of our glorious tongue'.

James loved other countries as well, especially France and Italy.

Throughout his life he was an ardent admirer of the 'genius' of the French, particularly their devotion to art and form, and he lived in France[5] a year before settling in England. He thought that Italy was 'really so much the most beautiful country in the world . . . that others must stand off and be hushed while she speaks',[6] and until almost the end of his life he made an annual visit to 'pluperfect Italy'. But England loomed largest in his consciousness; it was his spiritual home. London encompassed all. Because of its 'innumerable races and creeds', it was the 'epitome of the round world'[7] and 'the capital of the human race'. James, whose subject was the drama of life, chose London instead of Paris (the theatre capital of the world) for his home because he considered London 'the particular spot in the world which communicates the greatest sense of life'. The American literary man in particular needed to know London, to immerse himself in 'the largest social incarnation of the language, of the tradition'. He explained:

> For a man of letters who endeavours to cultivate, however modestly, the medium of Shakespeare and Milton, of Hawthorne and Emerson, who cherishes the notion of what it has achieved and what it may even yet achieve, London must ever have a great illustrative and suggestive value, and indeed a kind of sanctity.[8]

Living and writing in England gave James an opportunity to use literature, 'fiction in particular', as 'a magnificent arm' in the cause of Anglo-American understanding. He wrote to William:

> I can't look at the English-American world, or feel about them, any more, save as a big Anglo-Saxon total, destined to such an amount of melting together that an insistence on their differences becomes more and more idle and pedantic; and that melting together will come the faster the more one takes it for granted and treats the life of the two countries as continuous or more or less convertible. . . . Literature, fiction in particular, affords a magnificent arm for such taking for granted, and one may so do an excellent work with it.[9]

James was not the only literary man of his day who felt that our 'consecrated English speech' and our literary heritage demanded that the writer be acquainted with England; and he was not the only American to feel that the artistic temperament demanded the richer climate of Europe for its development. The list is an imposing one from the nineteenth century to the present, and it includes such American artists, educators, and writers as William Wetmore Story (whose biography James was to write), Charles Eliot Norton, Henry Adams, James Russell Lowell, Edith Wharton, F. Scott Fitzgerald, Willa Cather, T. S. Eliot, and Ernest Hemingway. Most of America's leading writers came under the spell of 'Our Old Home': Irving, Cooper, Emerson, Hawthorne, Holmes, and Howells, to mention only a few;[10] and all of them complained of the 'plain and scanty diet' in the New World as compared to the 'rich traditional and historic food' of the Old World. Emerson called England 'the best of actual nations'.[11] Hawthorne concluded that 'If England were all the world, it still would have been worth while for the Creator to have made it'.[12] He urged Longfellow to make his home in England: 'If I were in your position, I think I should make my home on this side of the water. . . . A man of individuality and refinement can certainly live far more comfortably here . . . than in New England.'[13] Holmes expressed the opinion and the 'hope' that Americans would eventually re-emigrate to England: 'the time may come when a New Englander will feel more as if he were among his own people in London than in one of our seaboard cities'.[14] Mark Twain – America's favourite son – during his first visit to England wrote home: 'There is nothing like it elsewhere on the globe . . . I would a good deal rather live here if I could get the rest of you over.'[15] He took great pride in the honorary degree which Oxford conferred upon him in 1907.

> I am quite well aware – and so is America, and so is the rest of Christendom – that an Oxford decoration is a loftier distinction than is conferrable by any other university on either side of the ocean, and is worth twenty-five of any other, whether foreign or domestic.[16]

There were scores of other Americans who felt the 'pull' of Europe, but of course not all preferred England. Some found France and Italy more to their liking,[17] but surely none of them admired these countries more than James.

Few writers took their travels or sojourns abroad more seriously than Henry James, and few had a more propitious background for their life's work.[18] Ostensibly, James had had a proper introduction to England. As 'a small American child' he had been 'a silent devotee of *Punch*' and to him '*Punch* was England; *Punch* was London'. Poring over the sketches of Leech, he became as familiar with 'the features of a world which he longed so to behold' as with the furniture in his own home.[19] He never forgot those pictures. When not poring over magazines, he was reading English books, burying his nose in half-open books just for the 'English smell', visiting bookshops in order to 'snuff up' fresh uncut volumes redolent with the 'taste of the very substance of London'. These English books, he perceived years later, were responsible for 'more fond dreams and glimmering pictures than any other one principle of growth'.[20] He devoured the novels of Dickens and Thackeray and George Eliot, and he was to cherish to the end of his days the privilege of meeting these illustrious authors. Later, when he looked at England, everything seemed to be scenes out of their novels.

Because the elder James wished to give his children a 'sensuous education', he took the family to Europe in 1855 for a three-year stay. Henry never forgot the summer of 1855 for it gave him his first meaningful glimpse of 'vast, portentous London' (he had been too young to remember his first visit, but it 'was a mystic satisfaction to him that he had lived in Piccadilly when he was a baby . . .'). All the impressions he had been gathering in America seemed in preparation for that hour. The ineffaceable stamp of that June afternoon ride through the streets of London, seated on a box beside the coachman, was of such 'extreme intensity' that it was to 'underlie, deep down, the whole mass of later observation'.[21] At long last he was to 'become personally and incredibly acquainted with Piccadilly and Richmond Park and Ham Common'. His childhood dream to 'go to Drury Lane to see a pantomime' was to become a reality, and he and William did see a pantomime which reminded them of Dickens. Dressed in 'little "high" black hats and inveterate gloves', they went as often as possible to the theatre. At The Olympic they saw Frederick Robson in *The Discreet Princess*; Charles Mathews in Sheridan's *The Critic*; and Alfred Wigan in *Still Waters*

*Run Deep*; and at the Princess Theatre, Charles Kean's presentation of *Henry the Eighth*. The latter was 'a momentous date' in their lives, and for days afterwards they enjoyed reproducing in water-colours scenes from the play.

Henry had always been interested in scenes, whether at the theatre or in the streets. 'I thought, I lisped, at any rate I composed, in scenes,' he later recalled; and the scenes he witnessed during his youth, particularly the 'horrors' in the 'squalid' street through which the carriage had to pass en route to the theatre or railway station, were indelibly stamped upon his memory. One scene, 'framed by the cab-window, of a woman reeling backward as a man felled her to the ground with a blow in the face', reminded him of Cruikshank (later he recognised that the scene had 'quite a Hogarth' side as well).[22] He never forgot the people he observed in the streets and their images are to be found throughout his travel writings as well as in his fiction. His observation of the 'working class' was particularly acute:

> the demureness of a maid-servant opening a street-door in Brompton, the top-heavy attitude of the small 'Ameliar-Ann', as she stands planted with the baby in her arms on the corner of a Westminster slum, the coal-heavers, the cabmen, the publicans, the butcher-boys, the flunkeys, the guardsmen, the policemen. . . .[23]

Every scene young Henry's eyes fell upon during these impressionable years reminded him not only of Dickens and Thackeray but also of drawings and paintings which he had seen reproduced in magazines and books. From the beginning the plastic arts were to mean almost as much to him as literature. During their youthful sojourn abroad, William and Henry strolled through the streets with sketchbooks tucked under their arms, stopping often to sketch an unusual building or scene. They gaped at paintings in London's National Gallery, 'haunted' the Pantheon to gaze at Haydon's huge canvases, attended exhibitions at the Royal Academy (one of the Pre – Raphaelites), delighted in the Vernon collection then on view at Marlborough House, and admired the architecture of buildings, churches and castles. When they crossed the Channel and visited the Louvre, Henry seemed to hear a voice that admonished: 'Art, art, art, don't you see? Learn, little gaping pilgrims, what *that* is!' Henry learned the lesson so well that on succeeding visits to Europe he spent much of his time gazing at the world's masterpieces and then writing critical articles for various magazines.[24]

After nearly three years in Europe, the James family returned to America for a brief stay in Newport, but in the autumn of 1859 they were back again in Europe for a sojourn in Switzerland and Germany. They returned to Newport at the end of 1860 in order that William might study under the celebrated American painter, William Morris Hunt. Henry, too, tried 'daubing' for a while, but he was soon aware that his efforts did not compare with William's. He began to neglect his brush in favour of literary discussions with his 'bookish' friends Thomas Sergeant Perry and John La Farge.[25] When William deserted his painting and entered Harvard (for a career in science), Henry once again followed his brother's lead and in 1862 registered at Harvard's Law School. He had little interest in the law, however, and spent most of his time reading, attending the theatre and writing short stories.[26] At Bonn, in 1860, he had felt that he was 'almost on the spot to commence author', and by the end of his year at Harvard, he at last was sure that all he ' "wanted to want" to be was . . . just *literary*'. Encouraged by La Farge (who introduced him to Balzac, Mérimée and Browning), he began sending reviews and stories to various periodicals.[27] Charles Eliot Norton, editor of the *North American Review*, held out the 'golden light of promise' to young Henry, which led to his 'positive consecration to letters'.[28] By the end of 1865 he could claim to be a man of letters; he had written at least eighteen reviews, criticisms and stories for four of the leading periodicals of the day.[29] The next year he added a fifth magazine, the *Galaxy*, and by the end of 1869 he had contributed sixty-nine literary pieces to various magazines.[30] But during the winter of 1867–1868, as he read William's letters from Europe, he felt again the old 'nostalgia for the "greater richness" of Europe'; and he concluded that to be 'literary' demanded, for him at least, a richer background than American life and letters offered at that time.[31]

In the spring of 1869, Henry once more set sail for Europe. It had been nearly ten years since he had been in Europe, and never had a more passionate pilgrim set foot on English soil. The arrival at Liverpool and the journey to London were to be described again and again in his letters, essays, memoirs and fiction.[32] Years later he found 'every small circumstance of those hours of approach and arrival still as vivid as if the solemnity of an opening era had breathed upon it'. Everywhere the 'sentimental tourist' looked, he was reminded (as he had been in 1855) of characters and scenes in books or paintings. Mrs William Morris had 'a mouth like the "Oriana" in our illustrated Tennyson'; she was straight 'out of one of Rossetti's or Hunt's pictures'. The countryside between Great Malvern and Worcester was 'thick-sown with good old English "effects" . . . suggestive of the opening chapters of half-remembered novels, devoured in infancy'.[33] The play of light and shade across the English landscape was that of Du Maurier's drawings.

Delighting in such literary and pictorial scenes, James went on to make the Grand Tour and to write letters that often were sheer poetry and certainly beautiful prose. Some of them, such as the one he wrote his father from Great Malvern, were embryonic travel essays. As he looked back upon his first adult tour, James recorded that he knew then that the experience 'represented at once a chain stretching off to heaven knew where, but far into one's future . . . and every link and pulse of which it was going accordingly to be indispensable, besides being delightful and wonderful, to recognise'. And in 1914 he did not feel that the harvest of that seed had yet 'all been gathered'.[34]

## II

When James returned to America at the end of May 1870, he was commissioned by *The Nation* to do a series of travel sketches of North American watering-places: Saratoga, Newport, Niagara and Quebec. These essays are 'delicious' bits of prose,[1] and the reader is as grateful for them as he is for the travel letters, which no doubt prompted the sketches.[2] These early American sketches in turn led to another commission from *The Nation* for a series of 'transatlantic sketches'. In May 1872, in company with his Aunt Kate (Miss Catherine Walsh) and his sister Alice, James embarked upon his second Grand Tour and his second professional tour as a writer of travel sketches. He began in England by making a leisurely tour of several cathedral towns; he crossed the Channel to France, strolled through Paris streets and sauntered through museums; collected observations in Switzerland; spent six months in Italy, and then returned to England by way of Germany, Holland, Belgium and France. During these peregrinations he developed certain habits which lend a human interest to his travel sketches and reveal a side of James's personality not readily apparent elsewhere.[3] He was still somewhat the 'gaping' pilgrim, but travel had now become an art for him and his habits as a traveller form a pattern as carefully 'composed' as his travel essays.

James, for example, had a predilection for arriving at his destination late in the afternoon or by moonlight. A place was more picturesque, quieter, more dramatic at the end of the day; he advised the 'discreet traveller' never to miss 'an opportunity to come into a great church at eventide'. He observed that the Norman stonework of Exeter Cathedral comes out best 'when the long June twilight turns at last to a deeper grey'. It is then that the 'little broken-visaged effigies of saints and kings and bishops . . . begin to peer sidewise out of their narrow recesses and to converse in some strange form of early English'. James could 'wish the traveller no better fortune than to stroll forth in the early evening' to visit Wells Cathedral, and he found that the Vicars' Close adjoining the Cathedral Green was 'adorably of another world and time' in the 'dimness of twilight'. Later, in 1877, he lingered at Rochester Cathedral 'for a long time, looking in the fading light at what was left' and mused that 'English ruins always come out peculiarly when the day begins to fail'; they turn 'paler in the twilight' and become 'consciously solemn and spectral'.

Part of the joy of visiting a cathedral or ruin by moonlight was that these historic places were then 'void of any human presence' and the traveller might observe in quietness and solitude. Wherever James went, he tried to visit a place at a time when there would not be a 'crush' of tourists. He enjoyed London in midsummer because most Londoners were then away on holiday. He bore the tourist no ill will, however; he simply wished to contemplate a scene and immerse himself in 'the sense of the past' without the intrusion of distracting elements. James was pleased that tourists were 'swarming' over Europe; he took 'a peculiar satisfaction in seeing them' there. He was glad that their presence gave him 'a lively impression of the quantity of luxury now diffused through the world' and that travelling was no longer the pastime of the 'lords and nabobs'. He was glad that 'honest folks' had 'a little more elevating amusement' than formerly and that they, too, found 'snow-peaks, and glaciers, and passes, and lakes, and chalets, and sunsets . . . prime necessities for six weeks every year'.[4] Always busy 'catching character' James welcomed every opportunity to observe these tourists. When his coach stopped at the little inn at Andermatt, it was not the evening meal but rather the national characteristics of the travellers who had 'bundled in to dinner' that interested him.

> The American gentleman in the banquette made the acquaintance of the Irish lady in the coupé, who talked of the weather as *foine*, and wore a Persian scarf twisted about her head. At the other end of the table sat an Englishman out of the intérieur, who bore a most extraordinary resemblance to the portraits of Edward VI's and Mary's reigns. He was a walking Holbein. It was fascinating, and he must have wondered why I stared at him.[5]

It was the average native of a country that interested James most when he travelled; not upper-class society.[6] Although he preferred to visit historic places in 'perfect solitude', he would ride crowded omnibuses and third-class carriages in order to observe the people of a country.[7] He went to Epsom Downs in a coach which was loaded with hampers, champagne-baskets and merry people whose social quality James 'made less of a point of testing'. The coaches were so thick on the road that progress was a bit hazardous, but James found 'the spectacle from the top of the coach proportionately absorbing'. He felt that he was getting 'for the first time a notion of the London population at large', which had 'piled itself into carts, into omnibuses, into every possible and impossible species of "trap" '. This glimpse of the 'popular revel' gave James the feeling that 'he was learning something more about the English people'. It afforded him an excellent opportunity to witness the 'unbuttoning of the popular straight-jacket'. While visiting Oxford, James had another chance to witness this sort of unbuttoning. He was a bit surprised at 'the boisterous conduct' of the young intellectuals but concluded that it was the same sort of 'carnival of "chaff" ' as the Epsom 'popular "lark" '. In spite of the difference in social status, it was 'the same race enjoying a certain definitely chartered licence'. Later, in order to obtain a fuller view of the manners and customs, the idiosyncrasies and social institutions of English middle-class society, James made a tour of various watering-places. He found Hastings and St. Leonards to be 'a kind of *résumé* of middle-class English civilisation'.

On these excursions James walked everywhere, not only within a village or city but from town to town. He never missed an opportunity to exchange a few words with the beggars he met along the way (a few of them were incorporated into his fiction) or with peasants, farmers, shepherds, waiters, laundresses, as well as with his fellow travellers. Walking across the Italian countryside gave him an opportunity to chat with a young Italian communist 'who took a hard, grim view of everything'.[8] But for the accident of his having gossiped with the young man, James would have had him 'do service . . . as an example of sensuous optimism !' While in France, James walked ten miles in the hot sun to see the races at Fécamp, and on one occasion he walked across the Alps into Italy. The habit of 'endlessly' walking, which he had begun as a youth, gave James many scenes and characters for his fiction.[9]

And wherever he went, whether walking or riding, James was always in a genial mood. He possessed an inordinate amount of patience and an extremely tolerant attitude toward his fellow man. He was never perturbed by delays in coach or train schedules. On the contrary, he seemed to welcome these delays, for they afforded an opportunity to sit behind his book or newspaper and observe his companions. He found railway stations a perpetual delight. London railway stations fascinated him; he liked them 'æsthetically' as well, and he enjoyed the evidence they offered 'of our larger way of looking at life'.

They remind me of all our reciprocities and activities, our energies and curiosities, and our being all distinguished together from other people by our great common stamp of perpetual motion, our passion for seas and deserts and the other side of the globe, the secret of the impression of strength – I don't say of social roundness and finish – that we produce in any collection of Anglo-Saxon types.[10]

In 'the beloved foggy season' he delighted 'in the spectacle of Paddington, Euston or Waterloo', where it was apparent that 'the English are immensely distinct from other people', as well as 'extremely distinct from each other' socially. The 'rich colouring of their differences' was even more striking 'in the fine flare of one of Mr W. H. Smith's bookstalls'. There was a 'glamour' about these 'glittering' booths which made literature seem 'a thing of splendour, of a dazzling essence', and the traveller always came away with a volume tucked under his arm.

James was as unperturbed by inadequate hotel accommodation and physical discomforts as he was by delays in train or bus schedules. He had long since realised that whichever hotel you select, you will wish 'very much that it had been the other'. The twin hotels at Saratoga had taught him that, and the lesson had been verified again at Arles. Years later when modern hotels with all their comforts sprang up all over Europe, James found himself preferring the 'ancient malodorous inn which somehow didn't matter, to that new type of polyglot caravanserai which everywhere insists on mattering . . . so much more than anything else'.[11] It was the local colour of hotels and restaurants that mattered to James. He 'retained a more vivid impression of the talk and the faces' at the excellent inn at Ilfracombe than of the 'joints and side-dishes'; conversation was 'uproarious almost', not at all in accord with 'the supposed national characteristics'. The analytical tourist was not sure whether the introduction of *table d'hôte* or a social earthquake was responsible for this 'suspension of a common social law', but ostensibly he preferred it to the banal drawing-room conversation about which he complained to his family[12] and which he satirised in his fiction.

It was 'a shame', James thought, to care for one's bodily comforts in an intellectual atmosphere 'so intense that you feel as if you ought to live on the mere atmosphere – the historic whisperings, the nameless romantic intimations'. He felt sure that most American travellers would be, like himself, too diverted by beautiful scenery and historic buildings to think of their 'inalienable right to be comfortable' or to mind the 'universal smell of strong *charcuterie*'[13] so prevalent in Europe. But of course he was forgetting Hawthorne, Howells and Twain on this subject; they were the forerunners of the modern tourist who demands all the comforts of home while travelling. From the beginning James had made up his mind to be 'but half comfortable' and to pay little attention whether a place was hot or cold or the air thick. It was not that James was unaware of these conditions. Indeed, he had a very keen sense of smell and his writings are replete with references to odours. Trying to wedge his way into Westminster Abbey for Easter services in 1877, he commented: 'The crowd was terribly compact, and beneath the Gothic arches the odour was not that of incense.' But 'the historic whisperings' were usually worth whatever unpleasantness he might endure.

Regardless of physical discomforts, poor accommodation or weather conditions, James, the traveller, kept to his planned itinerary and to his regular habits. He crossed the Alps in a creaking coach; he made precarious train journeys through flooded areas in France; he visited Switzerland in the autumn rather than the summer; he enjoyed travelling by night and strolling about the streets of a town in the moonlight. He rambled across the English countryside during rain and cold, and he even professed to love the 'friendly' English fog and English winters! He found that it was 'in the winter months that the imagination weaves . . . delights'. Certainly weather was never a deterrent to James; instead it served as an inspiration. His letters, his travel sketches, his novels and tales are a testimony to his love of sunsets, twilight, moonlight, fog and rain; his love of beauty in any form (particularly framed landscapes and lovely houses and gardens)[14] and his delight – sometimes his repugnance[15] – in the panorama of life which passed before his observing eyes. He longed to sketch it all, but he had to content himself with 'mental' sketches which he later turned into 'word-sketches'. His 'painter's eye' was often dissatisfied with his word-sketching, however, and more than once he remarked that 'a dozen pencil-strokes would be a better memento' of a place than his 'vague word-sketching'.

From 1869 to 1907 – his last journey to Italy – James maintained a healthy, philosophical attitude toward travel. The passionate pilgrim and sentimental tourist of 1869–1876 became the 'observant, analytical visitor' (sometimes the 'musing, mature visitor') of 1877–1888, and the 'brooding' and 'restless analyst' of the 1890's, and 1900's; but he never lost interest in 'the romance of travel' and he did not envy people who had 'outlived or outworn the simple entertainment of feeling settled to go somewhere, with bag and umbrella'. He liked 'nothing so much as moving about to see the world'. To travel was 'to go to the play', and a seat in a hansom cab was better than 'a box at the play' or 'any box at the opera'. Travel was a delightful, carefree experience as well, at least for a while: 'Responsibility is left at home, or, at the worst, packed away in the valise, in quite another part of the diligence, with the clean shirts and the writing-case'.[16]

III

The England James loved because of its literary associations, he turned back into literature: travel sketches, short stories, novels and plays, as well as all sorts of fugitive pieces. Before he accepted the commission from *The Nation*, James had already turned some of his travel experience into fiction. His early novels and tales read like literary travelogues, and indeed travel furnished the *donné*, in one way or another, for most of his works.[1] But James was not content with a fictionised re-telling of his impressions as a traveller. From 1870 until almost the end of his life, he spoke for himself through his travel essays. Although he wrote as fairly and objectively as possible, it is through these travel essays that we come to know James's personal opinions about a country and its people, its art and literature. His interest in the travel sketch was more than professional; he seemed to enjoy this personal method of explaining Europe to his American readers.[2] He found it a rather intimate way to keep in touch with his native land.

In writing travel essays James was following the *Zeitgeist* of his day. The travel essay was a significant literary *genre* during the nineteenth century, and magazines and newspapers of the time were quick to meet the demands of prospective tourists and arm-chair travellers. Not only

xxv

*The Nation* but other leading American magazines such as *Atlantic Monthly*, *Galaxy*, *Lippincott's*, *North American Review*, and *Scribner's* published travel sketches regularly, as well as all sorts of advice for the traveller such as Lewis Morris Iddings's 'The Art of Travel. By Land' and 'The Art of Travel. Ocean Crossings'.[3] Editors also published with alacrity short stories and novels based on travel. Book publishers like-wise took notice of the public's increasing interest in travel, and they soon brought out in book form travel essays, and stories based on travel, which had first appeared serially. They also supplied the traveller with the indispensable Baedeker or Murray, or some sort of travel-guide, and with the pocket-size (usually paper-bound) books [4] to read while waiting for trains or lying in steamer deck-chairs.

The literature of travel comprised quite an extensive library on both sides of the Atlantic long before Henry James's volumes began to appear.[5] European travellers of the nineteenth century were familiar with such travel accounts as those of Flaubert, Gautier, Taine and Stendhal, as well as those of Smollett, Sterne and Ruskin. American travellers used as virtual guidebooks Irving's *Sketch-Book*, Cooper's *Gleanings in Europe*, Emerson's *English Traits*, Hawthorne's *Our Old Home* and Holmes's *Our Hundred Days in Europe*. Also in demand were the illustrated travel books such as Nathaniel Parker Willis's *Pencillings By the Way* or Felix O. C. Darley's *Sketches Abroad With Pen and Pencil*. By the turn of the century not only Mark Twain's *Innocents Abroad* or *A Tramp Abroad* but also Howells's and James's numerous travel books had become 'best sellers'. James read avidly the travel accounts of other writers, and he advised the prospective traveller to do the same. He never overlooked pertinent information in the guide-books, and wherever he went he recalled what others had said about a place, a historic building or a work of art. He liked nothing better than to challenge the validity of Ruskin's *Mornings in Florence*[6] or to compare notes with Taine or Stendhal. He often re-viewed the travel books of other writers, and it is from these reviews[7] that we learn a good deal about his notions of the form and content of the travel sketch.

For his first English sketches of 1872, James followed the pattern which he had developed in his North American sketches. However, 'Chester' (remarkably similar to 'Quebec'), the first of these essays, reflects a greater attention to detail and an increasing interest in what lies beneath the surface of 'antiquities'. James concluded that Chester was 'a theme for the philosophers' and really 'too heavy' for his pen, but his pen was equal to that of the philosopher when he looked at the Rows:

> Fix one of them with your gaze, and it seems fairly to reek with mortality. Every stain and crevice seems to syllable some human record – a record of lives airless and unlighted. . . . Human life, surely, packed away behind those impenetrable lattices of lead and bottle-glass . . . can have expanded into scant freedom and bloomed into small sweetness.[8]

His pen was adequate, too, whenever he commented upon the 'fine differences in national manners'. The 'tone of things' in England was heavier than in America; 'manners and modes . . . more absolute and positive'. James was usually as objective as the philosopher, but on occasions his Americanism triumphed over his objective spirit. He had listened to a sermon unworthy of Chester's great Cathedral, which prompted him to remind his American readers that even though America did not have 'the scale of beauty' to be found in England, the tourist could at least hold up his head and 'reflect that so far as we *have* opportunities we mostly rise to them'.

Cathedrals are the centre of interest in the early English sketches, and they loom large in all James's travel writings. His 'church habit', he called it. Lichfield Cathedral he thought 'the finest, on the whole, of all cathedrals'. Exeter Cathedral prompted him to compare 'the pleasure of cathedral-hunting' with that of seeking out the great paintings of the world. The difficulty with 'fine pictures' is that they 'are terribly numerous, and have a troublesome way of crowding and jostling in the memory'. But cathedrals are smaller in number, which enables the traveller to retain in his memory 'a single broad image of the vast grey edifice, with its head and shoulders, its vessel and its towers, its tone of colour, and its still green precinct'. Equally vivid in James's memory were the castles and ruins he visited. Warwick Castle was 'the only great residence' James 'coveted as a home'; it satisfied 'the imagination without irritating the democratic conscience'. He particularly enjoyed the art treasures of the castle. While admiring the Van Dycks and Rembrandts, he was reminded 'afresh' that 'the best fortune for good pictures is not to be crowded into public collections . . . but to hang in largely spaced half-dozens on the walls of fine houses'. Ruined castles were of especial interest to James; he was 'somehow aware of a deeper note in the crumbled castle than any note of the solid one'. He found that in England 'the purest enjoyment of architecture was to be had among the ruins of great buildings'.

It was not only because of his interest in architecture and paintings that James went in search of castles and ruins. Most of them brought back memories of his reading as well: 'Miss Burney's and Miss Austen's heroines might perfectly well have had their first love-affair' in the shadow of Ludlow Castle, 'the most impressive and magnificent of ruins'. Haddon Hall, which was 'exactly Elizabethan', seemed 'the ideal *mise en scène* for portions of Shakespeare's comedies'. The ruins of Lynton were both poetry and picture. James spent two evenings until midnight on those 'pinnacles of stone', listening to 'the short, sharp cry of sea-mews and looking at 'the sullen calmness of the unbroken tide at the dreadful base of the cliffs'; he 'kept forever repeating, as if they contained a spell, half a dozen words from Tennyson's "Idylls of the King" – "On Wild Tintagil, by the Cornish Sea" '. The whole scene held 'the lurking signature of Gustave Doré.[9] Everywhere James went across the English countryside he was aware of 'thick-crowding literary and historical associations'. He noticed at Chester that the 'two hoary shells of masonry' which had been converted into museums were presided over by 'a couple of those grotesque creatures, *à la* Dickens, whom one finds squeezed into every cranny of English civilisation, scraping a thin subsistence, like mites in a mouldy cheese'. Loitering in the yew-shaded church at Porlock, 'betwixt the high-backed manorial pew and the battered tomb of a crusading knight and his lady', James expected at any moment to see 'Sir Roger de Coverley marching up the aisle'. He longed for the pen of Mr Addison 'to give a proper account of it all'.

Warwickshire, especially, was literature come to life. It was Shakespeare's country,[10] and the 'broad sloping pastures of velvet turf' seemed 'as deeply attuned to human needs' as 'the underlying morality of the poet'. But Warwickshire was also George Eliot's country. Watching a group of young women playing lawn tennis, James kept waiting to see George Eliot's Gwendolen 'step out of the muslin group'; and he recalled that 'It was in one of the old nestling farmhouses . . . that Hetty Sorrel smiled into her milk-pans as if she were looking for a reflection of her pretty face'. James was indeed a 'literary alchemist';[11] he even conjured up literary ghosts![12] Because he listened 'with proper credulity' at Haddon Hall, he seemed to hear the 'ghostly footfalls' of Dorothy Vernon and Lord John Manners 'on the flags of the castle court'. On occasions he 'did see' ghosts 'as we see ghosts nowadays'. Sometimes he was not sure whether his attitude toward ghosts was to be interpreted 'as a fond hope or a great fear'; nevertheless, he was always grateful that 'at least there were ghosts' to be met in the beautiful old houses which were deserted because the owners could no longer afford to live in them.

If England was literature, it was also painting. Everywhere James looked he saw landscapes that might have been painted by Turner, Claude, Berghem or Doré. The charm of England was that its scenery was so beautifully composed. There were 'no waste details'; everything was 'something particular'. English 'sacred piles' (abbeys and churches) possessed 'as pictures, a spacious and harmonious setting'. Each might have been the work of a painter. The 'hoary relics of Glastonbury . . . in their broken eloquence' reminded James 'of one of the other great ruins of the world – the *Last Supper* of Leonardo. A beautiful shadow, in each case, is all that remains; but that shadow is the soul of the artist'. Kenilworth Castle 'made a perfect picture', with its 'purple shadows and slowly shifting lights, with a soft-hued, bosky country for the middle distance'. The traveller would no more have thought of walking to the castle than he 'would have thought of walking to a purple-shadowed tower in the background of a Berghem or a Claude'. Both Rye and Winchelsea had 'the note of Turner and Claude', and Devon was a 'veritable landscape in water-colours'. The Isle of Wight, which was 'pure picture', existed only 'for exclamation and the water-colour brush'. Dissatisfied with his own word-sketches, James concluded that most places in England were 'a matter for the brush and not the pen'.

But he often sketched landscapes and portraits with a skill equal to that of the masters whom he admired.[13] In composition and colour, his Somerset landscape[14] rivals that of the plastic artist, and his portrait of the residents of an almshouse near St Cuthbert's[15] is as graphic as any painter's. Nowhere is there a better portrait of Dr Johnson than the one James sketched while in Lichfield. The reader remembers long afterward: 'the London coach facing towards Temple Bar with the young author of "Rasselas" scowling near-sightedly from the cheapest seat'.

## IV

James left England in 1872 with the feeling that the English did not 'half discern their good fortune, and that it takes passionate pilgrims, vague aliens and other disinherited persons to appreciate the "points" ' of their 'admirable country'. He went on to the Continent to complete his tour before returning to America; however, he was back in Europe again in 1875 as Paris correspondent for the *New York Tribune*.[1] It was not until the end of 1876, when he settled in London – at 3 Bolton Street – that he turned his hand once again to writing travel sketches of England. In spite of the fact that the winter of 1876 was 'the darkest and wettest' James could remember, he nevertheless was in 'a state of deep delight'; he read English books before an English fire; he had always known that London was 'the right place' for him, and now he knew that London was 'on the whole the most possible form of life'. He 'had complete liberty, and the prospect of profitable work', as well as a flat that was to become 'sacred' to him. Years later he looked back with nostalgia on that 'little shabby furnished apartment'; he had '*lived*' much there, felt much, thought much, learned much, produced much'.[2]

Although about half of the sketches James wrote during the period 1877–1901 follow the pattern of the earlier essays of 1870–1872 and reflect a continued interest in cathedrals, castles and ruins, an equal number demonstrate that the analytical observer (sometimes 'the would-be redresser of æsthetic wrongs') had become increasingly interested in a 'landscape with figures'. The first essay of this period, 'An English

Easter', establishes a new pattern, both in content and style, which was to culminate in the impressionistic sketches of *The American Scene*. It is the human scene that is the centre of interest in this Easter holiday essay. As James walked from Piccadilly to Westminster Abbey on a Good Friday, it was the national character of Britons that he observed: their love of convention, their holiday spirit, their church-going habits, their physiognomy, their treatment of 'radicals'. Everywhere he looked he saw evidences of the greatness of the Empire, and he observed that even 'a little puffing steamer' or a soldier in the sentry-box played a part in 'the imperial machinery of this great country'. But the mature analyst also saw much that was stupid, cruel and vulgar in the 'duskiest of modern Babylons'.

James chose the holiday seasons to analyse and evaluate English life, because these occasions gave him an excellent opportunity to watch the populace enjoying the parks ('the drawing-rooms and clubs of the poor'), departing from railway stations, or taking rides on penny-steamers. He enjoyed these rides himself; he considered the Thames 'an adjunct of London life, an expression of London manners'. He especially enjoyed London in August (when all the city departs); he had the sprawling city to himself then. In quietness and solitude he was able to observe the 'murky Babylon' more closely. He could see the 'ugliness' a little more clearly, and he could turn the glow of his lantern more easily 'on each successive facet of the jewel'. As he strolled around London or journeyed across the countryside, he was a good deal more aware of social conditions, economic inequalities, politics and even world affairs than is sometimes thought. He may not have analysed any of these subjects in detail (he was never a reformer), but he was quick to call attention to them or to any of the problems inherent in 'the essentially hierarchical plan of English society . . . the great and ever-present fact to the mind of a stranger'. He emphasised that a traveller should be more than a superficial observer, and he was disappointed that Gautier, in writing his travel essays, was not more analytical. He agreed with another critic (even though his remark had been 'somewhat uncivilly said') that Gautier's 'powers of reflection were about equivalent to those of an intelligent poodle'.[3]

In spite of his love for England, James did not close his eyes to any of her shortcomings, nor did he gloss over any of the injustices. He shared with his family a sensitiveness to any form of injustice, and he was as quick to comment upon an untenable situation as his sister Alice. At times he may have been subtle and indirect (often resorting to symbols), but frequently his trenchant satire and irony equalled that of the great satirists, American or European. He had tried to be 'very delicate' when he satirised 'inherited aristocracy' in *An International Episode*, but his English readers found the satire anything but delicate.[4] They reacted in much the same way as Americans reacted to 'Daisy Miller' and *The Bostonians*.[5] On several occasions James took the opportunity 'to stick a few pins' into England's 'closely graduated social hierarchy'. In such stories as 'Lady Barbarina', 'A London Life', *The Awkward Age*, *The Portrait of a Lady*, and *The Tragic Muse*, he directed very pointed barbs at the condescension, philistinism and intrigue (both social and political) so apparent in upper-class society.[6] Indeed, James saw the crack in the Golden Bowl; and not only in the Ververs' story but especially in *The Spoils of Poynton*, *The Wings of the Dove*, and *The Ivory Tower* he called attention to 'the black and merciless things that are behind great possessions'.[7] In his travel essays, James was, at times, extremely forthright with his barbs. Looking at a lovely old country house in Monmouthshire, he mused: 'It takes a great many plain people to keep a "perfect" gentleman going; it takes a great deal of wasted sweetness to make a saved property'. On another occasion he was pleased to observe that the British passion for sports had introduced 'the leaven of democracy into the most aristocratically constituted society in the world'. He noticed that when engaged in sport 'a "cad" may feel very much like a lord'; but he would not 'go so far as to say that a lord may feel like a cad'. He had some reservations, too, about the way in which English millionaires took over Scotland during the 'shooting' season. He did not find 'Mayfair among the heather' amusing.

> It seems to me that if I were a fervid Caledonian I should find something irritating, and even mortifying, in the sight of my beautiful little country parcelled out, on so immense a scale, into playgrounds for English millionaires. Was it for this that my ancestors bled with Wallace or flocked about Bruce?[8]

As James travelled around England, he was ever aware of the 'imperfect terms of intercourse' between the rich and poor. Although he devoted only one full-length novel to the plight of the lower classes (*The Princess Casamassima*, 1886), he had given the reader a glimpse of that world earlier in 'Gabrielle De Bergerac' (1869), a story of pre-revolutionary France.[9] James had been conscious of this 'strange underworld' since a child,[10] and the problem was in his mind when he contemplated the future evolution of 'the strangely mingled monster' London, and he wondered 'whether the poor will improve away the rich, or the rich expropriate the poor'. He wrote of the poor in a 'melancholy strain' when he described a 'party of the poor' in London's West End, and he ventured to 'drop a very soft sigh on the paper'. Londoners who dined out during the social season were transported in their broughams to the door of their hostesses. Watching the 'fine ladies' (so adequately treated in 'Lady Barbarina' and 'A London Life') step on to the carpets laid down for 'the footfall of the issuing if not the entering reveller' were groups of ragged children holding smaller sisters or brothers. As James observed 'these pathetic little gazing groups', who were 'by no means all children, but the lean mature also', he commented with characteristic – almost Swiftian – irony: 'They who dine only occasionally or never at all have plenty of time to contemplate those with whom the custom has more amplitude'.

A sociologist could not have written more poignantly than James of the children in 'a grim-looking charitable' workhouse in the North of England. He was reminded of 'the early pages of "Oliver Twist" ' as he watched the hundred and fifty little children march in to gaze at a Christmas tree which had been donated by a Lady Bountiful.

> They filed up and received their little offerings, and then they compressed themselves into a tight infantine bunch and, lifting up their small hoarse voices, directed a melancholy hymn toward their benefactress.[11]

The scene in 'the dying wintry light in the big bare, stale room' was a 'curious mixture of poetry and sordid prose' which James could not forget. Nor did he forget any of the 'great plump flourishing uglinesses' which offered 'themselves irresistibly as pin-cushions to criticism and irony'.[12] He thought Millbank Prison 'a worse act of violence than any it was erected to punish' and Charing Cross Station placed where it was 'a national crime'.

James had observed at Chester 'the steady rumble of that deep keynote of English manners . . . the economic struggle for existence', and on more than one occasion he gave his 'fictive' blessing to the struggle of the 'lower classes'. He was glad to see that the business depression of 1879, which had brought 'distress among the lower classes', also had 'its cheerful side'. The labourers had at least risen 'to the recreation of a strike'. He was also pleased to see that the *Daily News* had sent a correspondent to the great industrial regions in the North, and as a result every morning for three weeks 'the misery of certain parts of Yorkshire and Lancashire' was 'served up with the matutinal tea and toast'. He applauded this effort; he thought it 'eminently worth doing', for it appeared 'to have had a visible effect upon the purse-strings of the well-to-do'. Even though the suffering of the workers was being 'minimised by the gigantic poor-relief system . . . so characteristic a feature of English civilisation and . . . by private charity proportionately huge', James did not quite approve of England's 'science of distributing charity' and concluded: 'Truly there are aspects of England at which one can but darkly stare.'

If James pointed out the 'deplorable' conditions in England, he also gave the reader the other side of the picture. If he saw the ugly, he also looked long enough to find redeeming features. James had a discriminating mind and he saw all round a subject; he saw a subject whole, or as he put it, 'many wholes'. He might praise a people or a country ,but in the next moment he would make a statement as scathingly derogatory as the first might have been eulogistic. London was 'a mighty ogress who devours human flesh', but the ogress was at least human. London took away reputations, but she also formed character. In his travel essays James made use of an imaginary conversation or an inanimate speaker (a book, a picture, a city) in order to give both sides of the coin. If he grew too eulogistic about London, the city itself admonished him: 'Do you really take me so seriously as that, you dear, devoted, voluntary dupe, and don't you know what an immeasurable humbug I am?' Being a 'London-lover' (though it was 'almost ridiculous to talk of her as a lover talks of his mistress')[13], James delighted in every egalitarian manifestation. He observed that Green Park 'in spite of its being in the royal and military quarter and close to all kinds of stateliness' was 'perhaps the most democratic corner of London'. And in spite of London's 'brutalities' a general equality prevailed. Poverty was 'certainly not considered' a disgrace in London; money, of course, was 'immensely an advantage' but that was 'a very different thing from a disqualification in the lack of it'.

England's treatment of political radicals was another example of this general equality. On the day the Queen opened Parliament, James had witnessed a demonstration in Trafalgar Square 'which might easily have given on the nerves of a sensitive police department'. But the English police were unperturbed; they allowed the demonstrators to 'sun themselves' freely. James was struck by 'the frank good sense and the frank good humour and even the frank good taste of it', as well as by

> the fact that the mighty mob could march along and do its errand while the excellent quiet policeman – eternal, imperturbable, positively lovable reminders of the national temperament – stood by simply to see that the channel was kept clear and comfortable.[14]

It was political revolutionaries like this 'mighty mob' – as well as those he had witnessed in France – that James was remembering when he wrote *The Princess Casamassima*.[15]

Political affairs had always interested Henry James. As Paris correspondent for the *New York Tribune*, he had discussed French politics; and later in his travel essays he frequently commented upon current political questions. He often discussed political problems in his letters, and once he apologised to Grace Norton for being 'so beastly political!'[16] In a letter to his family, he lamented that the Irish question was being handled without imagination and without adequate knowledge. He found it difficult to talk about the matter: 'partly because one is sick of it . . . and one is still more sick of all the vain words on the subject, without knowledge or thought, that fill the air here'. And then he added: 'I don't see how the management of their own affairs can be kept away from them –

or why it should.'[17] A visit to Ireland confirmed his belief in the efficacy of home rule.[18]

Although James's English travel essays are by no means political, they do – like his letters – contain references to political affairs; and they do reflect his personal opinions regarding certain national and international problems. James did not enter actively into politics,[19] yet he saw long before many politicians that Egypt and Russia were the most important questions on the political scene. Before the turn of the century, he saw 'the threat from the East', and he recognised earlier than some political leaders that the status of Egypt was not simply a Middle-East question. He was astounded that Mr Gladstone could not see that what was happening in the Nile Valley was of consequence to the western world. The Prime Minister's statement 'that England had much more urgent duties than the occupation of Egypt: she had to attend to the great questions of . . . local taxation and the liquor laws!' sounded 'almost squalid' to James. Although he wrote to Howells in 1876 that he did not 'share the Russian eagerness for war',[20] James soon found himself preferring war to the 'machinations of Russia'. And in 1877 he longed to see England 'hurling definace at her foes'. Later, in 1882, James was glad to see that England was once 'again counting for something in Europe' because of 'her little Egyptian victories'.

Perhaps it was because James saw 'the threat from the East' that he spoke again and again for the unity of English-speaking peoples.[21] In 1878 he expressed his disappointment that America was 'assisting at the political decadence of our mighty mother-land'.[22] He recognised that petty jealousies and rivalries among English-speaking peoples were a threat to the democratic way of life. His plea for unity was in no way chauvinistic, however. The Anglo-American world – a world of 'shared instincts and ideals' – stood for the sovereignty of the individual, for freedom to think and to choose, and James believed that those who shared these ideals should strengthen their bonds. When he pondered the 'rumour' of the fading Empire, or looked at the crowded conditions in England, he reflected 'with a sort of physical relief on Australia, Canada, India'. He felt sure that if the political structure of the Empire did change, the ideals of the Anglo-Saxon world would survive in another form. He would have approved of the Commonwealth of Nations which has replaced the Empire, but he would not have been surprised. James saw also that 'social fusion' was taking place and that the cosmopolite spirit was triumphing over national prejudices.[23] 'The consequence of the cosmopolite spirit', he explained, 'is to initiate you into the merits of all peoples . . . and to make downright preference really very hard'.[24] Indeed James was a cosmopolite of the highest order, and his objective, charitable spirit pervades his travel essays, which is part of their charm.

Always sensitive to change, James perceived as early as 1872 that the twentieth century would be more interested in scientific and mechanical achievements than in castles, cathedrals and ruins. He recognised that the digging of the St Gothard Tunnel through the Alps was the forerunner of the scientific age. He saw that Nature was being superseded, that

> she must be reckoning up the years which may elapse before the cleverest of Ober-Ingénieurs decides that mountains are altogether superfluous, and has the Jungfrau melted down and the residuum carried away in balloons and dumped upon another planet.[25]

The Jungfrau still stands, but in the middle of the twentieth century we are blasting down mountains and trying to reach another planet. James realised as well that the world was becoming more materialistic and that the 'business man' would become 'the typical American figure' for the novelist and dramatist of the new age.[26] Not only did James see this type evolving as the chief literary protagonist, but he sketched the prototype of 'The Man in the Grey Flannel Suit' as early as 1878 in *An International Episode*. His analysis of the type in *The American Scene* (1907) has yet to be surpassed. Few things in the 1950's would have surprised Henry James, whether literary, social, economic or political. He foresaw fifty years ago that eventually Europe would have to deal with America: 'The painter of manners who neglects America is not thereby incomplete as yet; but a hundred years hence – fifty years perhaps – he will doubtless be accounted so.'[27] And James saw long before the advent of jet planes and space ships that the globe 'was fast shrinking . . . to the size of an orange'.[28] He did not, of course, use his travel writings either to instruct or to prophesy, but he did as a serious thinker discern the full import of whatever passed before his observing eyes.

James's travel sketches show us a mind perceptive and prophetic, analytical and æsthetic, tolerant and sympathetic; they show us James the observer and likewise the participant. And indeed he was more of the latter than is sometimes thought. His life in London was a round of 'parties, exhibitions, concerts, "private views", meetings . . . solitudes'. He complained that he 'knew too many people' and that he had 'gone in too much for society'. He was apologetic that he had dined out 107 times in one season. He spent endless hours attending the theatre or strolling through museums. He recommended that a traveller include the theatre in his itinerary, not only for the pleasure [29] he might derive from the dramatic form ('the ripest of all the arts') but also in order to observe the manners of a people.

> . . . They [theatres] offer him a great deal of interesting evidence upon the manners and customs of the people among whom he has come to dwell. They testify to the civilisation around him, and throw a great deal of light upon the ways of thinking, feeling, and behaving of the community.[30]

For the same reason James advised the traveller to visit England during the 'Picture Season'. English art, like the theatre, revealed the English mind, and the 'visitor from another country' would find in the numerous exhibitions something more than the merit of the art; equally important was 'the evidence they should offer as to the English mind and character – the English way of thinking and feeling about all things, art included'.[31] Such evidence he found in Gainsborough's 'Miss Boothby', which was 'rich with the morality of all the English nurseries'.[32]

In addition to the many hours James spent at the theatre and in galleries and museums, he also found time to see most of the 'regular prescribed' sights. Few travellers have been as energetic; yet he was often in pain.[33] From the start James had known that a novelist must pluck his material 'in the garden of life'; material grown elsewhere would be 'stale and uneatable'; and from his first visit to Europe until his last 'excursion' James 'looked at history . . . at society, manners, types, characters, possibilities and prodgies and mysteries of fifty sorts'.[34] The material he plucked while travelling accounts in a large measure for the 'air of reality' in James's fiction.[35] His American characters enjoy the moonlight as much as he; they go in search of castles and ruins; they look for ghosts; they wander through museums and analyse works of art; they attend the theatre and the opera; they comment upon the beauty of landscapes; they pause for meditation in churches and cathedrals; they visit most of the sights prescribed in guidebooks; and, like their author, they have a predilection for the picturesque and the 'mementoes and reverberations of greatness' to be found in Europe. A 'story-seeker' from the beginning, James always hoped that 'the object, the place, the person, the unreduced impression . . . should give out . . . something of a situation';[36] and indeed his observations gave out many situations. He was able to make something of his 'very own with them' all his life.

Certainly travel was basic to the writings of Henry James, and surely no writer ever served a more profitable apprenticeship than James in writing his travel sketches. He began in the literary tradition of Laurence Sterne's *Sentimental Journey Through France and Italy* (1768), but he finished by writing impressionistic sketches in the tradition of the French painters.[37] The 'very Gallic element' which James admired in the work of George Du Maurier, 'his fineness of perception, his remarkable power of specifying types, his taste, his grace, his lightness, a certain refinement of art,'[38] likewise characterises his own work. He had learned from La Farge 'that the arts were after all essentially one';[39] and even though he put down the brush in favour of the pen, he continued to be a painter in prose. He had always felt that 'the picture was still after all in essence one's aim'.[40] If we take the 'backward reach' to the early American sketches and come forward to *English Hours*, the 'picture' composes into a singularly beautiful one with green, yellow, sapphire blue, and the silvery grey of moonlight as background colours; and in the foreground the bright reds and blues of flowers, vestments, military uniforms, and peasant's rags, as well as the dull, musty 'unpolished silver' of old ruins. Some of the incidents James observed also compose into individual pictures 'with a magic for which the landscape painters have no corresponding art'. His visit to a little churchyard in Warwickshire was such an incident:

the sweetest evening stillness hung over the place, and the sunset was red behind a dark row of rook-haunted elms. The stillness seemed the greater because three or four rustic children were playing, with little soft cries, among the crooked, deep-buried grave-stones. One poor little girl, who seemed deformed, had climbed some steps that served as a pedestal for a tall, medieval-looking cross. She sat perched there and stared at me through the gloaming.[41]


## V


When James compiled *English Hours* in 1905, it became the fifth volume of his travel writings;[1] all except two of the essays had appeared earlier in *Transatlantic Sketches*, *Portraits of Places*, and *Essays in London and Elsewhere*. That James considered his travel essays significant literary pieces is evident by the time and patience he expended in writing them and by his careful and rather extensive revision of most of them for publication in book form. Whenever an essay appeared in book form for a second time, he usually made additional revisions. James seemed always to think of a better way, or a more precise way, of saying a thing. He was constantly revising and polishing his literary creations, and his travel essays were no exception.[2] As he reviewed his English travel sketches for inclusion in *English Hours*, he found several words and phrases 'susceptible of a better turn'. No longer a sentimental tourist, and aware of the changing taste of the twentieth century,[3] James deleted as often as possible the words 'picturesque' (which sometimes had appeared three or four times on a page), 'sentimental', 'beautiful', 'pretty', and 'delicious'. The passionate pilgrim of 1872 had quoted passages from Tennyson's 'Idylls of the King'; but the mature resident of 1905 deleted the quotation, and wrote instead that Lynton 'prompted one . . . to respouting, for sympathy and relief, some idyllic Tennysonian line that haunted one's destitute past and that seemed to speak of the conditions in spite of being false to them geographically'. The mature resident's love for England was likewise less passionate; yet in spite of much that he deplored, his admiration was more soundly based. It was with conviction that he changed the earlier 'our incomparable English speech' to 'our consecrated English speech'.

The revisions of the travel sketches reflect the same development in James's maturing style that is evident in his fiction. The composition, mood and tone of the early sketches of 1870–1875 are those of 'The Passionate Pilgrim', 'Travelling Companions' and *Roderick Hudson*. The emphasis in *Transatlantic Sketches* (1875) is upon detailed, factual information, particularly of landscapes, architecture and paintings; but the sketches of the next decade are less documentary. The mood and tone have changed, and the emphasis has shifted to the human scene and to the moral import of manners and customs. The essays in *Portraits of Places* (1883) have the ease and grace of James's 'middle period' from *The American* to *The Portrait of a Lady*. The sketches revised or written during the late 1880's and after 1900 are even more analytical, more philosophical, and they are replete with elaborate metaphors, intricate sentences,[4] and abundant punctuation so characteristic of James's 'mature' or 'later manner'. They are akin to *The Tragic Muse* and *The Golden Bowl*. The late revisions were in the interest of objectivity; the personal 'I' became 'we', and a particularly personal viewpoint was restated in general terms. Had James completed the projected two volume 'romantical-psychological-pictorial "social" ' *London Town*[5] (for which he began taking notes in 1905 just after seeing *English Hours* through the press), the style would no doubt have been as impressionistic, and perhaps as poetic, as *The American Scene* (1907) and *Italian Hours* (1909).[6] James's travel writings are an integral part of his total literary output;[7] they manifest the same changes in style as his letters, reviews, criticisms and fiction;[8] and they bear the same relation to his early fiction as the *Notebooks* to his later fiction. When James ceased to write travel sketches, he began to keep a fuller, more systematic notebook.

That James, the 'master', the celebrity so devoted to the 'art' of writing, so concerned with the moral view of life, should take time from his fiction and his autobiographical writings during his mature period to collect and revise his French and English sketches and to revise and enlarge his Italian sketches,[9] as well as to write the thoughtful, prophetic *American Scene*, is a tribute to his respect for the travel sketch and his love of 'the sweet mysteries of travel'.

## VI

Using his own experiences and observations, James began early to contrast the America he knew with the Europe of his travels. In his letters, his travel essays, his journalistic jottings, his novels and tales he set forth the sensitive American's reaction to the historical richness of older civilisations.[1] Europe held the roots of American culture, and James realised long before many of his countrymen that America must deal with Europe; it was part of the 'complex fate' of being an American.[2] He accepted the responsibility of interpreting Europe to America – occasionally the other way around – as a 'terrible burden', and he thought it a bit 'hard' that he felt compelled to do so 'whereas no European is obliged to deal in the least with America'.[3] But being an American permitted James the traveller, the observer, the brooding analyst to see Europe objectively. Throughout his travel sketches his contrasts of nationalities, whether of face, figure, customs or habits, and his philosophical musings are remarkably objective. And seeing Europe objectively enabled him to see America objectively. He felt sure that he had looked at America 'as Europe itself might be conceived so to look',[4] and he had tried to write so that the reader would not know whether he was an American or an Englishman.[5] By bringing his protagonists to Europe and contrasting them with Europeans, he was able in his fiction to present in 'bas relief' the moral quality which he considered inherent in the American character.[6] No American writer – not Mark Twain nor Walt Whitman – has written more candidly yet more praiseworthily of the American, 'the heir of all the ages', than Henry James.

Like their author, James's Americans long to live a full life; they have vitality, an insatiable curiosity, a keenness of perception; they are intellectually aware; they are naïve[7] and romantic; they are open-minded and warm-hearted. The qualities James found 'beguilingly American' belong as well to himself and his American protagonists: 'intrinsically and actively ample' with 'a mind incapable of the shut door in any direction'.[8] Some Americans in James's own day and since have decried his decision to live abroad as un-American,[9] but the very reverse is true. To such charges, James replied: 'I know what I am about, and I have always my eyes on my native land.'[10] He believed that 'one's supreme relation... was one's relation to one's country'. But by living and writing in Europe, James was able to extract the very essence of Americanism and 'throw it off in words'. From a distance he could see so much more clearly what it meant to be an American, and one could serve America best in the light of that knowledge. He was not one of his Europeanised Americans; he always insisted that Americans living abroad should 'be themselves'. He urged James Russell Lowell to return to London in order that he might continue his task of bettering Anglo-American relations, for that was the only way he could 'be a good American'. He explained: 'You can't look after it there: that is the function of an Englishman – and if *you* do it there they will call you one.'[11] Living in England gave James a broader view of the kind of democracy for which the Anglo-American world stood, a democracy which insisted upon 'the air of liberty to care for the things of the mind'. James's own Irish-Scots-English background[12] led him naturally to proclaim the ideals of the English-speaking world, but he knew that other Americans might have other visions. He was never doctrinaire; he never insisted upon his own viewpoint. But Henry James exercised his 'inalienable right', his democratic right, to speak for the way of life which he felt would preserve the freedom and dignity of the individual, the sort of dignity to which his heroes and heroines so adequately attest.

James emphasised that a writer of fiction should answer the question, 'How does he feel about life? What, in the last analysis, is his philosophy?' The reader in turn should find in a writer's mature work an exposition of his 'total view of the world' that he has been 'so actively observing'.[13] Certainly in his travel writings and in his fiction James set forth his 'total view' of the world; his devotion to his art,[14] his belief in the sanctity of the individual, his interest in Anglo-American unity,[15] his pride in the American character, his faith in the civilising influence of the fine arts, and his love of travel. For his contribution to the literary world, James received an honorary degree from Harvard in 1911 and another from Oxford in 1912; and in 1916 England bestowed upon him the Order of Merit, not only for his contribution to literature but also for his dedicated service in the cause of democracy during World War I.[16] Indeed, Henry James, the American, was 'all the while' a great ambassador both as a literary man and as an individual, and during his last days he was very close to the American Embassy in London. His decision to become a British subject[17] was the supreme example of what meant morally and spiritually to be an American. He took the step which he thought 'morally' to be right, and he proclaimed the American doctrine of spiritual freedom.[18]

England was America's literary heritage, and to James it was literature come to life. With his prolific pen he broadened that literature with numerous sketches and tales of the American in England – occasionally the other way around – and in the end he himself was literature come to life. He was Newman and Strether, the American and the Ambassador, an individual as 'finely aware' and 'richly responsible' as his protagonists.[19] He was likewise the 'sentimental tourist' and the 'analytical observer', and nowhere is James the American more intimately revealed than in his travel writings. Nowhere is his American idealism with its roots in British soil more evident than in *English Hours*.

ALMA LOUISE LOWE

Houston, Texas
*December* 1959

*Tower Bridge in the fog*

# London

## I

There is a certain evening that I count as virtually a first impression – the end of a wet, black Sunday, twenty years ago, about the first of March. There had been an earlier vision, but it had turned to grey, like faded ink, and the occasion I speak of was a fresh beginning.[1] No doubt I had mystic prescience of how fond of the murky modern Babylon I was one day to become; certain it is that as I look back I find every small circumstance of those hours of approach and arrival still as vivid as if the solemnity of an opening era had breathed upon it. The sense of approach was already almost intolerably strong at Liverpool, where, as I remember, the perception of the English character of everything was as acute as a surprise, though it could only be a surprise without a shock. It was expectation exquisitely gratified, superabundantly confirmed. There was a kind of wonder, indeed, that England should be as English as, for my entertainment, she took the trouble to be; but the wonder would have been greater, and all the pleasure absent, if the sensation had not been violent. It seems to sit there again like a visiting presence, as it sat opposite to me at breakfast at a small table in a window of the old coffee-room of the Adelphi Hotel – the unextended (as it then was), the unimproved, the unblushingly local Adelphi. Liverpool is not a romantic city, but that smoky Saturday returns to me as a supreme success, measured by its association with the kind of emotion in the hope of which, for the most part, we betake ourselves to far countries.

It assumed this character at an early hour – or rather, indeed, twenty-four hours before – with the sight, as one looked across the wintry ocean, of the strange, dark, lonely freshness of the coast of Ireland. Better still, before we could come up to the city, were the black steamers knocking about in the yellow Mersey, under a sky so low that they seemed to touch it with their funnels, and in the thickest, windiest light. Spring was already in the air, in the town; there was no rain, but there was still less sun – one wondered what had become, on this side of the world, of the big white splotch in the heavens; and the grey mildness, shading away into black at every pretext, appeared in itself a promise. This was how it hung about me, between the window and the fire, in the coffee-room of the hotel – late in the morning for breakfast, as we had been long disembarking. The other passengers had dispersed, knowingly catching trains for London (we had only been a handful); I had the place to myself, and I felt as if I had an exclusive property in the impression. I prolonged it, I sacrificed to it, and it is perfectly recoverable now, with the very taste of the national muffin, the creak of the waiter's shoes as he came and went (could anything be so English as his intensely professional back? it revealed a country of tradition), and the rustle of the newspaper I was too excited to read.

I continued to sacrifice for the rest of the day; it didn't seem to me a sentient thing, as yet, to inquire into the means of getting away. My curiosity must indeed have languished, for I found myself on the morrow in the slowest of Sunday trains, pottering up to London with an interruptedness which might have been tedious without the conversation of an old gentleman who shared the carriage with me, and to whom my alien as well as comparatively youthful character had betrayed itself. He instructed me as to the sights of London, and impressed upon me that

*Lavender Hill, Battersea:* '*So many rows of coal-scuttles*'

nothing was more worthy of my attention than the great cathedral of St Paul.[2] 'Have you seen St Peter's in Rome? St Peter's is more highly embellished, you know; but you may depend upon it that St Paul's is the better building of the two.'[3] The impression I began with speaking of was, strictly, that of the drive from Euston, after dark, to Morley's Hotel in Trafalgar Square. It was not lovely – it was in fact rather horrible; but as I move again through dusky, tortuous miles, in the greasy four-wheeler to which my luggage had compelled me to commit myself, I recognise the first step in an initiation of which the subsequent stages were to abound in pleasant things. It is a kind of humiliation in a great city not to know where you are going, and Morley's Hotel was then, to my imagination, only a vague ruddy spot in the general immensity. The immensity was the great fact, and that was a charm; the miles of house-tops and viaducts, the complication of junctions and signals through which the train made its way to the station had already given me the scale. The weather had turned to wet, and we went deeper and deeper into the Sunday night. The sheep in the fields, on the way from Liverpool, had shown in their demeanour a certain consciousness of the day; but this momentous cab-drive was an introduction to the rigidities of custom. The low black houses were as inanimate as so many rows of coal-scuttles, save where at frequent corners, from a gin-shop, there was a flare of light more brutal still than the darkness. The custom of gin – that was equally rigid, and in this first impression the public-houses counted or much.

Morley's Hotel proved indeed to be a ruddy spot; brilliant, in my recollection, is the coffee-room fire, the hospitable mahogany, the sense that in the stupendous city this, at any rate for the hour, was a shelter and a point of view. My remembrance of the rest of the evening – I was probably very tired – is mainly a remembrance of a vast four-poster. My little bedroom-candle, set in its deep basin, caused this monument to project a huge shadow and to make me think, I scarce knew why, of 'The Ingoldsby Legends'. If at a tolerably early hour the next day I found myself approaching St Paul's, it was not wholly in obedience to the old gentleman in the railway-carriage: I had an errand in the City, and the City was doubtless prodigious. But what I mainly recall is the romantic consciousness of passing under the Temple Bar, and the way two lines of 'Henry Esmond' repeated themselves in my mind as I drew near the masterpiece of Sir Christopher Wren. 'The stout, red-faced woman' whom Esmond had seen tearing after the staghounds over the slopes at Windsor was not a bit like the effigy 'which turns its stony back upon St Paul's and faces the coaches struggling up Ludgate Hill'. As I looked at Queen Anne over the apron of my hansom – she struck me as very small and dirty, and the vehicle ascended the mild incline without an effort – it was a thrilling thought that the statue had been familiar to the hero of the incomparable novel. All history appeared to live again, and the continuity of things to vibrate through my mind.

To this hour, as I pass along the Strand, I take again the walk I took there that afternoon. I love the place today, and that was the commence-ment of my passion. It appeared to me to present phenomena, and to contain objects of every kind, of an inexhaustible interest; in particular it struck me as desirable and even indispensable that I should purchase most of the articles in most of the shops. My eyes rest with a certain tenderness

4

*St Paul's Cathedral*

on the places where I resisted and on those where I succumbed. The fragrance of Mr Rimmel's establishment is again in my nostrils; I see the slim young lady (I hear her pronunciation) who waited upon me there. Sacred to me today is the particular aroma of the hair-wash that I bought of her. I pause before the granite portico of Exeter Hall (it was unexpectedly narrow and wedge-like), and it evokes a cloud of associations which are none the less impressive because they are vague; coming from I don't know where – from *Punch*, from Thackeray, from volumes of the *Illustrated London News* turned over in childhood; seeming connected with Mrs Beecher Stowe and 'Uncle Tom's Cabin'. Memorable is a rush I made into a glover's at Charing Cross – the one you pass, going eastward, just before you turn into the station; that, however, now that I think of it, must have been in the morning, as soon as I issued from the

5

hotel. Keen within me was a sense of the importance of deflowering, of despoiling the shop.

A day or two later, in the afternoon, I found myself staring at my fire, in a lodging of which I had taken possession on foreseeing that I should spend some weeks in London. I had just come in, and, having attended to the distribution of my luggage, sat down to consider my habitation. It was on the ground floor, and the fading daylight reached it in a sadly damaged condition. It struck me as stuffy and unsocial, with its mouldy smell and its decoration of lithographs and wax-flowers – an impersonal black hole in the huge general blackness. The uproar of Piccadilly hummed away at the end of the street, and the rattle of a heartless hansom passed close to my ears. A sudden horror of the whole place came over me, like a tiger-pounce of homesickness which had been watching its moment.[4] London was hideous, vicious, cruel, and above all overwhelming; whether or no she was 'careful of the type', she was as indifferent as Nature herself to the single life. In the course of an hour I should have to go out to my dinner, which was not supplied on the premises, and that effort assumed the form of a desperate and dangerous quest. It appeared to me that I would rather remain dinnerless, would rather even starve, than sally forth into the infernal town, where the natural fate of an obscure stranger would be to be trampled to death in Piccadilly and have his carcass thrown into the Thames. I did not starve, however, and I eventually attached myself by a hundred human links to the dreadful, delightful city. That momentary vision of its smeared face and stony heart has remained memorable to me, but I am happy to say that I can easily summon up others.

## II

It is, no doubt, not the taste of every one, but for the real London-lover the mere immensity of the place is a large part of its savour. A small London would be an abomination, as it fortunately is an impossibility, for the idea and the name are beyond everything an expression of extent and number. Practically, of course, one lives in a quarter, in a plot; but in imagination and by a constant mental act of reference the accommodated haunter enjoys the whole – and it is only of him that I deem it worth while to speak. He fancies himself, as they say, for being a particle in so unequalled an aggregation; and its immeasurable circumference, even though unvisited and lost in smoke, gives him the sense of a social, an intellectual margin. There is a luxury in the knowledge that he may come and go without being noticed, even when his comings and goings have no nefarious end. I don't mean by this that the tongue of London is not a very active member; the tongue of London would indeed be worthy of a chapter by itself. But the eyes which at least in some measure feed its activity are fortunately for the common advantage solicited at any moment by a thousand different objects. If the place is big, everything it contains is certainly not so; but this may at least be said, that if small questions play a part there, they play it without illusions about its importance. There are too many questions, small or great; and each day, as it arrives, leads its children, like a kind of mendicant mother, by the hand. Therefore perhaps the most general characteristic is the absence of insistence. Habits and inclinations flourish and fall, but intensity is never one of them. The spirit of the great city is not analytic and, as they come up, subjects rarely receive at its hands a treatment drearily earnest or tastelessly thorough. There are not many – of those of which London disposes with the assurance begotten of its large experience – that wouldn't lend themselves to a tenderer manipulation elsewhere. It takes a very great affair, a turn of the Irish screw or a divorce case lasting many days, to be fully threshed out. The mind of Mayfair, when it aspires to show what it really can do, lives in the hope of a new divorce case, and an indulgent providence – London is positively in certain ways the spoiled child of the world – abundantly recognises this particular apititude and humours the whim.

The compensation is that material does arise; that there is a great variety, if not morbid subtlety; and that the whole of the procession of events and topics passes across your stage. For the moment I am speaking of the inspiration there may be in the sense of far frontiers; the London-lover loses himself in this swelling consciousness, delights in the idea that the town which encloses him is after all only a paved country, a state by itself. This is his condition of mind quite as much if he be an adoptive as if he be a matter-of-course son. I am by no means sure even that he need be of Anglo-Saxon race and have inherited the birthright of English speech; though, on the other hand, I make no doubt that these advantages minister greatly to closeness of allegiance. The great city spreads her dusky mantle over innumerable races and creeds, and I believe there is scarcely a known form of worship that has not some temple there (have I not attended at the Church of Humanity, in Lamb's Conduit, in company with an American lady, a vague old gentleman, and several seamstresses?) or any communion of men that has not some club or guild. London is indeed an epitome of the round world, and just as it is a commonplace to say that there is nothing one can't 'get' there, so it is equally true that there is nothing one may not study at first hand.

One doesn't test these truths every day, but they form part of the air one breathes (and welcome, says the London-hater – for there be such perverse reasoners – to the pestilent compound). They colour the thick, dim distances which in my opinion are the most romantic town-vistas in the world; they mingle with the troubled light to which the straight, ungarnished aperture in one's dull, undistinctive housefront affords a passage and which makes an interior of friendly corners, mysterious tones and unbetrayed ingenuities, as well as with the low, magnificent medium of the sky, where the smoke and fog and the weather in general, the strangely undefined hour of the day and season of the year, the emanations of industries and the reflection of furnaces, the red gleams and blurs that may or may not be of sunset – as you never see any *source* of radiance you can't in the least tell – all hang together in a confusion, a complication, a shifting but irremovable canopy. They form the undertone of the deep, perpetual voice of the place. One remembers them when one's loyalty is on the defensive; when it is a question of introducing as many striking features as possible into the list of fine reasons one has sometimes to draw up, that eloquent catalogue with which one confronts the hostile indictment – the array of *other* reasons which may easily be as long as one's arm. According to these other reasons it plausibly and conclusively stands that, as a place to be happy in, London will never do. I don't say it is necessary to meet so absurd an allegation except for one's

8

personal complacency. If indifference, in so gorged an organism, is still livelier than curiosity, you may avail yourself of your own share in it simply to feel that since such and such a person doesn't care for real richness, so much the worse for such and such a person. But once in a while the best believer recognises the impulse to set his religion in order, to sweep the temple of his thoughts and trim the sacred lamp. It is at such hours as this that he reflects with elation that the British capital is the particular spot in the world which communicates the greatest sense of life.

### III

The reader will perceive that I do not shrink even from the extreme concession of speaking of our capital as British, and this in a shameless connection with the question of loyalty on the part of an adoptive son. For I hasten to explain that if half the source of one's interest in it comes from feeling that it is the property and even the home of the human race – Hawthorne,[5] that best of Americans, says so somewhere, and places it in this sense side by side with Rome – one's appreciation of it is really a large sympathy, a comprehensive love of humanity. For the sake of such a charity as this one may stretch one's allegiance; and the most alien of the cockneyfied, though he may bristle with every protest at the intimation that England has set its stamp upon him, is free to admit with conscious pride that he has submitted to Londonisation. It is a real stroke of luck for a particular country that the capital of the human race happens to be British. Surely every other people would have it theirs if they could. Whether the English deserve to hold it any longer might be an interesting field of inquiry; but as they have not yet let it slip, the writer of these lines professes without scruple that the arrangement is to his personal taste. For, after all, if the sense of life is greatest there, it is a sense of the life of people of our consecrated English speech. It is the headquarters of that strangely elastic tongue; and I make this remark with a full sense of the terrible way in which the idiom is misused by the populace in general, than whom it has been given to few races to impart to conversation less of the charm of tone. For a man of letters who endeavours to cultivate, however modestly, the medium of Shakespeare and Milton, of Hawthorne and Emerson, who cherishes the notion of what it has achieved and what it may even yet achieve, London must ever have a great illustrative and suggestive value, and indeed a kind of sanctity. It is the single place in which most readers, most possible lovers, are gathered together; it is the most inclusive public and the largest social incarnation of the language, of the tradition. Such a personage may well let it go for this and leave the German and the Greek to speak for themselves, to express the grounds of *their* predilection, presumably very different.

When a social product is so vast and various it may be approached on a thousand different sides, and liked and disliked for a thousand different reasons. The reasons of Piccadilly are not those of Camden Town, nor are the curiosities and discouragements of Kilburn the same as those of Westminster and Lambeth. The reasons of Piccadilly – I mean the friendly ones – are those of which, as a general thing, the rooted visitor remains most conscious; but it must be confessed that even these, for the most part, do not lie upon the surface. The absence of style, or rather of the intention of style, is certainly the most general characteristic of the face of London. To cross to Paris under this impression is to find one's self surrounded with far other standards. There everything reminds you that the idea of beautiful and stately arrangement has never been out of fashion, that the art of composition has always been at work or at play. Avenues and squares, gardens and quays, have been distributed for effect, and today the splendid city reaps the accumulation of all this ingenuity. The result is not in every quarter interesting, and there is a tiresome monotony of the 'fine' and the symmetrical above all, of the deathly passion for making things 'to match'. On the other hand the whole air of the place is architectural. On the banks of the Thames it is a tremendous chapter of accidents – the London-lover has to confess to the existence of miles upon miles of the dreariest, stodgiest commonness. Thousands of acres are covered by low black houses of the cheapest construction, without ornament, without grace, without character or even identity. In fact there are many, even in the best quarters, in all the region of Mayfair and Belgravia, of so paltry and inconvenient, especially of so diminutive a type (those that are let in lodgings – such poor lodgings as they make – may serve as an example), that you wonder what peculiarly limited domestic need they were constructed to meet. The great misfortune of London to the eye (it is true that this remark applies much less to the City) is the want of elevation. There is no architectura impression without a certain degree of height, and the London street-vista has none of that sort of pride.

All the same, if there be not the intention, there is at least the accident, of style, which, if one looks at it in a friendly way, appears to proceed from three sources. One of these is simply the general greatness, and the manner in which that makes a difference for the better in any particular spot; so that, though you may often perceive yourself to be in a shabby corner, it never occurs to you that this is the end of it. Another is the atmosphere, with its magnificent mystifications, which flatters and superfuses, makes everything brown, rich, dim, vague, magnifies distances and minimises details, confirms the inference of vastness by suggesting that, as the great city makes everything, it makes its own system of weather and its own optical laws. The last is the congregation of the parks, which constitute an ornament not elsewhere to be matched and give the place a superiority that none of its uglinesses overcome. They spread themselves with such a luxury of space in the centre of the town that they form a part of the impression of any walk, of almost any view, and, with an audacity altogether their own, make a pastoral landscape under the smoky sky. There is no mood of the rich London climate that is not becoming to them – I have seen them look delightfully romantic, like parks in novels, in the wettest winter – and there is scarcely a mood of the appreciative resident to which they have not something to say. The high things of London, which here and there peep over them, only make the spaces vaster by reminding you that you are, after all, not in Kent or Yorkshire; and these things, whatever they be – rows of 'eligible' dwellings, towers of churches, domes of institutions – take such an effective grey-blue tint that a clever water-colourist would seem to have put them in for pictorial reasons.

The view from the bridge over the Serpentine has an extraordinary nobleness, and it has often seemed to me that the Londoner twitted with his low standard may point to it with every confidence. In all the town-scenery of Europe there can be few things so fine; the only reproach it is open to is that it begs the question by seeming – in spite of its being the pride of five millions of people – not to belong to a town at all. The towers of Notre Dame, as they rise in Paris from the island that divides the Seine, present themselves no more impressively than those of West-minster as you see them looking doubly far beyond the shining stretch of Hyde Park water. Equally delectable is the large river-like manner in which the Serpentine opens away between its wooded shores. Just after you have crossed the bridge (whose very banisters, old and ornamental, of yellowish-brown stone, I am particularly fond of), you enjoy on your left, through the gate of Kensington Gardens as you go towards Bays-water, an altogether enchanting vista – a footpath over the grass, which loses itself beneath the scattered oaks and elms exactly as if the place were a 'chase'. There could be nothing less like London in general than this particular morsel, and yet it takes London, of all cities, to give you such an impression of the country.

IV

It takes London to put you in the way of a purely rustic walk from Notting Hill to Whitehall. You may traverse this immense distance – a most comprehensive diagonal – altogether on soft, fine turf, amid the song of birds, the bleat of lambs, the ripple of ponds, the rustle of admir-able trees. Frequently have I wished that, for the sake of such a daily luxury and of exercise made romantic, I were a government clerk living, in snug domestic conditions, in a Pembridge villa – let me suppose – and having my matutinal desk in Westminster. I should turn into Kensington Gardens at their north-west limit, and I should have my choice of a hundred pleasant paths to the gates of Hyde Park. In Hyde Park I should follow the water-side, or the Row, or any other fancy of the occasion; liking best perhaps, after all, the Row in its morning mood, with the mist hanging over the dark red course, and the scattered early riders taking an identity as the soundless gallop brings them nearer. I am free to admit that in the Season, at the conventional hours, the Row becomes a weariness (save perhaps just for a glimpse once a year, to remind one's self how much it is like Du Maurier); the preoccupied citizen eschews it and leaves it for the most part to the gaping barbarian. I speak of it now from the point of view of the pedestrian; but for the rider as well it is at its best when he passes either too early or too late. Then, if he be not bent on comparing it to its disadvantage with the bluer and boskier alleys of the Bois de Boulogne, it will not be spoiled by the fact that, with its surface that looks like tan, its barriers like those of the ring on which the clown stands to hold up the hoop to the young lady, its empty benches and chairs, its occasional orange peel, its mounted policemen patrolling at intervals like expectant supernumeraries, it offers points of real contact with a circus whose lamps are out. The sky that bends over it is frequently not a bad imitation of the dingy tent of such an establishment. The ghosts of past cavalcades seem to haunt the foggy arena, and somehow they are better company than the mashers and elongated beauties of current seasons. It is not without interest to remember that most of the salient figures of English society during the present century – and English society means, or rather has hitherto meant, in a large degree English history – have bobbed in the saddle between Apsley House and Queen's Gate. You may call the roll if you care to, and the air will be thick with dumb voices and dead names, like that of some Roman amphitheatre.

It is doubtless a signal proof of being a London-lover *quand même* that one should undertake an apology for so bungled an attempt at a great public place as Hyde Park Corner, It is certain that the improvements and embellishments recently enacted there have only served to call further attention to the poverty of the elements, and to the fact that this poverty is terribly illustrative of general conditions. The place is the beating heart of the great West End, yet its main features are a shabby, stuccoed hospital, the low park-gates in their neat but unimposing frame, the drawing-room windows of Apsley House, and of the commonplace frontages on the little terrace beside it; to which must be added, of course, the only item in the whole prospect that is in the least monumental – the arch spanning the private road beside the gardens of Buckingham Palace. This structure is now bereaved of the rueful effigy which used to surmount it – the Iron Duke in the guise of a tin soldier – and has not been enriched by the transaction as much as might have been expected.* There is a fine view of Piccadilly and Knightsbridge, and of the noble mansions, as the house-agents call them, of Grosvenor Place, together with a sense of generous space beyond the vulgar little railing of the Green Park; but, except for the impression that there would be room for something better, there is nothing in all this that speaks to the imagination: almost as much as the grimy desert of Trafalgar Square the prospect conveys the idea of an opportunity wasted.

None the less has it on a fine day in spring an expressiveness of which I shall not pretend to explain the source further than by saying that the flood of life and luxury is immeasurably great there. The edifices are mean, but the social stream itself is monumental, and to an observer not purely stolid there is more excitement and suggestion than I can give a reason for in the long, distributed waves of traffic, with the steady policemen marking their rhythm, which roll together and apart for so many hours. Then the great dim city becomes bright and kind, the pall of smoke turns into a veil of haze carelessly worn, the air is coloured and almost scented by the presence of the biggest society in the world, and most of the things that meet the eye – or perhaps I should say more of them, for the most in London is, no doubt, ever the realm of the dingy – present themselves as 'well-appointed'. Everything shines more or less, from the window-panes to the dog-collars. So it all looks, with its myriad variations and qualifications, to one who surveys it over the apron of a hansom, while that vehicle of vantage, better than any box at the opera, spurts and slackens with the current.

It is not in a hansom, however, that we have figured our punctual young man, whom we must not desert as he fares to the south-east, and who has only to cross Hyde Park Corner to find his way all grassy again. I have a weakness for the convenient, familiar, treeless, or almost treeless, expanse of the Green Park, and the friendly part it plays as a kind of encouragement to Piccadilly. I am so fond of Piccadilly that I am grateful

* The monument in the middle of the square, with Sir Edgar Boehm's four fine soldiers, had not been set up when these words were written.

to any one or anything that does it a service, and nothing is more worthy of appreciation than the southward look it is permitted to enjoy just after it passes Devonshire House – a sweep of horizon which it would be difficult to match among other haunts of men, and thanks to which, of a

*Victoria Tower, Westminster Abbey and Central Hall from St James's Park*

summer's day, you may spy, beyond the browsed pastures of the fore-ground and middle distance, beyond the cold chimneys of Buckingham Palace and the towers of Westminster and the swarming river-side and all the southern parishes, the hard modern twinkle of the roof of the Crystal Palace.

If the Green Park is familiar, there is still less of the exclusive in its pendant, as one may call it – for it literally hangs from the other, down the hill – the remnant of the former garden of the queer, shabby old palace whose black, inelegant face stares up St James's Street. This popular resort has a great deal of character, but I am free to confess that much of its character comes from its nearness to the Westminster slums. It is a park of intimacy, and perhaps the most democratic corner of London, in spite of its being in the royal and military quarter and close to all kinds of stateliness. There are few hours of the day when a thousand smutty children are not sprawling over it, and the unemployed lie thick on the grass and cover the benches with a brotherhood of greasy corduroys. If the London parks are the drawing-rooms and clubs of the poor – that is, of those poor (I admit it cuts down the number) who live near enough to them to reach them – these particular grass-plots and alleys may be said to constitute the very *salon* of the slums.

I know not why, being such a region of greatness – great towers, great names, great memories; at the foot of the Abbey, the Parliament, the fine fragment of Whitehall, with the quarters of the sovereign right and left – but the edge of Westminster evokes as many associations of misery as of empire. The neighbourhood has been much purified of late, but it still contains a collection of specimens – though it is far from unique in this – of the low, black element. The air always seems to me heavy and thick, and here more than elsewhere one hears old England – the panting, smoke-stained Titan of Matthew Arnold's fine poem – draw her deep breath with effort. In fact one is nearer to her heroic lungs, if those organs are figured by the great pinnacled and fretted talking-house on the edge of the river. But this same dense and conscious air plays such everlasting tricks to the eye that the Foreign Office, as you see it from the bridge, often looks romantic, and the sheet of water it over-hangs poetic – suggests an Indian palace bathing its feet in the Ganges. If our pedestrian achieves such a comparison as this he has nothing left but to go on to his work – which he will find close at hand. He will have come the whole way from the far north-west on the green – which is what was to be demonstrated.

## V

I feel as if I were taking a tone almost of boastfulness, and no doubt the best way to consider the matter is simply to say – without going into the treachery of reasons – that, for one's self, one likes this part or the other. Yet this course would not be unattended with danger, inasmuch as at the end of a few such professions we might find ourselves committed to a tolerance of much that is deplorable. London is so clumsy and so brutal, and has gathered together so many of the darkest sides of life, that it is almost ridiculous to talk of her as a lover talks of his mistress, and almost frivolous to appear to ignore her disfigurements and cruelties. She is like a mighty ogress who devours human flesh; but to me it is a mitigating circumstance – though it may not seem so to every one – that the ogress herself is human. It is not in wantonness that she fills her maw, but to keep herself alive and do her tremendous work. She has no time for fine discriminations, but after all she is as good-natured as she is huge, and the more you stand up to her, as the phrase is, the better she takes the joke of it. It is mainly when you fall on your face before her that she gobbles you up. She heeds little what she takes, so long as she has her stint, and the smallest push to the right or the left will divert her wavering bulk from one form of prey to another. It is not to be denied that the heart tends to grow hard in her company; but she is a capital antidote to the morbid, and to live with her successfully is an education of the temper, a consecration of one's private philosophy. She gives one a surface for which in a rough world one can never be too thankful. She may take away reputations, but she forms character. She teaches her victims not to 'mind', and the great danger for them is perhaps that they shall learn the lesson too well.

It is sometimes a wonder to ascertain what they do mind, the best-seasoned of her children. Many of them assist, without winking, at the most unfathomable dramas, and the common speech of others denotes a familiarity with the horrible. It is her theory that she both produces and appreciates the exquisite; but if you catch her in flagrant repudiation of both responsibilities and confront her with the shortcoming, she gives you a look, with a shrug of her colossal shoulders, which establishes a private relation with you for evermore. She seems to say: 'Do you really take me so seriously as that, you dear, devoted, voluntary dupe, and don't you know what an immeasurable humbug I am?' You reply that you shall know it henceforth; but your tone is good-natured, with a touch of the cynicism that she herself has taught you; for you are aware that if she makes herself out better than she is, she also makes herself out much worse. She is immensely democratic, and that, no doubt, is part of the manner in which she is salutary to the individual; she teaches him his 'place' by an incomparable discipline, but deprives him of complaint by letting him see that she has exactly the same lash for every other back. When he has swallowed the lesson he may enjoy the rude but unfailing justice by which, under her eye, reputations and positions elsewhere esteemed great are reduced to the relative. There are so many reputations, so many positions, that supereminence breaks down, and it is difficult to be so rare that London can't match you. It is a part of her good-nature and one of her clumsy coquetries to pretend sometimes that she hasn't your equivalent, as when she takes it into her head to hunt the lion or form a ring round a celebrity. But this artifice is so very transparent that the lion must be very candid or the celebrity very obscure to be taken by it. The business is altogether subjective, as the philosophers say, and the great city is primarily looking after herself. Celebrities are convenient – they are one of the things that people are asked to 'meet' – and lion-cutlets, put upon ice, will nourish a family through periods of dearth.

This is what I mean by calling London democratic. You may be in it, of course, without being of it; but from the moment you *are* of it – and on this point your own sense will soon enough enlighten you – you belong to a body in which a general equality prevails. However exalted however able, however rich, however renowned you may be, there are too many people at least as much so for your own idiosyncrasies to count. I think it is only by being beautiful that you may really prevail very much; for the loveliness of woman it has long been noticeable that London will go most out of her way. It is when she hunts that particular lion that she becomes most dangerous; then there are really moments when you would believe, for all the world, that she is thinking of what she can give, not of what she can get. Lovely ladies, before this, have paid for believing it, and will continue to pay in days to come. On the whole the people who are least deceived are perhaps those who have permitted themselves to believe, in their own interest, that poverty is not a disgrace. It is certainly not considered so in London, and indeed you can scarcely say where – in virtue of diffusion – it would more naturally be exempt. The possession of money is, of course, immensely an advantage, but that is a very different thing from a disqualification in the lack of it.

Good-natured in so many things in spite of her cynical tongue, and easy-going in spite of her tremendous pace, there is nothing in which the large indulgence of the town is more shown than in the liberal way she looks at obligations of hospitality and the margin she allows in these and cognate matters. She wants above all to be amused; she keeps her books loosely, doesn't stand on small questions of a chop for a chop, and if there be any chance of people's proving a diversion, doesn't know or remember or care whether they have 'called'. She forgets even if she herself have called. In matters of ceremony she takes and gives a long rope, wasting no time in phrases and circumvallations. It is no doubt incontestable that one result of her inability to stand upon trifles and consider details is that she has been obliged in some ways to lower rather portentously the standard of her manners. She cultivates the abrupt – for even when she asks you to dine a month ahead the invitation goes off like the crack of a pistol – and approaches her ends not exactly *par quatre chemins*. She doesn't pretend to attach importance to the lesson conveyed in Matthew Arnold's poem of 'The Sick King in Bokhara', that,

> Though we snatch what we desire,
> We may not snatch it eagerly.

London snatches it more than eagerly if that be the only way she can get it. Good manners are a succession of details, and I don't mean to say that she doesn't attend to them when she has time. She has it, however, but seldom – *que voulez-vous?* Perhaps the matter of note-writing is as good an example as another of what certain of the elder traditions inevitably have become in her hands. She lives by notes – they are her very heart-beats; but those that bear her signatures are as disjointed as the ravings of delirium, and have nothing but a postage-stamp in common with the epistolary art.

## VI

If she doesn't go into particulars it may seem a very presumptuous act to have attempted to do so on her behalf, and the reader will doubtless think I have been punished by having egregiously failed in my enumeration. Indeed nothing could well be more difficult than to add up the items – the column would be altogether too long. One may have dreamed of turning the glow – if glow it be – of one's lantern on each successive facet of the jewel; but, after all, it may be success enough if a confusion of brightness be the result. One has not the alternative of speaking of London as a whole, for the simple reason that there is no such thing as the whole of it. It is immeasurable – embracing arms never meet. Rather it is a collection of many wholes, and of which of them is it most important to speak? Inevitably there must be a choice, and I know of none more scientific than simply to leave out what we may have to apologise for. The uglinesses, the 'rookeries', the brutalities, the night-aspect of many of the streets, the gin-shops and the hour when they are cleared out before closing – there are many elements of this kind which have to be counted out before a genial summary can be made.

And yet I should not go so far as to say that it is a condition of such geniality to close one eye's upon the immense misery; on the contrary, I think it is partly because we are irremediably conscious of that dark gulf that the most general appeal of the great city remains exactly what it is, the largest chapter of human accidents. I have no idea of what the future evolution of the strangely mingled monster may be; whether the poor will improve away the rich, or the rich will expropriate the poor, or they will all continue to dwell together on their present imperfect terms of intercourse. Certain it is, at any rate, that the impression of suffering is a part of the general vibration; it is one of the things that mingle with all the others to make the sound that is supremely dear to the consistent London-lover – the rumble of the tremendous human mill. This is the note which, in all its modulations, haunts and fascinates and inspires him. And whether or no he may succeed in keeping the misery out of the picture, he will freely confess that the latter is not spoiled for him by some of its duskiest shades. We are far from liking London well enough till we like its defects: the dense darkness of much of its winter, the soot on the chimney-pots and everywhere else, the early lamplight, the brown blur of the houses, the splashing of hansoms in Oxford Street or the Strand on December afternoons.

There is still something that recalls to me the enchantment of children – the anticipation of Christmas, the delight of a holiday walk – in the way the shop-fronts shine into the fog. It makes each of them seem a little world of light and warmth, and I can still waste time in looking at them with dirty Bloomsbury on one side and dirtier Soho on the other. There are winter effects, not intrinsically sweet, it would appear, which somehow, in absence, touch the chords of memory, and even the fount of tears; as for instance the front of the British Museum on a black afternoon, or the portico, when the weather is vile, of one of the big square clubs in Pall Mall.[6] I can give no adequate account of the subtle poetry of such reminiscences; it depends upon associations of which we have often lost the thread. The wide colonnade of the Museum, its symmetrical wings, the high iron fence in its granite setting, the sense of the misty halls within, where all the treasures lie – these things loom patiently through atmospheric layers which instead of making them dreary impart to them something of a cheer of red lights in a storm. I think the romance of a winter afternoon in London arises partly from the fact that, when it is not altogether smothered, the general lamplight takes this hue of hospitality. Such is the colour of the interior glow of the clubs in Pall Mall, which I positively like best when the fog loiters upon their monumental staircases.

In saying just now that these retreats may easily be, for the exile, part of the phantasmagoria of homesickness, I by no means alluded simply to their solemn outsides. If they are still more solemn within, that does not make them any less dear, in retrospect at least, to a visitor much bent upon liking his London to the end. What is the solemnity but a tribute to your nerves, and the stillness but a refined proof of the intensity of life? To produce such results as these the balance of many tastes must be struck, and that is only possible in a very high civilisation. If I seem to intimate that this last abstract term must be the cheer of him who has lonely possession of a foggy library, without even the excitement of watching for some one to put down the magazine he wants, I am willing to let the supposition pass, for the appreciation of a London club at one of the empty seasons is nothing but the strong expression of a preference for the great city – by no means so unsociable as it may superficially appear – at periods of relative abandonment. The London year is studded with holidays, blessed little islands of comparative leisure – intervals of absence for good society. Then the wonderful English faculty for 'going out of town for a little change' comes into illimitable play, and families transport their nurseries and their bath-tubs to those rural scenes which form the real substratum of the national life. Such moments as these are the paradise of the genuine London-lover, for he then finds himself face to face with the object of his passion: he can give himself up to an intercourse which at other times is obstructed by his rivals. Then every one he knows is out of town, and the exhilarating sense of the presence of every one he doesn't know becomes by so much the deeper.

This is why I pronounce his satisfaction not an unsociable, but a positively affectionate emotion. It is the mood in which he most measures the immense humanity of the place, and in which its limits recede furthest into a dimness peopled with possible illustrations. For his acquaintance, however numerous it may be, is finite; whereas the other, the unvisited London, is infinite. It is one of his pleasures to think of the experiments and excursions he may make in it, even when these adventures don't particularly come off. The friendly fog seems to protect and enrich them – to add both to the mystery and security, so that it is most in the winter months that the imagination weaves such delights. They reach their climax perhaps during the strictly social desolation of Christmas week, when the country-houses are crowded at the expense of the capital. Then it is that I am most haunted with the London of Dickens, feel most as if it were still recoverable, still exhaling its queerness in patches perceptible to the appreciative. Then the big fires blaze in the lone twilight of the clubs, and the new books on the tables say 'Now at last you have time to read me,' and the afternoon tea and toast, and the torpid old gentleman who wakes up from a doze to order potash-water, appear to make the assurance good. It is not a small matter either, to a man of letters, that this is the best time for writing, and that during the lamplit days the white page he tries to blacken becomes, on his table, in the circle of the lamp, with the screen of the climate folding him in, more vivid and absorbent. Those to whom it is forbidden to sit up to work in the small hours may, between November and March, enjoy a semblance of this luxury in the morning. The weather makes a kind of sedentary midnight and muffles the possible interruptions. It is bad for the eyesight, but excellent for the image.

## VII

Of course it is too much to say that all the satisfaction of life in London comes from literally living there, for it is not a paradox that a great deal of it consists in getting away. It is almost easier to leave it than not to, and much of its richness and interest proceeds from its ramifications, the fact that all England is in a suburban relation to it. Such an affair it is in comparison to get away from Paris or to get into it. London melts by wide, ugly zones into the green country, and becomes pretty insidiously, inadvertently – without stopping to change. It is the spoiling, perhaps, of the country, but it is making of the insatiable town, and if one is a helpless and shameless cockney that is all one is obliged to look at. Anything is excusable which enlarges one's civic consciousness. It ministers immensely to that of the London-lover that, thanks to the tremendous system of coming and going, to the active, hospitable habits of the people, to the elaboration of the railway-service, the frequency and rapidity of trains, and last, though not least, to the fact that much of the loveliest scenery in England lies within a radius of fifty miles – thanks to all this he has the rural picturesque at his door and may cultivate unlimited vagueness as to the line of division between centre and circumference. It is perfectly open to him to consider the remainder of the United Kingdom, or the British empire in general, or even, if he be an American, the total of the English-speaking territories of the globe, as the mere margin, the fitted girdle.

Is it for this reason – because I like to think how great we all are together in the light of heaven and the face of the rest of the world, with the bond of our glorious tongue, in which we labour to write articles and books for each other's candid perusal, how great we all are and how great is the great city which we may unite fraternally to regard as the capital of our race – is it for this that I have a singular kindness for the London railway stations, that I like them æsthetically, that they interest and fascinate me, and that I view them with complacency even when I wish neither to depart nor to arrive? They remind me of all our reciprocities and activities, our energies and curiosities, and our being all distinguished together from other people by our great common stamp of perpetual motion, our passion for seas and deserts and the other side of the globe, the secret of the impression of strength – I don't say of social roundness and finish – that we produce in any collection of Anglo-Saxon types. If

*Battersea: 'London melts by wide, ugly zones into the green country'*

in the beloved foggy season I delight in the spectacle of Paddington,[7] Euston or Waterloo – I confess I prefer the grave northern stations – I am prepared to defend myself against the charge of puerility; for what I seek and what I find in these vulgar scenes is at bottom simply so much evidence of our larger way of looking at life. The exhibition of variety of type is in general one of the bribes by which London induces you to condone her abominations, and the railway platform is a kind of compendium of that variety. I think that nowhere so much as in London do people wear – to the eye of observation – definite signs of the sort of people they may be. If you like above all things to know the sort, you hail this fact with joy; you recognise that if the English are immensely distinct from other people they are also socially – and that brings with it, in England, a train of moral and intellectual consequences – extremely distinct from each other. You may see them all together, with the rich colouring of their differences, in the fine flare of one of Mr W. H. Smith's bookstalls – a feature not to be omitted in any enumeration of the charms of Paddington and Euston. It is a focus of warmth and light in the vast smoky cavern; it gives the idea that literature is a thing of splendour, of a dazzling essence, of infinite gas-lit red and gold. A glamour hangs over the glittering booth, and a tantalising air of clever new things. How brilliant must the books all be, how veracious and courteous the fresh, pure journals! Of a Saturday afternoon, as you wait in your corner of the compartment for the starting of the train, the window makes a frame for the glowing picture. I say of a Saturday afternoon because that is the most characteristic time – it speaks most of the constant circulation and in particular of the quick jump, by express, just before dinner, for the Sunday, into the hall of the country-house and the forms of closer friendliness, the prolonged talks, the familiarising walks which London excludes.

There is the emptiness of summer as well, when you may have the town to yourself, and I would discourse of it – counting the summer from the first of August – were it not that I fear to seem ungracious in insisting so much on the negative phases. In truth they become positive in another manner, and I have an endearing recollection of certain happy accidents attached to the only period when London life may be said to admit of accident. It is the most luxurious existence in the world, but of that especial luxury – the unexpected, the extemporised – it has in general too little. In a very tight crowd you can't scratch your leg, and in London the social pressure is so great that it is difficult to deflect from the perpendicular or to move otherwise than with the mass. There is too little of the loose change of time; every half-hour has its preappointed use, written down month by month in a little book. As I intimated, however, the pages of this volume exhibit from August to November an attractive blankness; they represent the season during which you may taste of that highest kind of inspiration, the inspiration of the moment.

This is doubtless what a gentleman had in mind who once said to me, in regard to the vast resources of London and its having something for every taste: 'Oh, yes; when you are bored, or want a little change, you can take the boat down to Blackwall.' I have never had occasion yet to resort to this particular remedy. Perhaps it's a proof that I have never been bored. Why Blackwall? I indeed asked myself at the time; nor have I yet ascertained what distractions the mysterious name represents.

My interlocutor probably used it generically, as a free, comprehensive allusion to the charms of the river at large. Here the London-lover goes with him all the way, and indeed the Thames is altogether such a wonderful affair that he feels he has distributed his picture very clumsily not to have put it in the very forefront. Take it up or take it down, it is equally an adjunct of London life, an expression of London manners.

From Westminster to the sea its uses are commercial, but none the less pictorial for that; while in the other direction – taking it properly a little further up – they are personal, social, athletic, idyllic. In its recreative character it is absolutely unique. I know of no other classic stream that is so splashed about for the mere fun of it. There is something almost droll and at the same time almost touching in the way that on the smallest pretext of holiday or fine weather the mighty population takes to the boats. They bump each other in the narrow, charming channel; between Oxford and Richmond they make an uninterrupted procession. Nothing is more suggestive of the personal energy of the people and their eagerness to take, in the way of exercise and adventure, whatever they can get. I hasten to add that what they get on the Thames is exquisite, in spite of the smallness of the scale and the contrast between the numbers and the space. In a word, if the river is the busiest suburb of London it is also by far the prettiest. That term applies to it less, of course, from the bridges down, but it is only because in this part of its career it deserves a larger praise. To be consistent, I like it best when it is all dyed and disfigured with the town, and you look from bridge to bridge – they seem wonderfully big and dim – over the brown, greasy current, the barges and the penny-steamers, the black, sordid, heterogeneous shores. This prospect, of which so many of the elements are ignoble, etches itself to the eye of the lover of 'bits' with a power that is worthy perhaps of a better cause.

The way that with her magnificent opportunity London has neglected to achieve a river-front is, of course, the best possible proof that she has rarely, in the past, been in the architectural mood which at present shows somewhat inexpensive signs of settling upon her. Here and there a fine fragment apologies for the failure which it doesn't remedy. Somerset House stands up higher, perhaps, than anything else on its granite pedestal, and the palace of Westminster reclines – it can hardly be said to stand – on the big parliamentary bench of its terrace. The Embankment, which is admirable if not particularly interesting, does what it can, and the mannered houses of Chelsea stare across at Battersea Park like eighteenth-century ladies surveying a horrid wilderness. On the other hand, the Charing Cross railway station, placed where it is, is a national crime; Millbank prison is a worse act of violence than any it was erected to punish, and the water-side generally a shameless renunciation of effect. We acknowledge, however, that its very cynicism is expressive; so that if one were to choose again – short of there being a London Louvre – between the usual English irresponsibility in such matters and some particular flight of conscience, one would perhaps do as well to let the case stand. We know what it is, the stretch from Chelsea to Wapping, but we know not what it might be. It doesn't prevent my being always more or less thrilled, of a summer afternoon, by the journey on a penny steamer to Greenwich.

## VIII

But why do I talk of Greenwich and remind myself of one of the un-executed vignettes with which it had been my plan that these desultory and, I fear, somewhat incoherent remarks should be studded? They will present to the reader no vignettes but those which the artist[8] who has kindly consented to associate himself with my vagaries may be so good as to bestow upon them. Why should I speak of Hampstead, as the question of summer afternoons just threatened to lead me to do after I should have exhausted the subject of Greenwich, which I may not even touch? Why should I be so arbitrary when I have cheated myself out of the space privately intended for a series of vivid and ingenious sketches of the particular physiognomy of the respective quarters of the town? I had dreamed of doing them all, with their idiosyncrasies and the signs by which you shall know them. It is my pleasure to have learned these signs – a deeply interesting branch of observation – but I must renounce the display of my lore.

I have not the conscience to talk about Hampstead, and what a pleasant thing it is to ascend the long hill which overhangs, as it were, St John's Wood and begins at the Swiss Cottage – you must mount from there, it must be confessed, as you can – and pick up a friend at a house of friendship on the top, and stroll with him on the rusty Heath, and skirt the garden walls of the old square Georgian houses which survive from the time when, near as it is today to London, the place was a kind of provincial centre, with Joanna Baillie for its muse, and take the way by the Three Spaniards – I would never miss that – and look down at the smoky city or across at the Scotch firs and the red sunset. It would never do to make a tangent in that direction when I have left Kensington unsung and Bloomsbury unattempted and have said never a word about the mighty eastward region – the queer corners, the dark secrets, the rich survivals and mementoes of the City. I particularly regret having sacrificed Kensington, the once-delightful, the Thackerayan, with its literary vestiges, its quiet, pompous red palace, its square of Queen Anne, its house of Lady Castlewood, its Greyhound tavern, where Henry Esmond lodged.

But I can reconcile myself to this when I reflect that I have also sacrificed the Season, which doubtless, from an elegant point of view, ought to have been the central *morceau* in the panorama. I have noted that the London-lover loves everything in the place, but I have not cut myself off from saying that his sympathy has degrees, or from remarking that the sentiment of the author of these pages has never gone all the way with the dense movement of the British carnival. That is really the word for the period from Easter to midsummer; it is a fine, decorous, expensive, Protestant carnival, in which the masks are not of velvet or silk, but of wonderful deceptive flesh and blood, the material of the most beautiful complexions in the world. Holding that the great interest of London is the sense the place gives us of multitudinous life, it is doubtless an inconsequence not to care most for the phase of greatest intensity. But there is life and life, and the rush and crush of these weeks of fashion is after all but a tolerably mechanical expression of human forces. Nobody would deny that it is a more universal, brilliant, spectacular one than can be seen anywhere else; and it is not a defect that these forces often take the form of women extremely beautiful. I risk the declaration that the London season brings together year by year an unequalled collection of handsome persons. I say nothing of the ugly ones; beauty has at the best been allotted to a small minority, and it is never, at the most, anywhere, but a question of the number by which that minority is least insignificant.

There are moments when one can almost forgive the follies of June for the sake of the smile which the sceptical old city puts on for the time and which, as I noted in an earlier passage of this disquisition, fairly breaks into laughter where she is tickled by the vortex of Hyde Park Corner. Most perhaps does she seem to smile at the end of the summer days, when the light lingers and lingers, though the shadows lengthen and the mists redden and the belated riders, with dinners to dress for, hurry away from the trampled arena of the Park. The population at that hour surges mainly westward and sees the dust of the day's long racket turned into a dull golden haze. There is something that has doubtless often, at this particular moment, touched the fancy even of the bored and the *blasés* in such an emanation of hospitality, of waiting dinners, of the festal idea, of the whole spectacle of the West End preparing herself for an evening six parties deep. The scale on which she entertains is stupendous, and her invitations and 'reminders' are as thick as the leaves of the forest.

For half an hour, from eight to nine, every pair of wheels presents the portrait of a diner-out. To consider only the rattling hansoms, the white neckties and 'dressed' heads which greet you from over the apron in a quick, interminable succession, conveys the overwhelming impression of a complicated world. Who are they all, and where are they all going, and whence have they come, and what smoking kitchens and gaping portals and marshalled flunkeys are prepared to receive them, from the southernmost limits of a loosely interpreted, an almost transpontine Belgravia, to the hyperborean confines of St John's Wood? There are broughams standing at every door, and carpets laid down for the foot-fall of the issuing if not the entering reveller. The pavements are empty now, in the fading light, in the big sallow squares and the stuccoed streets of gentility, save for the groups of small children holding others that are smaller – Ameliar-Ann intrusted with Sarah Jane – who collect, wherever the strip of carpet lies, to see the fine ladies pass from the carriage or the house. The West End is dotted with these pathetic little gazing groups; it is the party of the poor – *their* Season and way of dining out, and a happy illustration of 'the sympathy that prevails between classes.' The watchers,[9] I should add, are by no means all children, but the lean mature also, and I am sure these wayside joys are one of the reasons of an inconvenience much deplored – the tendency of the country poor to flock to London. They who dine only occasionally or never at all have plenty of time to contemplate those with whom the custom has more amplitude. However, it was not my intention to conclude these remarks in a melancholy strain, and goodness knows that the diners are a prodigious company. It is as moralistic as I shall venture to be if I drop a very soft sigh on the paper as I confirm that truth. Are they all illuminated spirits and is their conversation the ripest in the world? This is not to be expected, nor should I ever suppose it to be desired that an agreeable society should fail to offer frequent opportunity for intellectual rest. Such a shortcoming is not one of the sins of the London world in general, nor would it be just to complain of that world, on any side, on grounds of deficiency. It is not what London fails to do that strikes the observer, but the general fact that she does everything in excess. Excess is her highest reproach, and it is her incurable misfortune that there is really too much of her. She overwhelms you by quantity and number – she ends by making human life, by making civilisation, appear cheap to you. Wherever you go, to parties, exhibitions, concerts, 'private views', meetings, solitudes, there are already more people than enough on the field. How it makes you understand the high walls with which so much of English life is surrounded, and the priceless blessing of a park in the country, where there is nothing animated but rabbits and pheasants and, for the worst, the importunate nightingales! And as the monster grows and grows for ever, she departs more and more – it must be acknowledged – from the ideal of a convenient society, a society in which intimacy is possible, in which the associated meet often and sound and select and measure and inspire each other, and relations and combinations have time to form themselves. The substitute for this, in London, is the momentary concussion of a million of atoms. It is the difference between seeing a great deal of a few and seeing a little of every one. 'When did you come – are you "going on"?' and it is over; there is no time even for the answer. This may seem a perfidious arraignment, and I should not make it were I not prepared, or rather were I not eager, to add two qualifications. One of these is that, cumbrously vast as the place may be, I would not have had it smaller by a hair's-breadth, or have missed one of the fine and fruitful impatiences with which it inspires you and which are at bottom a heartier tribute, I think, than any great city receives. The other is that out of its richness and its inexhaustible good humour it belies the next hour any generalisation you may have been so simple as to make about it.

First published in *The Century Magazine*, XXXVII (December 1888), 219–39, with thirteen illustrations by Joseph Pennell. The essay was revised for *Essays in London and Elsewhere* (1893), but reprinted without Pennell's drawings. The latter version became the first essay in *English Hours* (1905).

# Browning in Westminster Abbey

The lovers of a great poet are the people in the world who are most to be forgiven a little wanton fancy about him, for they have before them, in his genius and work, an irresistible example of the application of the imaginative method to a thousand subjects. Certainly, therefore, there are many confirmed admirers of Robert Browning[1] to whom it will not have failed to occur that the consignment of his ashes to the great temple of fame of the English race was exactly one of those occasions in which his own analytic spirit would have rejoiced, and his irrepressible faculty for looking at human events in all sorts of slanting coloured lights have found a signal opportunity. If he had been taken with it as a subject, if it had moved him to the confused yet comprehensive utterance of which he was the great professor, we can immediately guess at some of the sparks he would have scraped from it, guess how splendidly, in the case, the pictorial sense would have intertwined itself with the metaphysical. For such an occasion would have lacked, for the author of *The Ring and the Book*, none of the complexity and convertibility that were dear to him. Passion and ingenuity, irony and solemnity, the impressive and the unexpected, would each have forced their way through; in a word, the author would have been sure to take the special, circumstantial view (the inveterate mark of all his speculation) even of so foregone a conclusion as that England should pay her greatest honour to one of her greatest poets. As they stood in the Abbey, at any rate, on Tuesday last, those of his admirers and mourners who were disposed to profit by his warrant for inquiring curiously may well have let their fancy range, with its muffled step, in the direction which *his* fancy would probably not have shrunk from following, even perhaps to the dim corners where humour and the whimsical lurk. Only, we hasten to add, it would have taken Robert Browning himself to render the multifold impression.

One part of it on such occasion is, of course, irresistible – the sense that these honours are the greatest that a generous nation has to confer and that the emotion that accompanies them is one of the high moments of a nation's life. The attitude of the public, of the multitude, at such hours, is a great expansion, a great openness to ideas of aspiration and achievement; the pride of possession and of bestowal, especially in the case of a career so complete as Mr Browning's, is so present as to make regret a minor matter. We possess a great man most when we begin to look at him through the glass plate of death; and it is a simple truth, though containing an apparent contradiction, that the Abbey never takes us so benignantly as when we have a valued voice to commit to silence there. For the silence is articulate after all, and in worthy instances the preservation great. It is the other side of the question that would pull most the strings of irresponsible reflection – all those conceivable postulates and hypotheses of the poetic and satiric mind to which we owe the picture of how the bishop ordered his tomb in St Praxed's. Macaulay's 'temple of silence nad reconciliation' – and none the less perhaps because he himself is now a presence there – strikes us, as we stand in it, not only as local but as social – a sort of corporate company; so thick, under its high arches, its dim transepts, and chapels, is the population of its historic names and figures. They are a company in possession, with a high standard of distinction, of immortality, as it were; for there is something serenely inexpugnable even in the position of the interlopers. As they look out, in the rich dusk, from the cold eyes of statues and the careful identity of tablets, they seem, with their converging faces, to scrutinise decorously the claims of each new recumbent glory, to ask each other how he is to be judged as an accession. How difficult to banish the idea that Robert Browning would have enjoyed prefiguring and playing with the mystifications, the reservations, even perhaps the slight buzz of scandal, in the Poets' Corner, to which his own obsequies might give rise! Would not his great relish, in so characteristic an interview with his crucible, have been his perception of the bewildering modernness, to much of the society, of the new candidate for a niche? That is the interest and the fascination, from what may be termed the inside point of view, of Mr Browning's having received, in this direction of becoming a classic, the only official assistance that is ever conferred upon English writers.

It is as classics on one ground and another – some members of it perhaps on that of not being anything less – that the numerous assembly in the Abbey holds together, and it is as a tremendous and incomparable modern that the author of *Men and Women* takes his place in it. He introduces to his predecessors a kind of contemporary individualism which surely for many a year they had not been reminded of with any such force. The tradition of the poetic character as something high, detached and simple, which may be assumed to have prevailed among them for a good while, is one that Browning has broken at every turn; so that we can imagine his new associates to stand about him, till they have got used to him, with rather a sense of failing measures. A good many oddities and a good many great writers have been entombed in the Abbey; but none of the odd ones have been so great and none of the great ones so odd. There are plenty of poets whose right to the title may be contested, but there is no poetic head of equal power – crowned and recrowned by almost importunate hands – from which so many people would withhold the distinctive wreath. All this will give the marble phantoms at the base of the great pillars and the definite personalities of the honorary slabs something to puzzle out until, by the quick operation of time, the mere fact of his lying there among the classified and protected makes even Robert Browning lose a portion of the bristling surface of his actuality.

For the rest, judging from the outside and with his contemporaries, we of the public can only feel that his very modernness – by which we mean the all-touching, all-trying spirit of his work, permeated with accumulations and playing with knowledge – achieves a kind of conquest, or at least of extension, of the rigid pale. We cannot enter here upon any account either of that or of any other element of his genius, though surely no literary figure of our day seems to sit more unconsciously for the painter. The very imperfections of this original are fascinating, for they never present themselves as weaknesses; they are boldnesses and overgrowths, rich roughnesses and humours, and the patient critic need not despair of digging to the primary soil from which so many disparities and contradictions spring. He may finally even put his finger on some explanation of the great mystery, the imperfect conquest of the poetic form by a genius in which the poetic passion had such volume and range, He may successfully say how it was that a poet without a lyre – for that is practically Browning's deficiency: he had the scroll, but not often the sounding strings – was nevertheless, in his best hours, wonderfully rich in the magic of his art, a magnificent master of poetic emotion. He will justify on behalf of a multitude of devotees[2] the great position assigned to a writer of verse of which the nature or the fortune has been (in proportion to its value and quantity) to be treated rarely as quotable. He will do all this and a great deal more besides; but we need not wait for it to feel that something of our latest sympathies, our latest and most restless selves, passed the other day into the high part – the show-part, to speak vulgarly – of our literature. To speak of Mr Browning only as he was in the last twenty years of his life, how quick such an imagination as his would have been to recognise all the latent or mystical suitabilities that, in the last resort, might link to the great Valhalla by the Thames a figure that had become so conspicuously a figure of London! He had grown to be intimately and inveterately of the London world; he was so familiar and recurrent, so responsible to all its solicitations, that, given the endless incarnations he stands for today, he would have been missed from the congregation of worthies whose memorials are the special pride of the Londoner. Just as his great sign to those who knew him[3] was that he was a force of health, of temperament, of tone, so what he takes into the Abbey is an immense expression of life – of life rendered with large liberty and free experiment, with an un-prejudiced intellectual eagerness to put himself in other people's place, to participate in complications and consequences; a restlessness of psychological research that might well alarm any pale company for their formal orthodoxies.

But the illustrious whom he rejoins may be reassured, as they will not fail to discover: in so far as they are representative it will clear itself up that, in spite of a surface unsuggestive of marble and a reckless in-dividualism of form, he is quite as representative as any of them. For the great value of Browning is that at bottom, in all the deep spiritual and human essentials, he is unmistakably in the great tradition – is, with all his Italianisms and cosmopolitanisms, all his victimisation by societies organised to talk about him, a magnificent example of the best and least dilettantish English spirit. That constitutes indeed the main chance for his eventual critic, who will have to solve the refreshing problem of how, if subtleties be not what the English spirit most delights in, the author of, for instance, *Any Wife to any Husband* made them his perpetual pasture, and yet remained typically of his race. He was indeed a wonderful mixture of the universal and the alembicated. But he played with the curious and the special, they never submerged him, and it was a sign of his robustness that he could play to the end. His voice sounds loudest, and also clearest, for the things that, as a race, we like best – the fascination of faith, the acceptance of life, the respect for its mysteries, the endurance of its charges, the vitality of the will, the validity of character, the beauty of action, the seriousness, above all, of the great human passion. If Browning had spoken for us in no other way, he ought to have been made sure of, tamed and chained as a classic, on account of the extraordinary beauty of his treatment of the special relation between man and woman. It is a complete and splendid picture of the matter, which somehow places it at the same time in the region of conduct and responsibility. But when we talk of Robert Browning's speaking 'for us' we go to the end of our privilege, we say all. With a sense of security, perhaps even a certain complacency, we leave our sophisticated modern conscience, and perhaps even our heterogeneous modern vocabulary, in his charge among the illustrious. There will possibly be moments in which these things will seem to us to have widened the allowance, made the high abode more comfortable, for some of those who are yet to enter it.

First published unsigned in *The Speaker*, I (4 January 1890), 10–12; reprinted in *Essays in London and Elsewhere* (1893), and *English Hours* (1905).

# Chester

If the Atlantic voyage be counted, as it certainly may, even with the ocean in a fairly good humour, an emphatic zero in the sum of one's better experience, the American traveller arriving at this venerable town finds himself transported, without a sensible gradation, from the edge of the New World to the very heart of the Old. It is almost a misfortune, perhaps, that Chester lies so close to the threshold of England; for it is so rare and complete a specimen of an antique town that the later-coming wonders of its sisters in renown – of Shrewsbury, Coventry, and York – suffer a trifle by comparison, and the tourist's appetite for the picturesque just loses its finer edge. Yet the first impressions of an observant American in England – of our old friend the sentimental tourist – stir up within him such a cloud of sensibility that while the charm is still unbroken he may perhaps as well dispose mentally of the greater as of the less, I have been playing at first impressions for the second time,[1] and have won the game against a cynical adversary. I have been strolling and restrolling along the ancient wall – so perfect in its antiquity – which locks this dense little city in its stony circle, with a certain friend who has been treating me to a bitter lament on the decay of his relish for the picturesque. 'I have turned the corner of youth,' is his ceaseless plaint; 'I suspected it, but now I know it – now that my heart beats but once where it beat a dozen times before, and that where I found sermons in stones and pictures in meadows, delicious revelations and intimations ineffable, I find nothing but the hard, heavy prose of British civilisation.'[2] But little by little I have grown used to my friend's sad monody, and indeed feel half indebted to it as a warning against cheap infatuations.

I defied him, at any rate, to argue successfully against the effect of the brave little walls of Chester. There could be no better example of that phenomenon so delightfully frequent in England – an ancient property or institution lovingly readopted and consecrated to some modern amenity. The good Cestrians may boast of their walls without a shadow of that mental reservation on grounds of modern ease which is so often the tax paid by the romantic; and I can easily imagine that, though most modern towns contrive to get on comfortably without this stony girdle, these people should have come to regard theirs as a prime necessity. For through it, surely they may know their city more intimately than their unbuckled neighbours – survey it, feel it, rejoice in it as many times a day as they please. The civic consciousness, sunning itself thus on the city's rim and glancing at the little swarming towered and gabled town within, and then at the blue undulations of the near Welsh border, may easily deepen to delicious complacency. The wall enfolds the place in a continuous ring, which, passing through innumerable picturesque vicissitudes, often threatens to snap, but never fairly breaks the link; so that, starting at any point, an hour's easy stroll will bring you back to your station, I have quite lost my heart to this charming creation, and there are so many things to be said about it that I hardly know where to begin. The great fact, I suppose, is that it contains a Roman substructure, rests for much of its course on foundations laid by that race of master-builders. But in spite of this sturdy origin, much of which is buried in the well-trodden soil of the ages, it is the gentlest and least offensive of ramparts; it completes its long irregular curve without a frown or menace in all its disembattled stretch. The earthy deposit of time has, indeed, in some places climbed so high about its base that it amounts to no more than a causeway of modest dimensions. It has everywhere, however, a rugged outer parapet and a broad hollow flagging, wide enough for two strollers abreast. Thus equipped, it wanders through its adventurous circuit; now sloping, now bending, now broadening into a terrace, now narrowing into an alley, now swelling into an arch, now dipping into steps, now passing some thorn-screened garden, and now reminding you that it was once a more serious matter than all this by the extrusion of a rugged, ivy-smothered tower. Its final hoary humility is enhanced, to your mind, by the freedom with which you may approach it from any point in the town. Every few steps, as you go, you see some little court or alley boring toward it through the close-pressed houses. It is full of that delightful element of the crooked, the accidental, the un-foreseen, which, to American eyes, accustomed to our eternal straight lines and right angles, is the striking feature of European street scenery. An American strolling in the Chester streets finds a perfect feast of crookedness – of those random corners, projections and recesses, odd domestic interspaces charmingly saved or lost, those innumerable architectural surprises and caprices and fantasies which lead to such refreshing exercise a vision benumbed by brown-stone fronts. An American is born to the idea that on his walks abroad it is perpetual level wall ahead of him, and such a revelation as he finds here of infinite accident and infinite effect gives a wholly novel zest to the use of his eyes. It produces, too, the reflection – superficial and fallacious one per-haps – that amid all this cunning chiaroscuro of its *mise en scéne*, life must have more of a certain homely entertainment. It is at least no fallacy to say that childhood – or the later memory of childhood – must borrow from such a background a kind of anecdotical wealth. We all know how in the retrospect of later moods the incidents of early youth 'compose', visibly, each as an individual picture, with a magic for which the greatest painters have no corresponding art. There is a vivid reflection of this magic in some of the early pages of Dickens' *Copperfield* and of George Eliot's *Mill on the Floss*, the writers having had the happiness of growing up among old, old things. Two or three of the phases of this rambling wall belong especially to the class of things fondly remembered. In one place it skirts the edge of the cathedral graveyard, and sweeps beneath the great square tower and behind the sacred east window of the choir. Of the cathedral there is more to say; but just the spot I speak of is the best standpoint for feeling how fine an influence in the architectural line – where theoretically, at least, influences are great – is the massive tower of an English abbey, dominating the homes of men; and for watching the eddying flight of swallows make vaster still to the eye the large calm fields of stonework. At another point, two battered and crumbling towers, decaying in their winding-sheets of ivy, make a prodigiously designed diversion. One inserted in the body of the wall and the other connected with it by a short crumbling ridge of masonry, they contri-bute to a positive jumble of local colour. A shaded wall wanders at the

*The Rows, Chester*

foot of the rampart; beside this passes a narrow canal, with locks and barges and burly watermen in smocks and breeches; while the venerable pair of towers, with their old red sandstone sides peeping through the gaps in their green mantles, rest on the soft grass of one of those odd fragments of public garden, a crooked strip of ground turned to social account, which one meets at every turn, apparently, in England – a tribute to the needs of the 'masses'. *Stat magni nominis umbra.* The quotation is doubly pertinent here, for this little garden strip is adorned with mossy fragments of Roman stonework, bits of pavement, altars, baths, disinterred in the local soil. England is the land of small economies, and the present rarely fails to find good use for the odds and ends of the past. These two hoary shells of masonry are therefore converted into 'museums', receptacles for the dustiest and shabbiest of tawdry back-parlour curiosities. Here preside a couple of those grotesque creatures, *à la* Dickens, whom one finds squeezed into every cranny of English civilisation, scraping a thin subsistence, like mites in a mouldy cheese.

Next after its wall – possibly even before it – Chester values its Rows, an architectural idiosyncrasy which must be seen to be appreciated. They are a sort of Gothic edition of the blessed arcades and porticoes of Italy, and consist, roughly speaking, of a running public passage tunnelled through the second story of the houses. The low basement is thus directly on the drive-way, to which a flight of steps descends, at frequent intervals, from this superincumbent veranda. The upper portion of the houses projects to the outer line of the gallery, where they are propped with pillars and posts and parapets. The shop-fronts face along the arcade and admit you to little caverns of traffic, more or less dusky according to their opportunities for illumination in the rear. If the picturesque be measured by its hostility to our modern notions of con-venience, Chester is probably the most romantic city in the world. This arrangement is endlessly rich in opportunities for amusing effect, but the full charm of the architecture of which it is so essential a part must be observed from the street below. Chester is still an antique town, and medieval England sits bravely under her gables. Every third house is a 'specimen' – gabled and latticed, timbered and carved, and wearing its years more or less lightly. These ancient dwellings present every shade and degree of historical colour and expression. Some are dark with neglect and deformity, and the horizontal slit admitting light into the lurking Row seems to collapse on its dislocated props like a pair of tooth-less old jaws. Others stand there square-shouldered and sturdy, with their beams painted and straightened, their plaster whitewashed, their carvings polished, and the low casement covering the breadth of the frontage adorned with curtains and flower-pots. It is noticeable that the actual townsfolk have bravely accepted the situation bequeathed by the past, and the large number of rich and intelligent restorations of the old façades makes an effective jumble of their piety and their policy. These elaborate and ingenious repairs attest a highly informed consciousness of the pictorial value of the city. I indeed suspect much of this revived innocence of having recovered a freshness that never can have been, of having been restored with usurious interest. About the genuine antiques there would be properly a great deal to say, for they are really a theme for the philosopher; but the theme is too heavy for my pen, and I can give them but the passing tribute of a sigh. They are cruelly quaint, dreadfully expressive. Fix one of them with your gaze, and it seems fairly to reek with mortality. Every stain and crevice seems to syllable some human record – a record of lives airless and unlighted. I have been trying hard to fancy them animated by the children of 'Merry England', but I am quite unable to think of them save as peopled by the victims of dismal old-world pains and fears. Human life, surely, packed away behind those impenetrable lattices of lead and bottle-glass, just above which the black outer beam marks the suffocating nearness of the ceiling, can have expanded into scant freedom and bloomed into small sweetness.[3]

Nothing has struck me more in my strolls along the Rows than the fact that the most zealous observation can keep but uneven pace with the fine differences in national manners. Some of the most sensible of these differences are yet so subtle and indefinable that one must give up the attempt to express them, though the omission leave but a rough sketch. As you pass with the bustling current from shop to shop, you feel local custom and tradition – another tone of things – pressing on you from every side. The tone of things is somehow heavier than with us; manners and modes are more absolute and positive; they seem to swarm and to thicken the atmosphere about you. Morally and physically it is a denser air than ours. We seem loosely hung together at home as compared with the English, every man of whom is a tight fit in his place. It is not an inferential but a palpable fact that England is a crowded country. There is stillness and space – grassy, oak-studded space – at Eaton Hall,[4] where the Marquis of Westminster dwells (or I believe can afford to humour his notion of not dwelling), but there is a crowd and a hubbub in Chester. Wherever you go the population has overflowed. You stroll on the walls at eventide and you hardly find elbow-room. You haunt the cathedral shades, and a dozen sauntering mortals temper your solitude. You glance up an alley or side-street, and discover populous windows and doorsteps. You roll along country roads and find countless humble pedestrians dotting the green waysides. The English landscape is always a 'landscape with figures'. And everywhere you go you are accompanied by a vague consciousness of the British child hovering about your knees and coat-skirts, naked, grimy, and portentous. You reflect with a sort of physical relief on Australia, Canada, India. Where there are many men, of course, there are many needs; which helps to justify to the philosophic stranger the vast number and the irresistible coquetry of the little shops which adorn these low-browed Rows. The shop-fronts have always seemed to me the most elegant things in England; and I waste more time than I should care to confess to in covetous contemplation of the vast, clear panes behind which the nether integuments of gentlemen are daintily suspended from glittering brass rods, The manners of the dealers in these comfortable wares seldom fail to confirm your agreeable impression. You are thanked with effusion for expending twopence – a fact of deep significance to the truly analytic mind, and which always seems to me a vague reverberation from certain of Miss Edgeworth's novels, perused in childhood. When you think of the small profits, the small jealousies, the long waiting, and the narrow margin for evil days implied by this redundancy of shops and shopmen, you hear afresh the steady rumble of that deep keynote of English manners, overscored so often, and with such sweet beguilement, by finer harmonies, but never extinguished – the economic struggle for existence.

The Rows are as 'scenic' as one could wish, and it is a pity that before the birth of their modern consciousness there was no English Balzac to introduce them into a realistic romance with a psychological commentary.[5] But the cathedral is better still, modestly as it stands on the roll of English abbeys. It is of moderate dimensions, and rather meagre in form and ornament; but to an American it expresses and answers for the type, producing thereby the proper vibrations. Among these is a certain irresistible regret that so much of its hoary substance should give place to the fine, fresh-coloured masonry with which Mr Gilbert Scott,[6] ruthless renovator, is so intelligently investing it. The red sandstone of the primitive structure, darkened and devoured by time, survives at many points in frowning mockery of the imputed need of tinkering.[7] The great tower, however – completely restored – rises high enough to seem to belong, as cathedral towers should, to the far-off air that vibrates with the chimes and the swallows, and to square serenely, east and west and south and north, its embossed and fluted sides. English cathedrals, within, are apt at first to look pale and naked; but after a while, if the proportions be fair and the spaces largely distributed, when you perceive the light beating softly down from the cold clerestory and your eye measures caressingly the tallness of columns and the hollowness of arches, and lingers on the old genteel inscriptions of mural marbles and brasses; and, above all, when you become conscious of that sweet, cool mustiness in the air which seems to haunt these places as the very climate of Episcopacy, you may grow to feel that they are less the empty shells of a departed faith than the abodes of a faith which may still affirm a presence and awaken echoes. Catholicism has gone, but Anglicanism has the next best music. So at least it seemed to me, a Sunday or two since, as I sat in the choir at Chester awaiting a discourse from Canon Kingsley. The Anglican service had never seemed to my profane sense so much an affair of magnificent intonations and cadences – of pompous effects of resonance and melody. The vast oaken architecture of the stalls[8] among which we nestled – somewhat stiffly and with a due apprehension of wounded ribs and knees – climbing vainly against the dizzier reach of the columns; the beautiful English voices of certain officiating canons; the little rosy 'king's scholars' sitting ranged beneath the pulpit, in white-winged surplices, which made their heads, above the pew-edges, look like rows of sleepy cherubs: every element in the scene gave it a great spectacular beauty. They suggested too what is suggested in England at every turn, that conservatism here has all the charm and leaves dissent and democracy and other vulgar variations nothing but their bald logic. Conservatism has the cathedrals, the colleges, the castles, the gardens, the traditions, the associations, the fine names, the better manners, the poetry; Dissent has the dusky brick chapels in provincial by-streets, the names out of Dickens, the uncertain tenure of the *h*, and the poor *mens sibi conscia recti*. Differences which in other countries are slight and varying, almost metaphysical, as one may say, are marked in England by a gulf. Nowhere else does the degree of one's respectability involve such solid consequences, and I am sure I don't wonder that the sacramental word which with us (and, in such correlatives as they possess, more or less among the continental races) is pronounced lightly and facetiously and as a quotation from the Philistines, is uttered here with a perfectly grave face. To have the courage of one's mere convictions is in short to have a prodigious deal of courage, and I think one must need as much to be a Dissenter as one needs patience not to be a duke. Perhaps the Dissenters (to limit the question to them) manage to stay out of the church by letting it all hang on the sermon. Canon Kingsley's discourse was one more example of the familiar truth – not without its significance to minds zealous for the good old fashion of 'making an effort' – that there is an odd link between large forms and small emanations. The sermon, beneath that triply consecrated vault, should have had a builded majesty. It had not; and I confess that a tender memory of ancient obligations to the author of *Westward Ho* and *Hypatia* forbids my saying more of it. An American, I think, is not incapable of taking a secret satisfaction in an incongruity of this kind. He finds with relief that even mortals reared as in the ring of a perpetual circus are only mortals. His constant sense of the beautiful scenic properties of English life is apt to beget a habit of melancholy reference to the dead-blank wall which forms the background of our own life-drama; and from doubting in this fantastic humour whether we have even that modest value in the scale of beauty that he has sometimes fondly hoped, he lapses into a moody scepticism as to our place in the scale of 'importance', and finds himself wondering vaguely whether this be not a richer race as well as a lovelier land. That of course will never do; so that when after being escorted down the beautiful choir in what, from the American point of view, is an almost gorgeous ecclesiastical march, by the Dean in a white robe trimmed with scarlet and black-robed sacristans carrying silver wands, the officiating canon mounts into a splendid canopied and pinnacled pulpit of Gothic stonework and proves – not an 'acting' Jeremy Taylor,[9] our poor sentimental tourist begins to hold up his head again and to reflect that so far as we *have* opportunities we mostly rise to them. I am not sure indeed that in the excess of his reaction he is not tempted to accuse his English neighbours of being impenetrable and uninspired, to affirm that they do not half discern their good fortune, and that it takes passionate pilgrims, vague aliens and other disinherited persons to appreciate the 'points' of this admirable country.

First of a series of four unsigned articles published under the title 'A European Summer', *The Nation*, XV (4 July 1872), 7–9; reprinted in *Transatlantic Sketches* (1875), *Foreign Parts* ( 1883), and *English Hours* (1905).

# Lichfield and Warwick

To write at Oxford of anything but Oxford requires, on the part of the sentimental tourist, no small power of mental abstraction. Yet I have it at heart to pay to three or four other scenes recently visited the debt of an enjoyment hardly less profound than my relish for this scholastic paradise. First among these is the cathedral city of Lichfield – the city, I say, because Lichfield has a character of its own apart from its great ecclesiastical feature. In the centre of its little market-place – dullest and sleepiest of provincial market-places – rises a huge effigy of Dr Johnson, the *genius loci*, who was constructed, humanly, with very nearly as large an architecture as the great abbey. The Doctor's statue, which is of some inexpensive composite painted a shiny brown, and of no great merit of design, fills out the vacant dullness of the little square in much the same way as his massive personality occupies – with just a margin for Garrick[1] – the record of his native town. In one of the volumes of Croker's *Boswell* is a steel plate of the old Johnsonian birth-house, by the aid of a vague recollection of which I detected the dwelling beneath its modernised frontage. It bears no mural inscription and, save for a hint of antiquity in the receding basement, with pillars supporting the floor above, seems in no especial harmony with Johnson's time or fame.[2] Lichfield in general appeared to me indeed to have little to say about her great son beyond the fact that the smallness and the sameness and the dullness, amid which it is so easy to fancy a great intellectual appetite turning sick with inanition, may help to explain the Doctor's subsequent almost ferocious fondness for London. I walked about the silent streets, trying to repeople them with wigs and short-clothes, and, while I lingered near the cathedral, endeavoured to guess the message of its Gothic graces to Johnson's ponderous classicism. But I achieved but a colourless picture at the best, and the most vivid image in my mind's eye was that of the

*Lichfield Cathedral*

London coach facing towards Temple Bar with the young author of *Rasselas*[3] scowling near-sightedly from the cheapest seat. With him goes the interest of Lichfield town. The place is stale without being really antique. It is as if that prodigious temperament had absorbed and appropriated its original vitality.

If every dull provincial town, however, formed but a girdle of quietude to a cathedral as rich as that of Lichfield, one would thank it for letting one alone. Lichfield Cathedral is great among churches, and bravely performs the prime duty of objects of its order – that of seeming for the time (to minds unsophisticated by architectural culture) the finest, on the whole, of all such objects. This one is rather oddly placed, on the slope of a hill, the particular spot having been chosen, I believe, because sanctified by the sufferings of certain primitive martyrs; but it is fine to see how its upper portions surmount any crookedness of posture and its great towers overtake in mid-air the conditions of perfect symmetry. The close is extraordinarily attractive; a long sheet of water expands behind it and, besides leading the eye off into a sweet green landscape, renders the inestimable service of reflecting the three spires as they rise above the great trees which mask the Palace and the Deanery. These august abodes edge the northern side of the slope, and behind their huge gate-posts and close-wrought gages the atmosphere of the Georgian era seems to abide. Before them stretches a row of huge elms, which must have been old when Johnson was young; and between these and the long-buttressed wall of the cathedral, you may stroll to and fro among as pleasant a mixture of influences (I imagine) as any in England. You can stand back here, too, from the west front further than in many cases, and examine at your ease its lavish decoration. You are perhaps a trifle too much at your ease; for you soon discover what a more cursory glance might not betray, that the immense façade has been covered with stucco and paint, that an effigy of Charles II, in wig and plumes and trunk-hose, of almost Gothic grotesqueness, surmounts the middle window; that the various other statues of saints and kings have but recently climbed into their niches; and that the whole expanse is in short an imposture. All this was done some fifty years ago, in the taste of that day as to restoration, and yet it but partially mitigates the impressiveness of the high façade, with its brace of spires, and the great embossed and image-fretted surface, to which the lowness of the portals (the too frequent reproach of English abbeys) seems to give a loftier reach. Passing beneath one of these low portals, however, I found myself gazing down as noble a church vista as any you need desire. The cathedral is of magnificent length, and the screen between nave and choir has been removed, so that from stem to stern, as one may say, of the great vessel of the church, it is all a mighty avenue of multitudinous slender columns, terminating in what seems a great screen of ruby and sapphire and topaz – one of the finest east windows in England. The cathedral is narrow in proportion to its length; it is the long-drawn aisle of the poet in perfection and there is something grandly elegant in the unity of effect produced by this unobstructed perspective. The charm is increased by a singular architectural fantasy. Standing in the centre of the doorway, you perceive that the eastern wall does not directly face you, and that from the beginning of the choir the receding aisle deflects slightly to the left, in reported suggestion of the droop of the Saviour's head on the cross. Here again Mr Gilbert Scott[4] has lately laboured to no small purpose of *un*doing, it would appear – undoing the misdeeds of the last century. This extraordinary period expended an incalculable amount of imagination in proving that it had none. Universal whitewash was the least of its offences. But this has been scraped away and the solid stone-work left to speak for itself, the delicate capitals and cornices disencrusted and discreetly rechiselled and the whole temple æsthetically re-dedicated. Its most beautiful feature, happily, has needed no repair, for its perfect beauty has been its safeguard. The great choir window of Lichfield is the noblest glass-work before the spell of which one's soul has become simple. I remember nowhere colours so chaste and grave, and yet so rich and true, or a cluster of designs so piously decorative and yet so vivified. Such a window as this seems to me the most sacred ornament of a great church; to be, not like vault and screen and altar, the dim contingent promise to the spirit, but the very redemption of the whole vow. This Lichfield glass is not the less interesting for being visibly of foreign origin. Exceeding so obviously as it does the range of English genius in this line, it indicates at least the heavenly treasure stored up in continental churches. It dates from the early sixteenth century, and was transferred hither sixty years ago from a decayed Belgian abbey.[5] This, however, is not all of Lichfield. You have not seen it till you have strolled and restrolled along the close on every side, and watched the three spires constantly change their relation as you move and pause. Nothing can well be finer than the combination of the two lesser ones soaring equally in front with the third riding tremendously the magnificently sustained line of the roof. At a certain distance against the sky this long ridge seems something infinite and the great spire to sit astride of it like a giant mounted on a mastodon. Your sense of the huge mass of the building is deepened by the fact that though the central steeple is of double the elevation of the others, you see it, from some points, borne back in a perspective which drops it to half their stature and lifts them into immensity.[6] But it would take long to tell all that one sees and fancies and thinks in a lingering walk about so great a church as this.

To walk in quest of any object that one has more or less tenderly dreamed of, to find your way, to steal upon it softly, to see at last, if it be church or castle, the tower-tops peeping above elms or beeches – to push forward with a rush, and emerge and pause and draw that first long breath which is the compromise between so many sensations: this is a pleasure left to the tourist even after the broad glare of photography has dissipated so many of the sweet mysteries of travel; even in a season when he is fatally apt to meet a dozen fellow pilgrims returning from the shrine, each as big a fool, so to speak, as he ever was, or to overtake a dozen more telegraphing their impressions down the line as they arrive. Such a pleasure I lately enjoyed quite in its perfection, in a walk to Haddon Hall, along a meadow path by the Wye, in this interminable English twilight which I am never weary of admiring watch in hand. Haddon Hall lies among Derbyshire hills, in a region infested, I was about to write, by Americans. But I achieved my own sly pilgrimage in perfect solitude; and as I described the grey walls among the rook-haunted elms I felt not like a dusty tourist, but like a successful adventurer. I have certainly had, as a dusty tourist, few more charming moments than some – such as any one, I suppose, is free to have – that I passed on a little ruined grey bridge which spans, with its single narrow arch, a trickling stream at the base of the eminence from which those walls and trees look down. The twilight deepened, the ragged battlements and the low, broad oriels glanced duskily from the foliage, the rooks wheeled and clamoured in the glowing sky; and if there had been a ghost on the premises I certainly ought to have seen it. In fact I did see it, as we see ghosts nowadays.[7] I felt the incommunicable spirit of the scene with the last, the right intensity. The old life, the old manners, the old figures seemed present again. The great *coup de théâtre* of the young woman who shows you the Hall – it is rather languidly done on her part – is to point out a little dusky door opening from a turret to a back terrace as the aperture through which Dorothy Vernon eloped with Lord John Manners.[8] I was ignorant of this episode, for I was not to enter the place till the morrow, and I am still unversed in the history of the actors. But as I stood in the luminous dusk weaving the romance of the spot, I recognised the inevitability of a Dorothy Vernon and quite understood a Lord John. It was of course on just such an evening that the romantic event came off, and by listening with the proper credulity, I might surely hear on the flags of the castle court ghostly footfalls and feel in their movements the old heart-beats. The only footfall I can conscientiously swear to, however, is the far from spectral tread of the damsel who led me through the mansion in the prosier light of the next morning. Haddon Hall,[9] I believe, is one of the sights in which it is the fashion to be 'disappointed'; a fact explained in a great measure by the absence of a formal approach to the house, which shows its low, grey front to every trudger on the high road. But the charm of the spot is so much less that of grandeur than that of melancholy, that it is rather deepened than diminished by this attitude of obvious survival and decay. And for that matter, when you have entered the steep little outer court through the huge thickness of the low gateway, the present seems effectually walled out and the past walled in, even as a dead man in a sepulchre. It is very dead, of a fine June morning, the genius of Haddon Hall; and the silent courts and chambers, with their hues of ashen grey and faded brown, seem as time-bleached as the dry bones of any mouldering mortality. The comparison is odd, but Haddon Hall reminded me perversely of some of the larger houses at Pompeii. The private life of the past is revealed in each case with very much the same distinctness and on a scale small enough not to stagger the imagination. This old dwelling, indeed, has so little of the mass and expanse of the classic feudal castle that it almost suggests one of those miniature models of great buildings which lurk in dusty corners of museums. But it is large enough to be delectably complete and to contain an infinite store of the poetry of grass-grown courts looked into by wide, jutting windows and climbed out of by crooked stone stairways mounting against the walls to little high-placed doors. The 'tone' of Haddon Hall, of all its walls and towers and stone-work, is the grey of unpolished silver, and the reader who has been in England need hardly be reminded of the sweet accord – to eye and mind alike – existing between all stony surfaces covered with the pale corrosions of time and the deep living green of the strong ivy which seems to feed on their slow decay. Of this effect and of a hundred others – from those that belong to low-browed, stone-paved empty rooms where life was warm and atmospheres thick, to those one may note where the dark tower stairway emerges at last, on a level with the highest beech-tops, against the cracked and sunbaked parapet which flaunted the castle standard over the castle woods – of every form of sad desuetude and picturesque decay Haddon Hall contains some delightful example. Its finest point is undoubtedly a certain court from which a stately flight of steps ascends to the terrace where that daughter of the Vernons whom I have mentioned took such happy thought for our requiring, as the phase is, a reference. These steps, with the terrace, its balustrade topped with great ivy-muffled knobs of stone and its high background of massed woods, form the ideal *mise en scène* for portions of Shakespeare's comedies. 'It's exactly Elizabethan,' said my companion. Here the Countess Olivia may have listened to the fantastic Malvolio, or Beatrix, superbest of flirts, have come to summon Benedick to dinner.

The glories of Chatsworth,[10] which lies but a few miles from Haddon, serve as a marked offset to its more delicate merits, just as they are supposed to gain, I believe, in the tourist's eyes, by contrast with its charming, its almost Italian shabbiness. But the glories of Chatsworth, incontestable as they are, were so effectually eclipsed to my mind, a couple of days later, that in future, when I think of an English mansion, I shall think only of Warwick, and when I think of an English park, only of Blenheim. Your run by train through the gentle Warwickshire land does much to prepare you for the great spectacle of the castle, which seems hardly more than a sort of massive symbol and synthesis of the broad prosperity and peace and leisure diffused over this great pastoral expanse. The Warwickshire meadows are to common English scenery what this is to that of the rest of the world. For mile upon mile you can see nothing but broad sloping pastures of velvet turf, overbrowsed by sheep of the most fantastic shagginess, and garnished with hedges out of the trailing luxury of whose verdure great ivy-tangled oaks and elms arise with a kind of architectural regularity. The landscape indeed sins by excess of nutritive suggestion; it savours of larder and manger; it is too

*Warwick Castle*

ovine, too bovine, it is almost asinine; and if you were to believe what you see before you this rugged globe would be a sort of boneless ball covered with some such plush-like integument as might be figured by the down on the cheek of a peach. But a great thought keeps you company as you go and gives character to the scenery. Warwickshire – you say it over and over – was Shakespeare's country. Those who think that a great genius is something supremely ripe and healthy and human may find comfort in the fact. It helps greatly to enliven my own vague conception of Shakespeare's temperament, with which I find it no great shock to be obliged to associate ideas of mutton and beef. There is something as final, as disillusioned of the romantic horrors of rock and forest, as deeply attuned to human needs in the Warwickshire pastures as there is in the underlying morality of the poet.

With human needs in general Warwick Castle may be in no great accord, but few places are more gratifying to the sentimental tourist. It is the only great residence he may have coveted as a home.[11] The fire that we heard so much of last winter in America appears to have consumed but an inconsiderable and easily spared portion of the house, and the great towers rise over the great trees and the town with the same grand air as before. Picturesquely, Warwick gains from not being sequestered, after the common fashion, in acres of park.[12] The village street winds about the garden walls, though its hum expires before it has had time to scale them. There can be no better example of the way in which stone walls, if they do not of necessity make a prison, may on occasions make a palace, than the prodigious privacy maintained thus about a mansion whose windows and towers form the main feature of a bustling town. At Warwick the past joins hands so stoutly with the present that you can hardly say where one begins and the other ends, and you rather miss the various crannies and gaps of what I just now called the Italian shabbiness of Haddon. There is a Cæsar's tower and a Guy's tower and half a dozen more, but they are so well-conditioned in their ponderous antiquity that you are at a loss whether to consider them parts of an old house revived or of a new house picturesquely superannuated. Such as they are, however, plunging into the grassed and gravelled courts from which their battlements look really feudal, and into gardens large enough for all delight and too small, as they should be, to be amazing; and with ranges between them of great apartments at whose hugely recessed windows you may turn from Vandyck and Rembrandt to glance down the cliff-like pile into the Avon, washing the base like a lordly moat, with its bridge, and its trees and its memories, they mark the very model of a great hereditary dwelling – one which amply satisfies the imagination without irritating the democratic conscience. The pictures at Warwick reminded me afresh of an old conclusion on this matter: that the best fortune for good pictures is not to be crowded into public collections – not even into the relative privacy of Salons Carrés and Tribunes – but to hang in largely spaced half-dozens on the walls of fine houses. Here the historical atmosphere, as one may call it, is almost a compensation for the often imperfect light. If this be true of most pictures it is especially so of the works of Vandyck, whom you think of, wherever you may find him, as having, with that thorough good breeding which is the stamp of his manner, taken account in his painting of the local conditions and predestined his picture to just the spot where it hangs. This is in fact an illusion as regards the Vandycks at Warwick, for none of them represent members of the house. The very finest perhaps after the great melancholy, picturesque Charles I – death, or at least the presentiment of death on the pale horse – is a portrait from the Brignole palace at Genoa; a beautiful noble matron in black, with her little son and heir. The last Vandycks I had seen were the noble company this lady had left behind her in the Genoese palace, and as I looked at her I thought of her mighty change of circumstance. Here she sits in the mild light of mid-most England; there you could almost fancy her blinking in the great glare sent up from the Mediterranean. Intensity for intensity – intensity of situation constituted – I hardly know which to choose.[13]

Second in the series 'A European Summer', *The Nation*, XV (25 July 1872), 57–8; reprinted in *Transatlantic Sketches* (1875), *Foreign Parts* (1883), and *English Hours* (1905).

# North Devon

For those fanciful observers to whom broad England means chiefly the perfection of the rural picturesque, Devonshire means the perfection of England. I, at least, had so complacently taken for granted here all the characteristic graces of English scenery, had built so boldly on their rank orthodoxy, that before we fairly crossed the border I had begun to look impatiently from the carriage window for the veritable landscape in water colours. Devonshire meets you promptly in all its purity, for the course of ten minutes you have been able to glance down the green vista of a dozen Devonshire lanes. On huge embankments of moss and turf, smothered in wild flowers and embroidered with the finest lace work of trailing ground ivy, rise solid walls of flowering thorn and glistening holly and golden broom, and more strong, homely shrubs than I can name, and toss their blooming tangle to a sky which seems to look down between them, in places, from but a dozen inches of blue. They are over-sown with lovely little flowers with names as delicate as their petals of gold and silver and azure – bird's-eye and king's finger and wandering sailor – and their soil, a superb dark red, turns in spots so nearly to crimson that you almost fancy it some fantastic compound purchased at the chemist's and scattered there for ornament.[1] The mingled reflection of this rich-hued earth and the dim green light which filters through the hedge is a masterpiece of produced beauty. A Devonshire cottage is no less striking an outcome of the ages and the seasons and the manners. Crushed beneath its burden of thatch, coated with a rough white stucco of a tone to delight a painter, nestling in deep foliage and garnished at door-step and wayside with various forms of chubby infancy, it seems to have been stationed there for no more obvious purpose than to keep a promise to your fancy, though it covers, I suppose, not a little of the sordid side of life which the fancy likes to slur over.

I rolled past lanes and cottages to Exeter, where I had counted upon the cathedral. When one has fairly tasted of the pleasure of cathedral-hunting the approach to each new possible prize of the chase gives a peculiarly agreeable zest to the curiosity. You are making a collection of great impressions, and I think the process is in no case so delightful as applied to cathedrals. Going from one fine picture to another is certainly good; but the fine pictures of the world are terribly numerous, and they have a troublesome way of crowding and jostling each other in the memory. The number of cathedrals is small, and the mass and presence of each specimen great, so that as they rise in the mind in individual majesty they dwarf all the commoner impressions of calculated effect. They form indeed but a gallery of vaster pictures; for when time has dulled the recollection of details you retain a single broad image of the vast grey edifice, with its head and shoulders, its vessel and its towers, its tone of colour, and its still green precinct. All this is especially true perhaps of one's sense of English sacred piles, which are almost alone in possessing, as pictures, a spacious and harmonious setting. The cathedral stands supreme, but the close makes, always, the *scene*. Exeter is not one of the grandest, but, in common with great and small, it has certain points in favour of which local learning discriminates.[2] Exeter indeed does itself injustice by a low, dark front, which not only diminishes the apparent altitude of the nave, but conceals, as you look eastward, two noble Norman towers. The front, however, which has a gloomy impressiveness, is redeemed by two fine features: a magnificent rose window, whose vast stone ribs (enclosing some very pallid last-century glass) are disposed with the most charming intricacy; and a long sculptured screen – a sort of stony band of images – which traverses the façade from side to side. The little brown-visaged effigies of saints and kings and bishops, niched in tiers along this hoary wall, are prodigiously black and quaint and primitive in expression; and as you look at them with whatever contemplative tenderness your trade of hard-working tourist may have left at your disposal, you fancy that they are broodingly conscious of their names, histories and misfortunes; that, sensitive victims of time, they feel the loss of their noses, their toes, and their crowns; and that, when the long June twilight turns at last to a deeper grey and the quiet of the close to a deeper stillness, they begin to peer sidewise out of their narrow recesses and to converse in some strange form of early English, as rigid, yet as candid, as their features and postures, moaning, like a company of ancient paupers round a hospital fire, over their aches and infirmities and losses, and the sadness of being so terribly old. The vast square transeptal towers of the church seem to me to have the same sort of personal melancholy. Nothing in all architecture expresses better, to my imagination, the sadness of survival, the resignation of dogged material continuance, than a broad expanse of Norman stonework, roughly adorned with its low relief of short columns and round arches and almost barbarous hatchet work, and lifted high into that mild English light which accords so well with its dull grey surface. The especial secret of the impressiveness of such a Norman tower I cannot pretend to have discovered. It lies largely in the look of having been proudly and sturdily built – as if the masons had been urged by a trumpet blast, and the stones squared by a battle-axe – contrasted with this mere idleness of antiquity and passive lapse into quaintness. A Greek temple preserves a kind of fresh immortality in its concentrated refinement, and a Gothic cathedral in its adventurous exuberance; but a Norman tower stands up like some simple strong man in his might, bending a melancholy brow upon an age which demands that strength shall be cunning.

The North Devon coast, whither it was my design on coming to Exeter to proceed, has the primary merit of being, as yet, virgin soil as to railways. I went accordingly from Barnstaple to Ilfracombe on the top of a coach, in the fashion of elder days; and, thanks to my position, I managed to enjoy the landscape in spite of the two worthy aboriginals before me who were reading aloud together, with a natural glee which might have passed for fiendish malice, the *Daily Telegraph's* painfully vivid account of the defeat of the Atalanta crew. It seemed to me, I remember, a sort of pledge and token of the invincibility of English muscle that a newspaper record of its prowess should have power to divert my companions' eyes from the bosky flanks of Devonshire combes. The little watering place of Ilfracombe is seated at the lower verge of one of these seaward-plunging valleys, between a couple of magnificent headlands which hold it in a hollow slope and offer it securely to the caress of the Bristol Channel. It is a very finished little specimen of its genus and I think that during my short stay there I expended as much attention on its manners and customs and its social physiognomy as on its cliffs and beach and great coast view. My chief conclusion perhaps, from all these things, was that the terrible 'summer question' which works annual anguish in so many American households would rage less hopelessly if we had a few Ilfracombes scattered along our Atlantic coast; and furthermore that the English are masters of the art of not losing sight of ease and convenience in the pursuit of the pastoral life – unlike our own people, who, when seeking rural beguilement, are apt but to find a new rudeness added to nature. It is just possible that at Ilfracombe ease and convenience weigh down the scale; so very substantial are they, so very officious and business-like. On the left of the town (to give an example) one of the great cliffs I have mentioned rises in a couple of massive peaks and presents to the sea an almost vertical face, all muffled in tufts of golden broom and mighty fern. You have not walked fifty yards away from the hotel before you encounter half a dozen little sign boards, directing your steps to a path up the cliff. You follow their indications and you arrive at a little gatehouse, with photographs and various local gimcracks exposed for sale. A most respectable person appears, demands a penny and, on receiving it, admits you with great civility to commune with nature. You detect, however, various little influences hostile to perfect communion. You are greeted by another sign board threatening legal pursuit if you attempt to evade the payment of the sacramental penny. The path, winding in a hundred ramifications over the cliff, is fastidiously solid and neat, and furnished at intervals of a dozen yards with excellent benches, inscribed by knife and pencil with the names of such visitors as do not happen to have been the elderly maiden ladies who now chiefly occupy them. All this is prosaic, and you have to subtract it in a lump from the total impression before the sense of the beguilement of nature becomes distinct. Your subtraction made, a great deal assuredly remains; quite enough, I found, to give me an ample day's refreshment; for English scenery, like most other English commodities, resists and rewards familiar use. The cliffs are superb, the play of light and shade upon them is a perpetual study, and the air a particular mixture of the breath of the hills and moors and the breath of the sea. I was very glad, at the end of my climb, to have a good bench to sit upon – as one must think twice in England before measuring one's length on the grassy earth; and to be able, thanks to the smooth footpath, to get back to the hotel in a quarter of an hour. But it occurred to me that if I were an Englishman of the period, and, after ten months of a busy London life, my fancy were turning to a holiday, to rest and change and oblivion of the ponderous social burden, it might find rather less inspiration than needful in a vision of the little paths of Ilfracombe, of the sign boards and the penny fee and the solitude tempered by old ladies and sheep. I wondered whether change perfect enough to be salutary does not imply something more pathless, more idle, more unreclaimed from that deep-bosomed nature to which the overwrought mind reverts with passionate longing; something after all attainable at a moderate distance from New York and Boston. I must add that I cannot find in my heart to object, even on grounds the most æsthetic, to the very beautiful and excellent inn at Ilfracombe, where such of my readers as are perchance actually wrestling with the question of 'where to go' may be interested to learn that they may live *en pension*, very well indeed, at a cost of ten shillings a day. I have paid the American hotel clerk a much heavier tax on a much lighter entertainment. I made the acquaintance at this establishment of that strange fruit of time the insular *table d'hôte*, but I confess that, faithful to the habit of a tourist open to the *arrière-pensée*, I have retained a more vivid impression of the talk and the faces than of our joints and side-dishes. I noticed here what I have often noticed before (the truth perhaps has never been duly recognised), that no people profit so eagerly as the English by the suspension of a common social law. A *table d'hôte*, being something abnormal and experimental, as it were, resulted apparently in a complete reversal of the supposed national characteristics. Conversation was universal – uproarious almost; old legends and ironies about the insular *morgue* seemed to see their ground crumble away. What social, what psychologic earthquake, in our own time, had occurred?[3]

These are meagre memories, however, compared with those which cluster about that place of pleasantness which is locally known as Lynton. I am afraid I may seem a mere professional gusher when I declare how common almost any term appears to me applied to Lynton with descriptive intent. The little village is perched on the side of one of the great mountain cliffs with which this whole coast is adorned, and on the edge of a lovely gorge through which a broad hill torrent foams and tumbles from the great moors whose heather-crested waves rise purple along the inland sky. Below it, close beside the beach where the little torrent meets the sea, is the sister village of Lynmouth. Here – as I stood on the bridge that spans the stream and looked at the stony backs and foundations and overclambering garden verdure of certain little grey old houses which plunge their feet into it, and then up at the tender green of scrub-oak and fern, at the colour of gorse and broom and bracken climbing the sides of the hills and leaving them bare-crowned to the sun like miniature mountains – I read an unnatural blueness into the northern sea, and the village below put on the grace of one of the hundred hamlets of the Riviera. The little Castle Hotel at Lynton is a spot so consecrated to supreme repose – to sitting with a book in the terrace garden, among blooming plants of aristocratic magnitude and rarity, and watching the finest piece of colour in all nature, the glowing red and green of the great cliffs beyond the little harbour mouth, as they shift and change and melt, the livelong day, from shade to shade and ineffable tone to tone – that I feel as if in helping it to publicity I were doing it rather a disfavour than a service. It is in fact a very deep and sure retreat, and I have never known one where purchased hospitality wore a more disinterested smile. Lynton is of course a capital centre for excursions, but two or three of which I had time to make. None is more beautiful than a simple walk along the running face of the cliffs to a singular rocky eminence whose curious abutments and pinnacles of stone have caused it to be named the Castle, It has a fantastic resemblance to some hoary feudal ruin, with crumbling towers and gaping chambers tenanted by wild sea-birds. The late afternoon light had a way, at this season, of lingering on until within a couple of hours of midnight; and I remember among the charmed moments of English travel none of a more vividly poetical tinge than a couple of evenings spent on the summit of this all but legendary pile in company with the slow-coming darkness and the short, sharp cry of the sea-mews. There are places whose very aspect is a story or a song. This jagged and pinnacled coast wall, with the rock-strewn valley behind it, the sullen calmness of the unbroken tide at the dreadful base of the cliffs (where they divide into low sea-caves, making pillars and pedestals for the fantastic imagery of their summits), prompted one to wanton reminiscence and outbreak, to a recall of some drawing of Gustave Doré's[4] (of his good time), which was a divination of the place and made one look for his signature under a stone, or, better still, to respouting, for sympathy, and relief, some idyllic Tennysonian line that haunted one's destitute past and that seemed to speak of the conditions in spite of being false to them geographically.[5]

The last stage in my visit to North Devon was the long drive along the beautiful remnant of coast and through the rich pastoral scenery of Somerset. The whole broad spectacle that one dreams of viewing in a foreign land to the homely music of a postboy's whip I beheld on this admirable drive – breezy highlands clad in the warm blue-brown of heather tufts as if in mantles of rusty velvet, little bays and coves curving gently to the doors of clustered fishing huts, deep pastures and broad forests, villages thatched and trellised as if to take a prize for improbability, manor tops peeping over rook-haunted avenues. I ought to make especial note of an hour I spent at midday at the village of Porlock in Somerset. Here the thatch seemed steeper and heavier, the yellow roses on the cottage walls more cunningly mated with the crumbling stucco, the dark interiors within the open doors more quaintly pictorial, than elsewhere; and as I loitered, while the horses rested, in the little cool old timber-steepled, yew-shaded church, betwixt the high-backed manorial pew and the battered tomb of a crusading knight and his lady, and listened to the simple prattle of a blue-eyed old sexton, who showed me where, as a boy, in scantier corduroys, he had scratched his name on the recumbent lady's breast, it seemed to me that this at last was old England indeed, and that in a moment more I should see Sir Roger de Coverley marching up the aisle. Certainly, to give a proper account of it all, I should need nothing less than the pen of Mr Addison.

Third essay in the series 'A Summer in Europe', *The Nation*, XV (8 August 1872), 86–7; reprinted in *Transatlantic Sketches* (1875), *Foreign Parts* (1883), and *English Hours* (1905).

*Wells Cathedral*

# Wells and Salisbury

The pleasantest thing in life is doubtless ever the pleasantness that has found one off one's guard – though if I was off my guard in arriving at Wells it could only have been by the effect of a frivolous want of information. I knew in a general way that this ancient little town had a great cathedral to produce, but I was far from suspecting the intensity of the impression that awaited me. The immense predominance of the Minster towers, as you see them from the approaching train over the clustered houses at their feet, gives you indeed an intimation of its character, suggests that the city is nothing if not sanctified; but I can wish the traveller no better fortune than to stroll forth in the early evening with as large a reserve of ignorance as my own, and treat himself to an hour of discoveries. I was lodged on the edge of the Cathedral lawn and had only to pass beneath one of the three crumbling Priory gates which enclose it, and cross the vast grassy oval, to stand before a minster-front which ranks among the first three or four in England.[1] Wells Cathedral is extremely fortunate in being approached by this wide green level, on which the spectator may loiter and stroll to and fro and shift his standpoint to his heart's content. The spectator who does not hesitate to avail himself of his privilege of unlimited fastidiousness might indeed pronounce it too isolated for perfect picturesqueness – too uncontrasted with the profane architecture of the human homes for which it pleads to the skies. But Wells is in fact not a city with a cathedral for central feature; it is a cathedral with a little city gathered at the base and forming hardly more than an extension of the spacious close. You feel everywhere the presence of the beautiful church; the place seems always to savour of a Sunday afternoon; and you imagine every house tenanted by a canon, a prebendary or a precentor, with 'backs' providing for choristers and vergers.

The great façade is remarkable not so much for its expanse as for its elaborate elegance. It consists of two great truncated towers, divided by a broad centre bearing, beside its rich fretwork of statues, three narrow lancet windows. The statues on this vast front are the great boast of the cathedral. They number, with the lateral figures of the towers, no less than three hundred; it seems densely embroidered by the chisel. They are disposed, in successive niches, along six main vertical shafts; the central windows are framed and divided by narrower shafts, and the wall above them rises into a pinnacled screen traversed by two superb horizontal rows. Add to these a close-running cornice of images along the line corresponding with the summit of the aisles and the tiers which complete the decoration of the towers on either side, and you have an immense system of images governed by a quaint theological order and most impressive in its completeness. Many of the little high-lodged effigies are mutilated, and not a few of the niches are empty, but the injury of time is not sufficient to diminish the noble serenity of the building. The injury of time is indeed being actively repaired, for the front is partly masked by a slender scaffolding. The props and platforms are of the most delicate structure, and look in fact as if they were meant to facilitate no more ponderous labour than a fitting-on of noses to dis-featured bishops and a rearrangement of the mantle-folds of straitlaced queens discomposed by the centuries. The main beauty of Wells Cathedral, to my mind, is not its more or less visible wealth of detail, but its singularly charming tone of colour. An even, sober, mouse-coloured grey invests it from summit to base, deepening nowhere to the melancholy black of your truly romantic Gothic, but showing as yet none of the spotty brightness of renovation. It is a wonderful fact that the great towers, from their lofty outlook, see never a factory chimney – those cloud-compelling spires which so often break the charm of the softest English horizons; and the general atmosphere of Wells seemed to me, for some reason, peculiarly luminous and sweet. The cathedral has never been discoloured by the moral malaria of a city with an independent secular life. As you turn back from its portal and glance at the open lawn before it, edged by the mild grey seventeenth-century deanery and the other dwellings, hardly less stately, which seem to reflect in their comfortable fronts the rich respectability of the church, and then up again at the beautiful clear-hued pile, you may fancy it less a temple for man's needs than a monument of his pride – less a fold for the flock than for the shepherds; a visible token that, besides the actual assortment of heavenly thrones, there is constantly on hand a 'full line' of cushioned cathedral stalls. Within the cathedral this impression is not diminished. The interior is vast and massive, but it lacks incident – the incident of monuments, sepulchres and chapels – and it is too brilliantly lighted for picturesque, as distinguished from strictly architectural, interest. Under this latter head it has, I believe, great importance. For myself, I can think of it only as I saw it from my place in the choir during afternoon service of a hot Sunday.[2] The Bishop sat facing me, enthroned in a stately Gothic alcove and clad in his crimson band, his lawn sleeves and his lavender gloves; the canons, in their degree, with still other priestly forms, reclined comfortably in the carven stalls, and the scanty congregation fringed the broad aisle. But though scanty, the congregation was select; it was unexceptionably black-coated, bonneted and gloved. It savoured intensely in short of that inexorable gentility which the English put on with their Sunday bonnets and beavers and which fills me – as a mere taster of produced tastes – with a sort of fond reactionary remembrance of those animated bundles of rags which one sees kneeling in the churches of Italy.[3] But even here, as taster of tastes, I found my account. You always do if you throw yourself confidently enough, in England, on the chapter of accidents. Before me and beside me sat a row of the comeliest young men, clad in black gowns and wearing on their shoulders long hoods trimmed with white fur. Who and what they were I know not, for I preferred not to learn, lest by chance they should not be so medieval as they looked.

My fancy found its account even better in the singular quaintness of the little precinct known as the Vicars' Close. It directly adjoins the Cathedral Green, and you enter it beneath one of the solid old gatehouses which form so striking an element in the ecclesiastical furniture of Wells. It consists of a narrow, oblong court, bordered on each side with thirteen small dwellings, and terminating in a ruinous little chapel. Here formerly dwelt a congregation of minor priests, established in the thirteenth century to do curates' work for the canons. The little houses are very much modernised; but they retain their tall chimneys, with carven tablets in the face, their antique compactness and neatness, and a certain little sanctified air as of cells in a cloister. The place is adorably of another world and time, and, approaching it as I did in the first dimness of twilight, it looked to me, in its exaggerated perspective, like one of those conventional streets represented on the stage, down whose impossible vista the heroes and confidants of romantic comedies come swaggering arm-in-arm and hold amorous converse with heroines perched at second-story windows. But though the Vicars' Close is a curious affair enough, the great boast of Wells is its episcopal Palace. The Palace loses nothing from being seen for the first time in the kindly twilight, and from being approached with an uncautioned mind. To reach it (unless you go from within the cathedral by the cloisters), you pass out of the Green by another ancient gateway into the market-place, and thence back again through its own peculiar portal. My own first glimpse of it had all the felicity of a *coup de théâtre*. I saw within the dark archway an enclosure bedimmed at once with the shadows of trees and heightened with the glitter of water. The picture was worthy of this agreeable promise. Its main feature is the little grey-walled island on which the Palace stands, rising in feudal fashion out of a broad, clear moat, flanked with round towers and approached by a proper drawbridge. Along the outer side of the moat is a short walk beneath a row of picturesquely stunted elms; swans and ducks disport themselves in the current and ripple the bright shadows of the overclambering plants from the episcopal gardens and masses of wallflower lodged on the hoary battlements. On the evening of my visit the haymakers were at work on a great sloping field in the rear of the Palace, and the sweet perfume of the tumbled grass in the dusky air seemed all that was wanting to fix the scene for ever in the memory. Beyond the moat and within the grey walls dwells my lord Bishop, in the finest seat of all his order. The mansion dates from the thirteenth century; but, stately dwelling though it is, it occupies but a subordinate place in its own grounds. Their great ornament, picturesquely speaking, is the massive ruin of a banqueting-hall erected by a free-living medieval bishop and more or less demolished at the Reformation. With its still perfect towers and beautiful shapely windows, hung with those green tapestries so stoutly woven by the English climate, it is a relic worthy of being locked away behind an embattled wall. I have among my impressions of Wells, besides this picture of the moated Palace, half a dozen memories of the romantic sort, which I lack space to transcribe. The clearest impression perhaps is that of the beautiful church of St Cuthbert, of the same date as the cathedral, and in very much the same style of elegant, temperate Early English. It wears one of the high-soaring towers for which Somerset-shire is justly celebrated, as you may see from the window of the train in rolling past its almost top-heavy hamlets. The beautiful old church, surrounded with its green graveyard, and large enough to be impressive, without being too large (a great merit, to my sense) to be easily com-passed by a deplorably unarchitectural eye, wore a native English expression to which certain humble figures in the foreground gave additional point. On the edge of the churchyard was a low gabled house, before which four old men were gossiping in the eventide. Into the front of the house was inserted an antique alcove in stone, divided into three shallow little seats, two of which were occupied by extraordinary specimens of decrepitude. One of these ancient paupers had a huge protuberant forehead, and sat with a pensive air, his head gathered pain-fully upon his twisted shoulders and his legs resting across his crutch. The other was rubicund, blear-eyed and frightfully besmeared with snuff. Their voices were so feeble and senile that I could scarcely under-stand them, and only just managed to make out the answer to my inquiry[4] of who and what they were – 'We're Still's Almshouse, sir.'

One of the lions, almost, of Wells (whence it is but five miles distant) is the ruin of the famous Abbey of Glastonbury, on which Henry VIII, in the language of our day, came down so heavily. The ancient splendour of the architecture survives but in scattered and scanty fragments, among influences of a rather inharmonious sort. It was cattle-market in the little town as I passed up the main street, and a savour of hoofs and hide seemed to accompany me through the easy labyrinth of the old arches and piers. These occupy a large back yard, close behind the street, to which you are most prosaically admitted by a young woman who keeps a wicket and sells tickets. The continuity of tradition is not altogether broken, however, for the little street of Glastonbury has rather an old-time aspect, and one of the houses at least must have seen the last of the abbots ride abroad on his mule. The little inn is a capital bit of character, and as I waited for the 'bus under its low dark archway (in something of the mood, possibly, in which a train was once waited for at Coventry), and watched the barmaid flirting her way to and fro out of the heavy-browed kitchen and among the lounging young appraisers of colts and steers and barmaids, I might have imagined that the Merry England of the Tudors had not utterly passed away.[5] A beautiful England this must have been as well, if it contained many such abbeys as Glastonbury. Such of the ruined columns and portals and windows as still remain are of admirable design and finish. The doorways are rich in marginal ornament – ornament within ornament, as it often is; for the dainty weeds and wild flowers overlace the antique tracery with their bright arabesques and deepen the grey of the stone-work as it brightens their bloom. The thousand flowers which grow among English ruins deserve a chapter to themselves. I owe them, as an observer, a heavy debt of satisfaction, but I am too little of a botanist to pay them in their own coin. It has often seemed to me in England that the purest enjoyment of architecture was to be had among the ruins of great buildings. In the perfect building one is rarely sure that the impression is simply architectural: it is more or less pictorial and romantic; it depends partly upon association and partly upon various accessories and details which, however they may be wrought into harmony with the architectural idea, are not part of its essence and spirit. But in so far as beauty of structure is beauty of line and curve, balance and harmony of masses and dimensions, I have seldom relished it as deeply as on the grassy nave of some crumbling church, before lonely columns and empty windows where the wild flowers were a cornice and the sailing clouds a roof. The arts certainly hang together in what they do for us. These hoary relics of Glastonbury reminded me in their broken eloquence of one of the other great ruins of the world – the *Last Supper* of Leonardo. A beautiful shadow, in each case, is all that remains; but that shadow is the soul of the artist.

Salisbury Cathedral, to which I made a pilgrimage on leaving Wells, is the very reverse of a ruin, and you take your pleasure there on very different grounds from those I have just attempted to define. It is perhaps the best-known typical church in the world, thanks to its shapely spire;[6] but the spire is so simply and obviously fair that when you have respectfully made a note of it you have anticipated æsthetic analysis. I had seen it before and admired it heartily, and perhaps I should have done as well to let my admiration rest. I confess that on repeated inspection it grew to seem to me the least bit *banal*, or even *bête*, since I am talking French, and I began to consider whether it does not belong to the same range of art as the Apollo Belvedere or the Venus de' Medici. I am inclined to think that if I had to live within sight of a cathedral and encounter it in my daily

*Salisbury Cathedral*

71

comings and goings I should grow less weary of the rugged black front of Exeter than of the sweet perfection of Salisbury. There are people by temperament easily sated with beauties specifically fair, and the effect of Salisbury Cathedral architecturally is equivalent to that of flaxen hair and blue eyes physiognomically.[7] The other lions of Salisbury, Stonehenge and Wilton House, I revisited with undiminished interest. Stonehenge is rather a hackneyed shrine of pilgrimage. At the time of my former visit a picnic-party was making libations of beer on the dreadful altar sites. But the mighty mystery of the place has not yet been stared out of countenance; and as on this occasion there were no picnickers we were left to drink deep of all its ambiguities and intensities. It stands as lonely in history as it does on the great plain whose many-tinted green waves, as they roll away from it, seem to symbolise the ebb of the long centuries which have left it so portentously unexplained. You may put a hundred questions to these rough-hewn giants as they bend in grim contemplation of their fallen companions; but your curiosity falls dead in the vast sunny stillness that enshrouds them, and the strange monument, with all its unspoken memories, becomes simply a heart-stirring picture in a land of pictures. It is indeed immensely vague and immensely deep. At a distance you see it standing in a shallow dell of the plain, looking hardly larger than a group of ten-pins on a bowling-green. I can fancy sitting all a summer's day watching its shadows shorten and lengthen again, and drawing a delicious contrast between the world's duration and the feeble span of individual experience. There is something in Stonehenge almost reassuring to the nerves; if you are disposed to feel that the life of man has rather a thin surface, and that we soon get to the bottom of things, the immemorial grey pillars may serve to represent for you the pathless vaults beneath the house of history. Salisbury is indeed rich in antiquities. Wilton House,[8] a delightful old residence of the Earls of Pembroke, contains a noble collection of Greek and Roman marbles. These are ranged round a charming cloister occupying the centre of the house, which is exhibited in the most liberal fashion. Out of the cloister opens a series of drawing-rooms hung with family portraits, chiefly by Vandyck, all of superlative merit. Among them hangs supreme, as the Vandyck *par excellence*, the famous and magnificent group of the whole Pembroke family of James I's time. This splendid work has every pictorial merit – design, colour, elegance, force and finish, and I have been vainly wondering to this hour what it needs to be the finest piece of portraiture, as it surely is one of the most ambitious, in the world. What it lacks, characteristically, in a certain uncompromising veracity, it recovers in the beautiful dignity of its position – unmoved from the stately house in which its author sojourned and wrought, familiar to the descendants of its noble originals.

Fourth essay in the series 'A Summer in Europe', *The Nation*, XV (22 August 1872), 117–19; reprinted in *Transatlantic Sketches* (1875), *Foreign Parts* (1883), and *English Hours* (1905).

*Stonehenge*

# An English Easter

## I

It may be said of the English, as is said of the council of war in Sheridan's farce of *The Critic*[1] by one of the spectators of the rehearsal, that when they *do* agree, their unanimity is wonderful. They differ among themselves greatly just now as regards the machinations of Russia,[2] the derelictions of Turkey,[3] the merits of the Reverend Arthur Tooth, the genius of Mr Henry Irving,[4] and a good many other matters; but neither just now nor at any other time do they fail to conform to those social observances on which respectability has set her seal. England is a country of curious anomalies, and this has much to do with her being so interesting to foreign observers. The national, the individual character is very positive, very independent, very much made up according to its own sentiment of things, very prone to startling eccentricities; and yet at the same time it has beyond any other this peculiar gift of squaring itself with fashion and custom. In no other country, I imagine, are so many people to be found doing the same thing in the same way at the same time – using the same slang, wearing the same hats and neckties, collecting the same china plates, playing the same game of lawn tennis or of polo, admiring the same professional beauty. The monotony of such a spectacle would soon become oppressive if the foreign observer were not conscious of this latent capacity in the performers for great freedom of action; he finds a good deal of entertainment in wondering how they reconcile the traditional insularity of the private person with this perpetual tribute th usage. Of course in all civilised societies the tribute to usage is constantly paid: if it is less apparent in America than elsewhere the reason is not, I think, because individual independence is greater, but because usage is more sparsely established. Where custom can be ascertained people certainly follow it; but for one definite precedent in American life there are fifty in English. I am very far from having discovered the secret; I have not in the least learned what becomes of that explosive personal force in the English character which is compressed and corked down by social conformity. I look with a certain awe at some of the manifestations of the conforming spirit, but the fermenting idiosyncrasies beneath it are hidden from my vision. The most striking example, to foreign eyes, of the power of custom in England is certainly the universal church-going. In the sight of the English people getting up from its tea and toast of a Sunday morning and brushing its hat, and drawing on its gloves, and taking its wife on its arm, and making its offspring march before, and so, for decency's, respectability's, propriety's sake, wending its way to a place of worship appointed by the State, in which it repeats the formulas of a creed to which it attaches no positive sense and listens to a sermon over the length of which it explicitly haggles and grumbles – in this exhibition there is something very impressive to a stranger, something which he hardly knows whether to estimate as a great force or as a great futility. He inclines on the whole to pronounce the spectacle sublime, because it gives him the feeling that whenever it may become necessary for a people trained in these manœuvres to move all together under a common direction, they will have it in them to do so with tremendous weight and cohesiveness. We hear a good deal about the effect of the Prussian military system in consolidating the German people and making them available for a particular purpose; but I really think it not fanciful to say that the military punctuality which characterises the English observance of Sunday ought to be appreciated in the same fashion. A nation which has passed through such a mill will certainly have been stamped by it. And here, as in the German military service, it is really the whole nation. When I spoke just now of paterfamilias and his *entourage* I did not mean to limit the statement to him. The young unmarried men go to church, the gay bachelors, the irresponsible members of society. (That last epithet must be taken with a grain of allowance. No one in England is literally irresponsible; that perhaps is the shortest way of expressing a stranger's, certainly an American's, sense of their cohesion. Every one is free and every one is responsible. To say what it is people are responsible *to* is of course a great extension of the question: briefly, to social expectation, to propriety, to morality, to 'position', to the conventional English conscience, which is, after all, such a powerful factor. With us there is infinitely less responsibility; but there is also, I think, less freedom.)

The way in which the example of the more luxurious classes imposes itself upon the less luxurious may of course be noticed in smaller matters than church-going; in a great many matters which it may seem trivial to mention. If one is bent upon observation nothing, however, is trivial. So I may cite the practice of banishing the servants from the room at breakfast. It is the fashion, and accordingly, through the length and breadth of England, every one who has the slightest pretension to standing high enough to feel the way the social breeze is blowing conforms to it. It is awkward, unnatural, troublesome for those at table, it involves a vast amount of leaning and stretching, of waiting and perambulating, and it has just that vice against which, in English history, all great movements have been made – it is arbitrary. But it flourishes for all that, and all genteel people, looking into each other's eyes with the desperation of gentility, agree to endure it for gentility's sake. My instance may seem feeble, and I speak honestly when I say I might give others, forming part of an immense body of prescriptive usage, to which a society possessing in the largest manner, both by temperament and education, the sense of the 'inalienable' rights and comforts of the individual, contrives to accommodate itself. I do not mean to say that usage in England is always uncomfortable and arbitrary. On the contrary, few strangers can be unfamiliar with that sensation ( a most agreeable one) which consists in perceiving in the rigidity of a tradition which has struck one at first as mechanical a reason existing in the historic 'good sense' of the English race. The sensation is frequent, though in saying so I do not mean to imply that even superficially the presumption is against the usages of English society. It is not, for instance, necessarily against the custom of which I had it more especially in mind to speak in writing these lines. The stranger in London is forewarned that at Easter all the world goes out of town, and that if he have no mind to be left to some fate that universal terror of which half allures half appals his curiosity, he too had better make arrangements for a temporary absence. It must be admitted that there is a sort of unexpectedness in this prompt re-emigration of a body of people who but a week before were apparently devoting much energy to settling down for the season. Half of them have but lately come back from the country, where they have been spending the winter, and they have just had time, it may be supposed, to collect the scattered threads of town life. Presently, however, the threads are dropped and society is dispersed as if it had taken a false start. It departs as Holy Week draws to a close, and remains absent for the following ten days. Where it goes is its own affair; a good deal of it goes to Paris. Spending last winter in that city, I remember how, when I woke up on Easter Monday and looked out of my window, I found the street covered overnight with a sort of snow-fall of disembarked Britons. They made for other people an uncomfortable week of it. One's customary table at the restaurant, one's habitual stall at the Théâtre Français, one's usual fiacre on the cab-stand, were very apt to have suffered estrangement. I believe the pilgrimage to Paris was this year of the usual proportions; and you may be sure that people who did not cross the Channel were not without invitations to quiet old places in the country, where the pale fresh primroses were beginning to light up the dark turf and the purple bloom of the bare tree-masses to be freckled here and there with verdure. In England country-life is the obverse of the medal, town-life the reverse, and when an occasion comes for quitting London there are few members of what the French call the 'easy class' who have not a collection of dull, moist, verdant resorts to choose from. Dull I call them, and I fancy not without reason, though at the moment I speak of their dullness must have been mitigated by the unintermittent presence of the keenest and liveliest of east winds. Even in mellow English country homes Easter-tide is a period of rawness and atmospheric acridity – the moment at which the frank hostility of winter, which has at last to give up the game, turns to peevishness and spite. This is what makes it arbitrary, as I said just now, for 'easy' people to go forth to the wind-swept lawns and the shivering parks. But nothing is more striking to an American than the frequency of English holidays and the large way in which occasions for a 'little change' are made use of. All this speaks to Americans of three things which they are accustomed to see allotted in scantier measure. The English have more time than we, they have more money, and they have a much higher relish for active leisure. Leisure, fortune, and the love of sport are felicities encountered in English society at every turn. It was a very small number of weeks before Easter that Parliament met, and yet a ten days' recess was already, from the luxurious Parliamentary point of view, a necessity. A short time hence we shall be having the Whitsuntide holidays, which I am told are even more of a season of revelry than Easter, and from this point to midsummer, when everything stops, is an easy journey. The men of business and the professional men partake in equal measure of these agreeable diversions, and I was interested in hearing a lady whose husband was an active member of the bar say that, though he was leaving town with her for ten days, and though Easter was a very nice 'little break', they really amused themselves more during the later festival, which would come on toward the end of May. I thought this highly probable, and admired in their career such an effect of breeze-blown light and shade. If my phrase has a slightly ironical sound, this is purely accidental. A large appetite for holidays, the ability not only to take them but to know what to do with them when taken, is the sign of a robust people, and judged by this measure we Americans are sadly inexpert. Such holidays as we take are taken very often in Europe, where it is sometimes noticeable that our privilege is rather heavy on our hands. Acknowledgment made of English industry, however (our own stands in no need of compliments), it must be added that for those same easy classes I just spoke of things are very easy indeed. The number of persons obtainable for purely social purposes at all times and seasons is infinitely greater than among ourselves; and the ingenuity of the arrangements permanently going forward to disembarrass them of their superfluous leisure is as yet in America an undeveloped branch of civilisation. The young men who are preparing for the stern realities of life among the grey-green cloisters of Oxford are obliged to keep their terms but half the year; and the rosy little cricketers of Eton and Harrow are let loose upon the parental home for an embarrassing number of months. Happily the parental home is apt to be an affair of gardens, lawns and parks.

## II

Passion Week, in London, is distinctly an ascetic period; there is really an approach to sackcloth and ashes. Private dissipation is suspended; most of the theatres and music-halls are closed; the huge dusky city seems to take on a still sadder colouring and a half-hearted hush steals over its mighty uproar. At such a moment, for a stranger, London is not cheerful. Arriving there, during the past winter, about Christmas-time, I encountered three British Sundays in a row – a spectacle to strike terror into the stoutest heart. A Sunday and a 'bank holiday', if I remember aright, had joined hands with a Christmas Day and produced the portentous phenomenon to which I allude. I betrayed, I suppose, some apprehension of its oppressive character, for I remember being told in a consolatory way that I needn't fear; it would not come round again for another year. This information was given me on the occasion of that surprising interruption of one's relations with the laundress which is apparently characteristic of the period. I was told that all the washer-women were intoxicated and that, as it would take them some time to revive, I must not count upon a relay of 'fresh things'. I shall not forget the impression made upon me by this statement; I had just comes from Paris and it almost sent me spinning back. One of the incidental *agréments* of life in the latter city had been the knock at my door on Saturday evenings of a charming young woman with a large basket protected by a snowy napkin on her arm, and on her head a frilled and fluted muslin cap which was an irresistible advertisement of her art. To say that my admirable *blanchisseuse* was not in liquor is altogether too gross a com-pliment; but I was always grateful to her for her russet cheek, her frank expressive eye, her talkative smile, for the way her charming cap was poised upon her crisp, dense hair and her well-made dress adjusted and worn. I talked with her; I *could* talk with her; and as she talked she moved about and laid out her linen with a delightful modest ease. Then her light step carried her off again, talking, to the door, and with a brighter smile and an 'Adieu, monsieur!' she closed it behind her, leaving one to think how stupid is prejudice and how poetic a creature a washerwoman may be. London, in December, was livid with sleet and fog, and against this dismal background was offered me the vision of a horrible old woman in a smoky bonnet, lying prone in a puddle of whisky! She seemed to assume a kind of symbolic significance and almost frightened me away.

I mentioned this trifle, which is doubtless not creditable to my fortitude, because I found that the information given me was not strictly accurate and that at the end of three months I had another array of London Sundays to face. On this occasion, however, nothing occurred to suggest again the dreadful image I have just sketched, though I devoted a good deal of time to observing the manners of the lower orders.[5] From Good Friday to Easter Monday, inclusive, they were very much *en evidence*, and it was an excellent occasion for getting an impression of the British populace. Gentility had retired to the background, and in the West End all the blinds were lowered; the streets were void of carriages, and well-dressed pedestrians were rare; but the 'masses' were all abroad and making the most of their holiday, so that I strolled about and watched them at their gambols. The heavens were most unfavourable, but in an English 'outing' there is always a margin left for a drenching, and throughout the vast smoky city, beneath the shifting gloom of the sky, the grimy crowds wandered with a kind of weatherproof stolidity. The parks were full of them, the railway stations overflowed, the Thames embankment was covered. The 'masses', I think, are usually an entertaining spectacle, even when observed through the distorting medium of London bad weather. There are indeed few things in their way more impressive than a dusky London holiday; it suggests so many and such interestingly related reflections. Even looked at superficially the capital of the Empire is one of the most appealing of cities, and it is perhaps on such occasions as this that I have most felt its appeal. London is ugly, dusky, dreary, more destitute than any European city of graceful and decorative incident; and though on festal days, like those I speak of, the populace is massed in large numbers at certain points, many of the streets are empty enough of human life to enable you to perceive their intrinsic want of charm. A Christmas Day or a Good Friday uncovers the ugliness of London. As you walk along the streets, having no fellow pedestrians to look at, you look up at the brown brick house walls, corroded with soot and fog, pierced with their straight stiff window-slits, and finished, by way of a cornice, with a little black line resembling a slice of curb-stone. There is not an accessory, not a touch of architectural fancy, not the narrowest concession to beauty. If I were a foreigner it would make me rabid; being an Anglo-Saxon I find in it what Thackerary found in Baker Street – a delightful proof of English domestic virtue, of the sanctity of the British home. There are miles and miles of these edifying monuments, and it would seem that a city made up of them should have no claim to that larger effectiveness of which I just now spoke. London, however, is not made up of them; there are architectural combinations of a statelier kind, and the impression more-over does not rest on details. London is pictorial in spite of details – from its dark green, misty parks, the way the light comes down leaking and filtering from its cloud ceiling, and the softness and richness of tone which objects put on in such an atmosphere as soon as they begin to recede. Nowhere is there such a play of light and shade, such a struggle of sun and smoke, such aerial gradations and confusions. To eyes addicted to such contemplations this is a constant diversion, and yet this is only part of it. What completes the effect of the place is its appeal to the feelings, made in so many ways, but made above all by agglomerated immensity. At any given point London looks huge; even in narrow corners you have a sense of its hugeness, and petty places acquire a certain interest from their being parts of so mighty a whole. Nowhere else is so much human life gathered together, and nowhere does it press upon you with so many suggestions. These are not all of an exhilarating kind; far from it. But they are of every possible kind, and that is the interest of London. Those that were most forcible during the showery Easter season were certain of the more perplexing and depressing ones; but even with these was mingled a brighter strain.

I walked down to Westminster Abbey on Good Friday afternoon – walked from Piccadilly across the Green Park and through that of St James. The parks were densely filled with the populace – the elder people shuffling about the walks and the poor little smutty-faced children sprawling over the dark damp turf. When I reached the Abbey I found a dense group of people about the entrance, but I squeezed my way

through them and succeeded in reaching the threshold. Beyond this it
was impossible to advance, and I may add that it was not desirable. I put
my nose into the church and promptly withdrew it. The crowd was
terribly compact, and beneath the Gothic arches the odour was not that
of incense. I gradually gave it up, with that very modified sense of disappointment that one feels in London at being crowded out of a place.
This is a frequent form of philosophy, for you soon learn that there are,
selfishly speaking, too many people. Human life is cheap; your fellow
mortals are too numerous. Wherever you go you make the observation.
At the theatre, at a concert, an exhibition, a reception, you always find
that, before you arrive, there are people enough in the field. You are a
tight fit in your place, wherever you find it; you have too many companions and competitors. You feel yourself at times in danger of thinking
meanly of the human personality; numerosity, as it were, swallows up
quality, and the perpetual sense of other elbows and knees begets a
yearning for the desert. This is the reason why the perfection of luxury
in England is to own a 'park' – an artificial solitude. To get one's self into
the middle of a few hundred acres of oak-studded turf and to keep off the
crowd by the breadth, at least, of the grassy shade, is to enjoy a comfort
which circumstances make peculiarly precious. But I walked back
through the profane pleasure grounds of London, in the midst of
'superfluous herds', and I found the profit of vision that I never fail to
derive from a great English assemblage. The English are, on the whole,
to my eyes so appreciably the handsomest people in Europe – remembering always, of course, that when we talk of the frequency of beauty anywhere we talk of a minor quantity, more small or less small – that it takes
some effort of the imagination to believe that the appearance requires
demonstration. I never see a large number of them without feeling this
impression confirmed; though I hasten to add that I have sometimes felt
it to be much shaken in the presence of a limited group. I suspect that a
great English crowd would yield a larger percentage of *regular* faces and
tall figures than any other. With regard to the upper class I suppose this is
generally granted; but, with all abatements, I should extend it to the
people at large. Certainly, if the English populace strike the observer as
regular, nature, in them, must have clung hard to the higher ideal. They

are as ill-dressed as their betters are well-dressed, and their garments have that sooty surface which has nothing in common with the continental costume of labour and privation. It is the hard prose of misery – an ugly and hopeless imitation of respectable attire. This is especially noticeable in the battered and bedraggled bonnets of the women, which look as if their husbands had stamped on them, in hob-nailed boots, as a hint of what may be in store for their wearers. Then it is not too much to say that two-thirds of the London faces, as the streets present them, bear in some degree or other the traces of alcoholic action. The proportion of flushed, empurpled, eruptive masks is considerable; a source of depression, for the spectator, not diminished by the fact that many of the faces thus disfigured have evidently been planned on lines of high superficial decency. A very large allowance is to be made, too, for the people who bear the distinctive stamp of that physical and mental degradation which comes from the slums and purlieus of this duskiest of modern Babylons – the pallid, stunted, misbegotten and in every way miserable figures. These people swarm in every London crowd, and I know of none in any other place that suggest an equal depth of degradation. But when such exceptions are taken the observer still notes the quantity and degree of facial finish, the firmness of type, if not always its fineness, the clearnesses and symmetries, the modelled brows and cheeks and chins, the immense contribution made to his impression, above all, by the elements of complexion and stature. The question of expression is another matter, and one must admit at the outset, to have done with it, that expression here in general lacks, even to strangeness, any perceptible intensity, though it often has among the women, and adorably among the children, an indescribable shy delicacy. I have it at heart, however, to add that if the English are handsomer than ourselves they are also very much uglier. Indeed I think all the European peoples more richly ugly than the American: we are far from producing those magnificent types of facial eccentricity which flourish on soils socially more rank. American ugliness is on the side of physical poverty and meanness; English on that of redundancy and monstrosity. In America there are few grotesques; in England there are many – and some of them have a high plastic, historic, romantic value.

## III

The element of the grotesque was very noticeable to me in the most marked collection of the shabbier English types that I had seen since I came to London. The occasion of my seeing them was the funeral of Mr George Odger, which befell some four or five weeks before the Easter period. Mr George Odger, it will perhaps be remembered, was an English Radical agitator of humble origin, who had distinguished himself by a perverse desire to get into Parliament. He exercised, I believe, the useful profession of shoemaker, and he knocked in vain at the door that opens but to the refined. But he was a useful and honourable man, and his own people gave him an honourable burial. I emerged accidentally into Piccadilly at the moment they were so engaged, and the spectacle was one I should have been sorry to miss. The crowd was enormous, but I managed to squeeze through it and to get into a hansom cab that was drawn up beside the pavement, and here I looked on as from a box at the play. Though it was a funeral that was going on I will not call it a tragedy; but it was a very serious comedy. The day happened to be magnificent – the finest of the year. The ceremony had been taken in hand by the classes who are socially unrepresented in Parliament, and it had the character of a great popular manifestation. The hearse was followed by very few carriages, but the *cortège* of pedestrians stretched away in the sunshine, up and down the classic decorum of Piccadilly, on a scale highly impressive. Here and there the line was broken by a small brass band – apparently one of those bands of itinerant Germans that play for coppers beneath lodging-house windows; but for the rest it was compactly made up of what the newspapers call the dregs of the population. It was the London rabble, the metropolitan mob, men and women, boys and girls, the decent poor and the indecent, who had scrambled into the ranks as they gathered them up on their passage, and were making a sort of solemn 'lark' of it. Very solemn it all was – perfectly proper and undemonstrative. They shuffled along in an interminable line, and as I looked at them out of the front of my hansom I seemed to be having a sort of panoramic view of the under side, the wrong side,

*Rochester Castle*

of the London world. The procession was filled with figures which seemed never to have 'shown out', as the English say, before; of strange, pale, mouldy paupers who blinked and stumbled in the Piccadilly sunshine, I have no space to describe them more minutely, but I found the whole affair vaguely yet portentously suggestive. My impression rose not simply from the radical, or, as I may say for the sake of colour, the revolutionary, emanation of this dingy concourse, lighted up by the ironic sky; but from the same causes I had observed a short time before, on the day the Queen went to open Parliament, when in Trafalgar Square, looking straight down into Westminster and over the royal procession, were gathered a group of banners and festoons inscribed in big staring letters with mottoes and sentiments which might easily have given on the nerves of a sensitive police department. They were mostly in allusion to the Tichborne claimant, whose release from his dungeon they peremptorily demanded and whose cruel fate was taken as a pretext for several sweeping reflections on the social arrangements of the time and country. These signals of unreason were allowed to sun themselves as freely as if they had been the manifestoes of the Irish Giant or the

Oriental Dwarf at a fair. I had lately come from Paris, where the authorities have a shorter patience and where revolutionary placards at the base of the obelisk in the Place de la Concorde fall in with no recognised scheme – such is the effect of the whirligig of time – of the grand style or of monumental decorum. I was therefore the more struck on both of the occasions I speak of with the admirable English practice of letting people alone – with the frank good sense and the frank good humour and even the frank good taste of it. It was this that I found impressive as I watched the manifestation of Mr Odger's underfed partisans – the fact that the mighty mob could march along and do its errand while the excellent quiet policemen – eternal, imperturbable, positively lovable reminders of the national temperament – stood by simply to see that the channel was kept clear and comfortable.

When Easter Monday came it was obvious that every one (save Mr Odger's friends – three or four million or so) had gone out of town.

*The Tower of London*

There was hardly a pair of shutters in the West End that was not closed; there was not a bell that it was any use to pull. The weather was destestable, the rain incessant, and the fact that all your friends were away gave you plenty of leisure to reflect that the country must be the reverse of enlivening. But all your friends had gone thither (this is the unanimity I began by talking about), and to restrict as much as possible the proportions of that game of hide-and-seek of which, at the best, so much of London social life consists, it seemed wise to bring within the limits of the dull season any such excursion as might have been projected in commemoration of the first days of spring. After due cogitation I paid a little visit to Canterbury and Dover, taking Rochester by the way, and it was of this momentous journey that I proposed, in beginning these remarks, to give an account. But I have dallied so much by the way that I have come almost to my rope's end without reaching my first stage. I should have begun, artistically, by relating that I put myself in the humour for remote adventure by going down the Thames on a penny steamboat to the towers of Julius. This was on the Saturday before Easter, and the City was as silent as the grave. 'London's lasting shame' was a memory of my childhood, and, having theory that from such memories the dust of the ages had better not be shaken, I had not retraced my steps to its venerable walls. But the Tower – *the* Tower – is very good, and much less cockneyfied than I supposed it would seem to my maturer vision; very grey and historical, with the look that vivifies (rather lividly indeed), the past. I could not get into it, as it had been closed for Passion Week, but I was consequently relieved from the obligation to march about with a dozen fellow starers in the train of a didactic beefeater, and I strolled at will through the courts and the garden, sharing them only with the lounging soldiers of the garrison, who seemed to connect the place, for the backward-reaching fancy, with important events.

## IV

At Rochester I stopped for the sake of its castle,[6] which I espied from the railway train as it perched on a grassy bank beside the widening

Medway. There were other beguilements as well; the place has a small cathedral, and, leaving the creators of Falstaff and of the tale-telling Pilgrims out of the question, one had read about it in Dickens, whose house of Gadshill was a couple of miles from the town. All this Kentish country, between London and Dover, figures indeed repeatedly in Dickens; he expresses to a certain extent, for our later age, the spirit of the land. I found this to be quite the case at Rochester. I had occasion to go into a little shop kept by a talkative old woman who had a photograph

*Chatham*

of Gadshill lying on her counter. This led to my asking her whether the illustrious master of the house had often, to her old-time vision, made his appearance in the town. 'Oh, bless you, sir,' she said, 'we every one of us knew him to speak to. He was in this very shop on the Tuesday with a party of foreigners – as he was dead in his bed on the Friday.' (I should remark that I probably do not repeat the days of the week as she gave them.) 'He'ad on his black velvet suit, and it always made him look so 'andsome. I said to my 'usband, "I *do* think Charles Dickens looks so nice in that black velvet suit." But he said he couldn't see as he looked any way particular. He was in this very shop on the Tuesday, with a party of foreigners.' Rochester consists of little more than one long street, stretching away from the castle and the river toward neighbouring Chatham, and edged with low brick houses, of intensely provincial aspect, most of which have some small, dull smugness or quaintness of gable or window. Nearly opposite to the shop of the old lady with the snubby husband is a little dwelling with an inscribed slab set into its face, which must often have provoked a smile in the great master of the comic. The slab relates that in the year 1579 Richard Watts here established a charity which should furnish 'six poor travellers, not rogues or proctors', one night's lodging and entertainment gratis, and fourpence in the morning to go on their way withal, and that in memory of his 'munificence' the stone has lately been renewed. The inn at Rochester had small hospitality, and I felt strongly tempted to knock at the door of Mr Watts's asylum, under plea of being neither a rogue nor a proctor. The poor traveller who avails himself of the testamentary fourpence may easily resume his journey as far as Chatham without breaking his treasure. Is not this the place where little Davy Copperfield slept under a cannon on his journey from London to Dover to join his aunt Miss Trotwood? The two towns are really but one, which forms an interminable crooked thoroughfare, lighted up in the dusk, as I measured it up and down, with the red coats of the vespertinal soldier quartered at the various barracks of Chatham.

The cathedral of Rochester[7] is small and plain, hidden away in rather an awkward corner, without a verdant close to set it off. It is dwarfed and effaced by the great square Norman keep of the adjacent castle. But within it is very charming, especially beyond the detestable wall, the vice of almost all the English cathedrals, which shuts in the choir and breaks the sacred perspective of the aisle. Here, as at Canterbury, you ascend a high range of steps, to pass through the small door in the wall. When I speak slightingly, by the way, of the outside of Rochester cathedral, I intend my faint praise in a relative sense. If we were so happy as to have this secondary pile within reach in America we should go barefoot to see it; but here it stands in the great shadow of Canterbury, and that makes it humble. I remember, however, an old priory gateway

which leads you to the church, out of the main street; I remember a kind
of haunted-looking deanery, if that be the technical name, at the base of
the eastern walls; I remember a fluted tower that took the afternoon
light and let the rooks and the swallows come circling and clamouring
around it. Better still than these things I remember the ivy-muffled
squareness of the castle, a very noble and imposing ruin. The old walled
precinct has been converted into a little public garden, with flowers and
benches and a pavilion for a band, and the place was not empty, as such
places in England never are. The result is agreeable, but I believe the
process was barbarous, involving the destruction and dispersion of many
interesting portions of the ruin. I lingered there for a long time, looking
in the fading light at what was left. This rugged pile of Norman masonry
will be left when a great many solid things have departed; it mocks, ever
so monotonously, at destruction, at decay. Its walls are fantasticlly
thick; their great time-bleached expanses and all their rounded roughnesses, their strange mixture of softness and grimness, have an un-
definable fascination for the eye. English ruins always come out peculiarly
when the day begins to fail. Weather-bleached, as I say they are, they
turn even paler in the twilight and grow consciously solemn and spectral.
I have seen many a mouldering castle, but I remember in no single mass
of ruin more of the helpless, bereaved, amputated look.

It is not the absence of a close that damages Canterbury; the cathedral
stands amid grass and trees, with a cultivated margin all round it, and is
placed in such a way that, as you pass out from under the gatehouse, you
appreciate immediately its grand feature – its extraordinary and
magnificent length. None of the English cathedrals seems to sit more
gravely apart, to desire more to be shut up to itself. It is a long walk,
beneath the walls, from the gateway of the close to the farther end of the
last chapel. Of all that there is to observe in this upward-gazing stroll I
can give no detailed account; I can, in my fear to pretend to dabble in the
esoteric constructional question – often so combined with an absence of
other felt relations – speak only of the picture, the mere builded *scene*.
This is altogether delightful. None of the rivals of Canterbury has a
more complicated and elaborate architecture, a more perplexing inter-
mixture of periods, a more charming jumble of Norman arches and

English points and perpendiculars. What makes the side view superb, moreover, is the double transepts, which produce the finest agglomeration of gables and buttresses. It is as if two great churches had joined forces toward the middle – one giving its nave and the other its choir, and each keeping its own great cross-aisles. Astride of the roof, between them sits a huge Gothic tower, which is one of the latest portions of the building, though it looks like one of the earliest, so tempered and tinted, so thumb-marked and rubbed smooth is it, by the handling of the ages and the breath of the elements. Like the rest of the structure it has a magnificent colour – a sort of rich dull yellow, a sort of personal accent of tone that is neither brown nor grey. This is particularly appreciable from the cloisters on the further side of the church – the side, I mean, away from the town and the open garden-sweep I spoke of; the side that looks toward a damp old clerical house, lurking behind a brown archway through which you see young ladies in Gainsborough hats playing something on a patch of velvet turf; the side, in short, that is somehow intermingled with a green quadrangle – a quadrangle serving as a playground to a King's School and adorned externally with a very precious and picturesque old fragment of Norman staircase. This cloister is not 'kept up'; it is very dusky and mouldy and dilapidated, and of course very sketchable. The old black arches and capitals are various and handsome, and in the centre are tumbled together a group of crooked gravestones, themselves almost buried in the deep soft grass. Out of the cloister opens the chapter-house, which is not kept up either, but which is none the less a magnificent structure; a noble, lofty hall, with a beautiful wooden roof, simply arched like that of a tunnel, without columns or brackets. The place is now given up to dust and echoes; but it looks more like a banqueting-hall than a council-room of priests, and as you sit on the old wooden bench, which, raised on two or three steps, runs round the base of the four walls, you may gaze up and make out the faint ghostly traces of decorative paint and gold upon the brown ceiling. A little patch of this has been restored 'to give an idea'. From one of the angles of the cloister you are recommended by the verger to take a view of the great tower, which indeed detaches itself with tremendous effect. You see it base itself upon the roof as broadly as if it were striking roots in

earth, and then pile itself away to a height which seems to make the very swallows dizzy as they drop from the topmost shelf. Within the cathedral you hear a great deal, of course, about poor great Thomas A'Becket,[8] and the special sensation of the place is to stand on the spot where he was murdered and look down at a small fragmentary slab which the verger points out to you as a bit of the pavement that caught the blood-drops of the struggle. It was late in the afternoon when I first entered the church; there had been a service in the choir, but that was well over, and I had the place to myself. The verger, who had some pushing-about of benches to attend to, turned me into the locked gates and left me to wander through the side aisles of the choir and into the great chapel beyond it. I say I had the place to myself; but it would be more decent to affirm that I shared it, in particular, with another gentleman. This personage was stretched upon a couch of stone, beneath a quaint old canopy of wood; his hands were crossed upon his breast, and his pointed toes rested upon a little griffin or leopard. He was a very handsome fellow and the image of a gallant knight. His name was Edward Plantagenet, and his sobriquet was the Black Prince. '*De la mort ne pensai-je mye*,' he says in the beautiful inscription embossed upon the bronze base of his image; and I too, as I stood there, lost the sense of death in a momentary impression of personal nearness to him. One had been further off, after all, from other famous knights. In this same chapel, for many a year, stood the shrine of St Thomas of Canterbury, one of the richest and most potent in Christendom. The pavement which lay before it has kept its place, but Henry VIII swept away everything else in his famous short cut to reform. Becket was originally buried in the crypt of the church; his ashes lay there for fifty years, and it was only little by little that his martyrdom was made a 'draw'. Then he was transplanted into the Lady Chapel; every grain of his dust became a priceless relic, and the pavement was hallowed by the knees of pilgrims. It was on this errand of course that Chaucer's story-telling cavalcade came to Canterbury. I made my way down into the crypt, which is a magnificent maze of low, dark arches and pillars, and groped about till I found the place where the frightened monks had first shuffled the inanimate victim of Moreville and Fitzurse out of the reach of further desecration. While I stood there a violent thunderstorm broke over the cathedral; great rumbling gusts and rain-drifts came sweeping through the open sides of the crypt and, mingling with the darkness which seemed to deepen and flash in corners and with the potent mouldy smell, made me feel as if I had descended into the very bowels of history. I emerged again, but the rain had settled down and spoiled the evening, and I splashed back to my inn and sat, in an uncomfortable chair by the coffee-room fire, reading Dean Stanley's agreeable *Memorials of Canterbury* and wondering over the musty appointments and meagre resources of so many English hostels. This establishment had entitled itself in (compliment to the Black Prince, I suppose) the 'Fleur-de-Lis'. The name was very pretty (I had been foolish enough to let it attract me to the inn), but the lily was sadly deflowered.

First published in *Lippincott's Magazine*, XX (July 1877), 50–60; reprinted in *Portraits of Places* (1883), and *English Hours* (1905).

*Canterbury Cathedral*

# London at Midsummer

I believe it is supposed to require a good deal of courage to confess that one has spent the month of so-called social August in London; and I will therefore, taking the bull by the horns, plead guilty at the very outset to this poorness of spirit. I might attempt some ingenious extenuation of it; I might say that my remaining in town had been the most unexpected necessity or the merest inadvertence; I might pretend I liked it – that I had done it in fact for the perverse love of the thing; I might claim that you don't really know the charms of London until on one of the dog-days you have imprinted your boot-sole in the slumbering dust of Belgravia, or, gazing along the empty vista of the Drive, in Hyde Park, have beheld, for almost the first time in England, a landscape without figures. But little would remain of these specious apologies save the bald circumstance that I had distinctly failed to pack and be off – either on the first of August with the ladies and children, or on the thirteenth with the members of Parliament, or on the twelfth when the grouse-shooting began. (I am not sure that I have got my dates right to a day, but these were about the proper opportunities.) I have, in fact, survived the departure of everything genteel, and the three millions of persons who remained behind with me have been witnesses of my shame.

I cannot pretend, on the other hand, that, having lingered in town, I have found it a very odious or painful experience. Being a stranger, I have not felt it necessary to incarcerate myself during the day and steal abroad only under cover of the darkness – a line of conduct imposed by public opinion, if I am to trust the social criticism of the weekly papers (which I am far from doing), upon the native residents who allow themselves to be overtaken by the unfashionable season. I have indeed always held that few things are pleasanter, during very hot weather, than to have a great city, and a large house within it, quite to one's self. Yet these majestic conditions have not embellished my own metropolitan sojourn, and I have received an impression that in London it would be rather difficult for a visitor not having the command of a good deal of powerful machinery to find them united. English summer weather is rarely hot enough to make it necessary to darken one's house and denude one's person. The present year has indeed in this respect been 'exceptional', as any year is, for that matter, that one spends anywhere. But the manners of the people are, to alien eyes, a sufficient indication that at the best (or the worst) even the highest flights of the thermometer in the United Kingdom betray a broken wing. People live with closed windows in August very much as they do in January, and there is to the eye no appreciable difference in the character – that is in the thickness and stiffness – of their coats and boots. A 'bath' in England, for the most part, all the year round, means a little portable tin tub and a sponge. Peaches and pears, grapes and melons, are not a more obvious ornament of the market at midsummer than at Christmas. This matter of peaches and melons, by the way, offers one of the best examples of that fact to which a commentator on English manners from afar finds himself constantly recurring, and to which he grows at last almost ashamed of alluding – the fact that the beauty and luxury of the country, that elaborate system known and revered all over the world as 'English comfort', is a limited and restricted, an essentially private, affair. I am not one of those irreverent strangers who talk of English fruit as a rather audacious *plaisanterie*, though I could see very well what was meant a short time since by an anecdote related to me in a tone of contemptuous generalisation by a couple of my fellow countrywomen. They had arrived in London in the dog-days, and, lunching at their hotel, had asked to be served with some fruit. The hotel was of the stateliest pattern, and they were waited upon by a functionary whose grandeur was proportionate. This personage bowed and retired, and, after a long delay, reappearing, placed before them with an inimitable gesture a dish of gooseberries and currants. It appeared upon investigation that these acrid vegetables were the only things of succulence that the establishment could undertake to supply; and it seemed to increase the irony of the situation that the establishment was as near as possible to Buckingham Palace. I say that the heroines of my anecdote seemed disposed to generalise: this was sufficiently the case, I mean, to give me a pretext for assuring them that on a thousand fine properties the most beautiful peaches and melons were at that moment ripening either under glass or in warm old walled gardens. My auditors tossed their heads of course at the fine properties, the glass and the walled gardens; and indeed at their place of privation close to Buckingham Palace such a piece of knowledge was but scantily consoling.

It is to a more public fund of entertainment that the desultory stranger in any country chiefly appeals, especially in summer weather; and as I have implied that there is little encouragement in England to such an appeal it may appear remarkable that I should not have felt London, at this season, void of all beguilement. But one's liking for London – a stranger's liking at least – has at the best a kind of perversity and infirmity often rather difficult to reduce to a statement. I am far from meaning by this that there are not in this mighty metropolis a thousand sources of interest, entertainment and delight: what I mean is that, for one reason and another, with all its social resources, the place lies heavy on the imported consciousness. It seems grim and lurid, fierce and unmerciful. And yet the imported consciousness accepts it at last with an active satisfaction and finds something warm and comfortable, something that if removed would be greatly missed, in its portentous pressure. It must be admitted, however, that, granting that every one is out of town, your choice of pastimes is not embarrassing. If you have happened to spend a certain amount of time in places where public manners have more frankness London will seem to you but scantily provided with innocent diversions. This indeed brings us back simply to that question of the absence of a 'public fund' of amusement to which reference was just now made. You must give up the idea of going to sit somewhere in the open air, to eat an ice and listen to a band of music. You will find neither the seat, the ice, nor the band; but on the other hand, faithful at once to your interest and your detachment, you may supply the place of these delights by a little private meditation on the deep-lying causes of the English indifference to them. In such reflections nothing is idle – every grain of testimony counts; and one need therefore not be accused of

jumping too suddenly from small things to great if one traces a connection between the absence of ices and music and the essentially
hierarchical plan of English society. This hierarchical[1] plan of English
society is the great and ever-present fact to the mind of a stranger: there
is hardly a detail of life that does not in some degree betray it. It is really
only in a country in which a good deal of democratic feeling prevails that
people of 'refinement', as we say in America, will be willing to sit at little
round tables, on a pavement or a gravel-walk, at the door of a café. The
better sort are too 'genteel' and the inferior sort too base. One must
hasten to add too, in justice, that the better sort are, as a general thing,
quite too well furnished with entertainments of their own; they have
those special resources to which I alluded a moment since. They are
persons for whom the private machinery of ease has been made to work
with extraordinary smoothness. If you can sit on a terrace overlooking
gardens and have your *café noir* handed you in old Worcester cups by
servants who are models of consideration, you have hardly a decent
pretext for going to a public house. In France and Italy, in Germany and
Spain, the count and countess will sally forth and encamp for the evening,
under a row of coloured lamps, upon the paving-stones, but it is ten to
one that the count and countess live on a single floor and up several pair
of stairs. They are, however, I think, not appreciably affected by considerations which operate potently in England. An Englishman who
should propose to sit down, in his own country, at a café door would
find himself remembering that he is pretending to participations,
contacts, fellowships the absolute impracticability of which is expressed
in all the rest of his doings.

The study of these reasons, however, would lead us very far from the
potential little tables for ices in – where shall I say ? – in Oxford Street.
But, after all, there is no reason why our imagination should hover
about any such articles of furniture. I am afraid they would not strike us
as at the best happily situated. In such matters everything hangs together,
and I am certain that the customs of the Boulevard des Italiens and the
Piazza Colonna would not harmonise with the scenery of the great
London thoroughfare. A gin-palace right and left and a detachment of
the London rabble in an admiring semicircle – these strike one as some of

the more obvious features of the affair. Yet at the season of which I write one's social studies must at the least be studies of low life, for wherever one may go for a stroll or to spend the summer afternoon the comparatively sordid side of things is uppermost. There is no one in the parks

*Greenwich*

save the rough characters who are lying on their faces in the sheep-polluted grass. These people are always tolerably numerous in the Green Park, through which I frequently pass, and are always an occasion for deep wonder. But your wonder will go far if it begins to bestir itself on behalf of the recumbent British tramp. You perceive among them some rich possibilities. Their velveteen legs and their colossal high-lows, their purple necks and ear-tips, their knotted sticks and little greasy hats, make them look like stage-villains of realistic melodrama. I may do them injustice, but consistent character in them mostly requires that they shall have had a taste of penal servitude – that they shall have paid the penalty of stamping on some weaker human head with those huge square heels that are turned up to the summer sky. Actually, however, they are innocent enough, for they are sleeping as peacefully as the most accomplished philanthropist, and it is their look of having walked over half England, and of being pennilessly hungry and thirsty, that constitutes their romantic attractiveness. These six square feet of brown grass are their present sufficiency; but how long will they sleep, whither will they go next, and whence did they come last? You permit yourself to wish that they might sleep for ever and go nowhere else at all.

The month of August is so uncountenanced in London that, going a few days since to Greenwich, that famous resort, I found it possible to get but half a dinner. The celebrated hotel had put out its stoves and locked up its pantry. But for this discovery I should have mentioned the little expedition to Greenwich as a charming relief to the monotony of a London August. Greenwich and Richmond are, classically, the two suburban dining-places. I know not how it may be at this time with Richmond, but the Greenwich incident brings me back (I hope not once too often) to the element of what has lately been called 'particularism' in English pleasures. It was in obedience to a perfectly logical argument that the Greenwich hotel had, as I say, locked up its pantry. All well-bred people leave London after the first week in August, *ergo* those who remain behind are not well-bred, and cannot therefore rise to the conception of a 'fish dinner'. Why then should we have anything ready? I had other impressions, fortunately, of this interesting suburb, and I hasten to declare that during the period of good-breeding the dinner at Greenwich is the most amusing of all dinners. It begins with fish and it continues with fish: what it ends with – except songs and speeches and affectionate partings – I hesitate to affirm. It is a kind of mermaid reversed; for I do know, in a vague way, that the tail of the creature is elaborately and interminably fleshy. If it were not grossly indiscreet I should risk an allusion to the particular banquet which was the occasion of my becoming acquainted with the Greenwich *cuisine*. I would try to express how pleasant it may be to sit in a company of clever and distinguished men before the large windows that look out upon the broad brown Thames. The ships swim by confidently, as if they were part of the entertainment and put down in the bill; the light of the afternoon fades ever so slowly. We eat all the fish of the sea, and wash them down with liquids that bear no resemblance to salt water. We partake of any number of those sauces with which, according to the French adage, one could swallow one's grandmother with a good conscience. To touch on the identity of my companions would indeed be indiscreet, but there is nothing indelicate in marking a high appreciation of the frankness and robustness of English conviviality. The stranger – the American at least – who finds himself in the company of a number of Englishmen assembled for a convivial purpose becomes conscious of an indefinable and delectable something which, for want of a better name, he is moved to call their superior richness of temperament. He takes note of the liberal share of the individual in the magnificent temperament of the people. This seems to him one of the finest things in the world, and his satisfaction will take a keener edge from such an incident as the single one I may permit myself to mention. It was one of those little incidents which can occur only in an old society – a society in which every one that a newly arrived observer meets strikes him as having in some degree or other a sort of historic identity, being connected with some one or something that he has heard of, that he has wondered about. If they are not the rose they have lived more or less near it. There is an old English songwriter whom we all know and admire – whose songs are sung wherever the language is spoken. Of course, according to the law I just hinted at, one of the gentlemen sitting opposite must needs be his great-grandson. After dinner there are songs, and the gentleman trolls out one of his ancestral ditties with the most charming voice and the most finished art.

I have still other memories of Greenwich, where there is a charming old park, on a summit of one of whose grassy undulations the famous observatory is perched. To do the thing completely you must take passage upon one of the little grimy sixpenny steamers that ply upon the Thames, perform the journey by water, and then, disembarking, take a stroll in the park to get up an appetite for dinner. I find an irresistible charm in any sort of river navigation, but I scarce know how to speak of the little voyage from Westminster Bridge to Greenwich. It is in truth the most prosaic possible form of being afloat, and to be recommended rather to the inquiring than to the fastidious mind. It initiates you into the duskiness, the blackness, the crowdedness, the intensely commercial character of London. Few European cities have a finer river than the Thames, but none certainly has expended more ingenuity in producing a sordid river-front. For miles and miles you see nothing but the sooty backs of warehouses, or perhaps they are the sooty faces: in buildings so utterly expressionless it is impossible to distinguish. They stand massed together on the banks of the wide turbid stream, which is fortunately of too opaque a quality to reflect the dismal image. A damp-looking, dirty blackness is the universal tone. The river is almost black, and is covered with black barges; above the black housetops, from among the far-stretching docks and basins, rises a dusky wilderness of masts. The little puffing steamer is dingy and gritty – it belches a sable cloud that keeps you company as you go. In this carboniferous shower your companions, who belong chiefly, indeed, to the classes bereft of lustre, assume an harmonious greyness; and the whole picture, glazed over with the glutinous London mist, becomes a masterly composition. But it is very impressive in spite of its want of lightness and brightness, and though it is ugly it is anything but trivial. Like so many of the aspects of English civilisation that are untouched by elegance or grace, it has the merit of expressing something very serious. Viewed in this intellectual light the polluted river, the sprawling barges, the dead-faced warehouses, the frowsy people, the atmospheric impurities become richly suggestive. It sounds rather absurd, but all this smudgy detail may remind you of nothing less than the wealth and power of the British Empire at large; so that a kind of metaphysical magnificence hovers over the scene, and supplies what may be literally wanting. I don't exactly understand the association, but I know that when I look off to the left at the East India Docks, or pass under the dark hugely piled bridges, where the railway trains and the human processions are for ever moving, I feel a kind of imaginative thrill. The tremendous piers of the bridges, in especial, seem the very pillars of the Empire aforesaid.

It is doubtless owing to this habit of obtrusive and unprofitable reverie that the sentimental tourist thinks it very fine to see the Greenwich observatory lifting its two modest little brick towers. The sight of this useful edifice gave me a pleasure which may at first seem extravagant. The reason was simply that I used to see it as a child, in woodcuts, in school geographies, and in the corners of large maps which had a glazed, sallow surface and which were suspended in unexpected places, in dark halls and behind doors. The maps were hung so high that my eyes could reach only to the lower corners, and these corners usually contained a print of a strange-looking house perched among trees upon a grassy bank that swept down before it with the most engaging steepness. I used always to think of the joy it must be to roll at one's length down this curved incline. Close at hand was usually something printed about something being at such and such a number of degrees 'east of Greenwich'. Why east of Greenwich? The vague wonder that the childish mind felt on this point gave the place a mysterious importance and seemed to put it into relation with the difficult and fascinating parts of geography – the countries of unintentional outline and the lonely looking pages of the atlas. Yet there it stood the other day, the precise point from which the great globe is measured; there was the plain little façade with the old-fashioned cupolas; there was the bank on which it would be so delightful not to be able to stop running. It made me feel terribly old to find that I was not even tempted to begin. There are indeed a great many steep banks in Greenwich Park, which tumbles up and down in the most adventurous fashion. It is a charming place, rather shabby and footworn, as befits a strictly popular resort, but with a character all its own. It is filled with magnificent foreign-looking trees, of which I know nothing but that they have a vain appearance of being chestnuts, planted in long, convergent avenues, with trunks of extraordinary girth and limbs that fling a dusky shadow far over the grass; there are plenty of benches, and there are deer as tame as sleepy children; and from the tops of the bosky hillocks there are views of the widening Thames and the moving ships and the two classic inns by the waterside and the great pompous buildings, designed by Inigo Jones, of the old Hospital, which have been despoiled of their ancient pensioners and converted into a naval academy.

Taking note of all this, I arrived at a far-away angle in the wall of the park, where a little postern door stood ajar. I pushed the door open and found myself, by a thrilling transition, upon Blackheath Common. One had often heard, in vague, irrecoverable, anecdotic connections, of Blackheath: well, here it was – a great green, breezy place where lads in corduroys were playing cricket. I am, as a rule, moved to disproportionate ecstasy by an English common; it may be curtailed and cockneyfied, as this one was – which had lamp-posts stuck about on its turf and a fresh-painted banister all around – but it generally abounds in the note of English breeziness, and you always seem to have seen it water-coloured or engraved. Even if the turf be too much trodden there is to foreign eyes an intimate insular reference in it and in the way the high-piled, weather-bearing clouds hang over it and drizzle down their grey light. Still further to identify this spot, here was the British soldier[2] emerging from two or three of the roads, with his cap upon his ear, his white gloves in one hand and his foppish little cane in the other. He wore the uniform of the artillery, and I asked him where he had come from. I learned that he had walked over from Woolwich and that this feat might be accomplished in half an hour. Inspired again by vague associations I proceeded to accomplish its equivalent. I bent my steps to Woolwich, a place which I knew, in a general way, to be a nursery of British valour. At the end of my half-hour I emerged upon another common, where the water-colour bravery had even a higher pitch. The scene was like a chapter of some forgotten record. The open grassy expanse was immense, and, the evening being beautiful, it was dotted with strolling soldiers and townsfolk. There were half a dozen cricket matches, both civil and military. At one end of this peaceful *campus martius*, which stretches over a hilltop, rises an interminable façade – one of the fronts of the Royal Artillery barracks. It has a very honourable air, and more windows and doors, I imagine, than any building in Britain. There is a great clean parade before it, and there are many sentinels pacing in front of neatly kept places of ingress to officers' quarters. Everything it looks out upon is in the smartest military trim – the distinguished college (where the poor young man whom it would perhaps be premature to call the last of the Bonapartes lately studied the art of war) on one side; a sort of model camp, a collection of the tidiest plank huts, on the other; a hospital, on a well-ventilated site, at the remoter end. And then in the town below there are a great many more military matters: barracks on an immense scale; a dockyard that presents an interminable dead wall to the street; an arsenal which the gatekeeper (who refused to admit me) declared to be 'five miles' in circumference; and, lastly, grogshops enough to inflame the most craven spirit. These

*Grand Depot Barracks*

latter institutions I glanced at on my way to the railway station at the bottom of the hill; but before departing I had spent half an hour in strolling about the common in vague consciousness of certain emotions that are called into play (I speak but for myself) by almost any glimpse of the imperial machinery of this great country. The glimpse may be of the slightest; it stirs a peculiar sentiment. I know not what to call this sentiment unless it be simply an admiration for the greatness of England. The greatness of England; that is a very off-hand phrase, and of course I don't pretend to use it analytically. I use it romantically, as it sounds in the ears of any American who remounts the stream of time to the head-waters of his own loyalties. I think of the great part that England has played in human affairs, the great space she has occupied, her tremendous might, her far-stretching rule. That these clumsily general ideas should be suggested by the sight of some infinitesimal fraction of the English administrative system may seem to indicate a cast of fancy too hysterical; but if so I must plead guilty to the weakness. Why should a sentry-box more or less set one thinking of the glory of this little island, which has

*Royal Artillery, Woolwich*

found in her mere genius the means of such a sway? This is more than I can tell; and all I shall attempt to say is that in the difficult days that are now elapsing a sympathetic stranger finds his meditations singularly quickened. It is the imperial element in English history that he has chiefly cared for, and he finds himself wondering whether the imperial epoch is completely closed. It is a moment when all the nations of Europe seem to be doing something, and he waits to see what England, who has done so much, will do. He has been meeting of late a good many of his country people – Americans who live on the Continent and pretend to speak with assurance of continental ways of feeling. These people have been passing through London, and many of them are in that irritated condition of mind which appears to be of the portion of the American sojourner in the British metropolis when he is not given up to the delights of the historic sentiment. They have declared with assurance that the continental nations have ceased to care a straw for what England thinks, that her traditional prestige is completely extinct and that the affairs of Europe will be settled quite independently of her action and still more of her inaction. England will do nothing, will risk nothing; there is no cause bad enough for her not to find a selfish interest in it – there is no cause good enough for her to fight about it. Poor old England is defunct; it is about time she should seek the most decent burial possible. To all this the sympathetic stranger replies that in the first place he doesn't believe a word of it, and in the second doesn't care a fig for it – care, that is, what the continental nations think. If the greatness of England were really waning it would be to him as a personal grief; and as he strolls about the breezy common of Woolwich, with all those mementoes of British dominion around him, he vibrates quite too richly to be distracted by such vapours.[3]

He wishes nevertheless, as I said before, that England would *do* something – something striking and powerful, which should be at once characteristic and unexpected. He asks himself what she can do, and he remembers that this greatness of England which he so much admires was formerly much exemplified in her 'taking' something. Can't she 'take' something now? There is the *Spectator*, who wants her to occupy Egypt: can't she occupy Egypt? The *Spectator* considers this her moral duty – inquires even whether she has a right *not* to bestow the blessings of her beneficent rule upon the down-trodden Fellaheen. I found myself in company with an acute young Frenchman a day or two after this eloquent plea for a partial annexation of the Nile had appeared in the supersubtle sheet. Some allusion was made to it, and my companion of course pronounced it the most finished example conceivable of insular hypocrisy. I don't know how powerful a defence I made of it, but while I read it I had found the hypocrisy contagious. I recalled it while I pursued my contemplations, but I recalled at the same time that sadly prosaic speech of Mr Gladstone's to which it had been a reply. Mr Gladstone[4] had said that England had much more urgent duties than the occupation of Egypt: she had to attend to the great questions of—— What were the great questions? Those of local taxation and the liquor-laws! Local taxation and the liquor-laws! The phrase, to my ears, just then, sounded almost squalid. These were not the things I had been thinking of; it was not as she should bend anxiously over these doubtless interesting subjects that the sympathising stranger would seem to see

England in his favourite posture – that, as Macaulay says, of hurling defiance at her foes. Mr Gladstone may perhaps have been right, but Mr Gladstone was far from being a sympathising stranger.

First published in *Lippincott's Magazine*, XX (November 1877), 603–11; reprinted in *Portraits of Places* (1883), and *English Hours* (1905).

# Two Excursions

## I

They differed greatly from each other, but there was something to be said for each. There seemed in respect to the first a high consensus as to its being a pity that any stranger should ever miss the Derby day. Every one assured me that this was the great festival of the English people and that one didn't really know them unless one had seen them at it. So much, since it had to do with horse-flesh, I could readily believe. Had not the newspapers been filled for weeks with recurrent dissertations upon the animals concerned in the ceremony? and was not the event, to the nation at large, only imperceptibly less momentous than the other great question of the day – the fate of empires and the reapportionment of the East? The space allotted to sporting intelligence in a compact, eclectic, 'intellectual' journal like the *Pall Mall Gazette*, had seemed for some time past a measure of the hold of such questions upon the native mind. These things, however, are very natural in a country in which in 'society' you are liable to make the acquaintance of some such syllogism as the following. You are seated at dinner[1] next a foreign lady who has on her other hand a communicative gentleman through whom she is under instruction in the art of the right point-of-view for English life. I profit by their conversation and I learn that this point-of-view is apparently the saddle. 'You see, English life,' says the gentleman, 'is really English country life. It's the country that is the basis of English society. And you see, country life is – well, it's the *hunting*. It's the hunting that is at the bottom of it all.' In other words 'the hunting' is the basis of English society. Duly impressed with this explanation, the American observer is prepared for the huge proportions of the annual pilgrimage to Epsom. This pilgrimage, however, I was assured, though still well worth taking part in, is by no means so characteristic as in former days. It is now per-formed in a large measure by rail, and the spectacle on the road has lost many of its earlier and most of its finer features. The road has been given up more and more to the populace and the strangers and has ceased to be graced by the presence of ladies. Nevertheless, as a man and a stranger, I was strongly recommended to take it, for the return from the Derby is still, with all its abatements, a classic show.

I mounted upon a four-horse coach, a charming coach with a yellow body and handsome, clean-flanked leaders; placing myself beside the coachman, as I had been told this was the point of vantage. The coach was one of the vehicles of the new fashion – the fashion of public convey-ances driven, for the entertainment of themselves and of the public, by gentlemen of leisure. On the Derby day all the coaches that start from the classic headquarters – 'The White Horse' in Piccadilly – and stretch away from London toward a dozen different and well-selected goals, had been dedicated to the Epsom road. The body of the vehicle is empty, as no one thinks of occupying any but one of the thirteen places on the top. On the Derby day, however, a properly laden coach carries a company of hampers and champagne baskets in its inside places. I must add that on this occasion my companion was by exception a professional whip, who proved a friendly and amusing cicerone. Other companions there were, perched in the twelve places behind me, whose social quality I made less of a point of testing – though in the course of the expedition their various characteristics, under the influence of champagne, expanded so freely as greatly to facilitate the process. We were a society of exotics – Spaniards, Frenchmen, Germans. There were only two Britons, and these, accord-ing to my theory, were Australians – an antipodal bride and groom on a centripetal wedding-tour.

The drive to Epsom, when you get well out of London, is sufficiently pretty; but the part of it which most took my fancy was a district pre-eminently suburban – the classic community of Clapham. The vision of Chapham had been a part of the furniture of one's milder historic consciousness – the vision of its respectable common, its evangelical society, its rich drab humanity, its goodly brick mansions of the Georgian era. I now seemed really to focus these elements for the first time, and I thought them very charming. This epithet indeed scarcely applies to the evangelical society, which naturally, on the morning of the Derby day and during the desecrating progress of the Epsom revellers, was not much in the foreground. But all around the verdant if cockney-fied common are ranged commodious houses of a sober red complexion, from under whose neo-classic pediments you expect to see a mild-faced lady emerge – a lady in a cottage-bonnet and mittens, distributing tracts from a green silk satchel. It would take, however, the very ardour of the missionary among cannibals to stem the current of heterogeneous vehicles which at about this point takes up its metropolitan affluents and bears them in its rumbling, rattling tide. The concourse of wheeled conveyances of every possible order here becomes dense, and the spectacle from the top of the coach proportionately absorbing. You begin to perceive that the brilliancy of the road has in truth departed, and that a sustained high tone of appearance is not the note of the conditions. But when once you have grasped this fact your entertainment is con-tinuous. You perceive that you are 'in' for the vulgar on an unsurpassable scale, something blatantly, unimaginably, heroically shocking to timid 'taste'; all that is necessary is to accept this situation and look out for illustrations. Beside you, before you, behind you, is the mighty London populace taking its *ébats*. You get for the first time a notion of the London population at large. It has piled itself into carts, into omnibuses, into every possible and impossible species of 'trap'. A large proportion of it is of course on foot, trudging along the perilous margin of the middle way in such comfort as may be gathered from fifteen miles' dodging of broken shins. The smaller the vehicle, the more rat-like the animal that drags it, the more numerous and ponderous its human freight; and as every one is nursing in his lap a parcel of provender as big as himself, wrapped in ragged newspaper, it is not surprising that roadside halts are frequent and that the taverns all the way to Epsom (it is wonderful how many there are) are encompassed by dense groups of dusty pilgrims, indulging liberally in refreshment for man and beast. And when I say man I must by no means be understood to exclude woman. The female contingent on the Derby day is not the least remarkable part of the London outpouring. Every one is prepared for 'larks', but the women are even more brilliantly and resolutely prepared than the men; there is no better chance to follow the range of type – not that it is to be called large – of the British female of the lower orders. The lady in question is usually not ornamental. She is useful, robust, prolific, excellently fitted to play the somewhat arduous part allotted to her in the great scheme of English civilisation, but she has not those graces which enable her to lend herself easily to the decoration of life. On smaller holidays – or on simple working days – in London crowds, I have often thought she had points to contribute to the primary fine drawing, as to head and shoulders, of the Briton of the two sexes as the race at large sketches them. But at Epsom she is too stout, too hot, too red, too thirsty, too boisterous, too strangely accoutred. And yet I wish to do her justice; so I must add that if there is something to which an American cannot refuse a tribute of admiration in the gross plebeian jollity of the Derby day, it is not evident why these dowdy Bacchantes should not get part of the credit of it. The striking thing, the interesting thing, both on the outward drive and on the return, was that the holiday was so frankly, heartily, good-humouredly taken. The people that of all peoples is habitually the most governed by decencies, proprieties, rigidities of conduct, was for one happy day un-buttoning its respectable straight-jacket and affirming its large and simple sense of the joy of life. In such a spectacle there was inevitably much that was unlucky and unprofitable; these things came uppermost chiefly on the return, when demoralisation was supreme, when the temperament of the people had begun really to take the air. For the rest, to be dressed with a kind of brutal gaudiness, to be very thirsty and violently flushed, to laugh perpetually at everything and at nothing, thoroughly to enjoy, in short, a momentous occasion – all this is not, in simple persons of the more susceptible sex, an unpardonable crime.

The course at Epsom is in itself very pretty, and disposed by nature herself in sympathetic prevision of the sporting passion. It is something like the crater of a volcano without the mountain. The outer rim is the course proper; the space within it is a vast, shallow, grassy concavity in which vehicles are drawn up and beasts tethered and in which the greater part of the multitude – the mountebanks, the betting men and the myriad hangers-on of the scene – are congregated. The outer margin of the uplifted rim in question is occupied by the grand stand, the small stands, the paddock. The day was exceptionally beautiful; the charming sky was spotted over with little idle-looking, loafing, irresponsible clouds; the Epsom Downs went swelling away as greenly as in a coloured sporting-print, and the wooded uplands, in the middle distance, looked as innocent and pastoral as if they had never seen a policeman or a rowdy. The crowd that spread itself over this immense expanse was as rich a representation of human life off its guard as one need see. One's first fate after arriving, if one is perched upon a coach, is to see the coach guided, by means best known to the coachman himself, through the tremendous press of vehicles and pedestrians, introduced into a precinct roped off and guarded from intrusion save under payment of a fee, and then drawn up alongside of the course, as nearly as possible opposite the grand stand and the winning post. Here you have only to stand up in your place – on tiptoe, it is true, and with a good deal of stretching – to see the race fairly well. But I hasten to add that seeing the race is indifferent entertainment. In the first place you *don't* see it, and in the second – to be Irish on the occasion of a frolic – you perceive it to be not much worth the seeing. It may be fine in quality, but in quantity it is inappreciable. The horses and their jockeys first go dandling and cantering along the course to the starting-point, looking as insubstantial as sifted sunbeams. Then there is a long wait, during which, of the sixty thousand people present (my figures are imaginary), thirty thousand declare positively that they have started, and thirty thousand as positively deny it. Then the whole sixty thousand are suddenly resolved into unanimity by the sight of a dozen small jockey heads whizzing along a very distant sky-line. In a shorter space of time than it takes me to write it, the whole thing is before you, and for the instant it is anything but beautiful. A dozen furiously revolving arms – pink, green, orange, scarlet, white – whacking the flanks of as many straining steeds; a glimpse of this, and the spectacle is over. The spectacle, however, is of course an infinitesimally small part of the purpose of Epsom and the interest of the Derby. The finer vibration resides presumably in having money on the affair.

When the Derby Stakes had been carried off by a horse of which I confess I am barbarous enough to have forgotten the name, I turned my back to the running, for all the world as if I too were largely 'interested', and sought entertainment in looking at the crowd.[2] The crowd was very animated; that is the most succinct description I can give of it. The horses of course had been removed from the vehicles, so that the pedestrians were free to surge against the wheels and even to a certain extent to scale and overrun the carriages. This tendency became most pronounced when, as the mid-period of the day was reached, the process of lunching began to unfold itself and every coach top to become the scene of a picnic. From this moment, at the Derby, demoralisation begins. I was in a position to observe it, all around me, in the most characteristic forms. The whole affair, as regards the conventional rigidities I spoke of a while since, becomes a real *dégringolade*. The shabbier pedestrains bustle about the vehicles, staring up at the lucky mortals who are perched in a kind of tormentingly near empyrean – a region in which dishes of lobster-salad are passed about and champagne-corks cleave the air like celestial meteors. There are nigger-minstrels and beggars and mountebanks and spangled persons on stilts and gipsy matrons, as genuine as possible, with glowing Oriental eyes and dropping their *h*'s; these last offer you for sixpence the promise of everything genteel in life except the aspirate. On a coach drawn up beside the one on which I had a place, a party of opulent young men were passing from stage to stage of the higher beatitude with a zeal which excited my admiration. They were accompanied by two or three young ladies of the kind that usually shares the choicest pleasures of youthful British opulence – young ladies in whom nothing has been neglected that can make a complexion superlative. The whole party had been drinking deep, and one of the young men, a pretty lad of twenty, had in an indiscreet moment staggered down as best he could to the ground. Here his cups proved too many for him, and he collapsed and rolled over. In plain English he was beastly drunk. It was the scene that followed that arrested my observation. His companions on the top of the coach called down to the people herding under the wheels to pick him up and put him away inside. These people were the grimiest of the rabble, and a couple of men who looked like coal-heavers out of work undertook to handle this hapless youth. But their task was difficult; it was impossible to imagine a young man more drunk. He was a mere bag of liquor – at once too ponderous and too flaccid to be lifted. He lay in a helpless heap under the feet of the crowd – the best intoxicated young man in England. His extemporised chamberlains took him first in one way and then in another; but he was like water in a sieve. The crowd hustled over him; every one wanted to see; he was pulled and shoved and fumbled. The spectacle had a grotesque side, and this it was that seemed to strike the fancy of the young man's comrades. They had not done lunching, so they were unable to bestow upon the incident the whole of that consideration which its high comicality deserved. But they did what they could. They looked down very often, glass in hand, during the half-hour that it went on, and they stinted neither their generous, joyous laughter nor their appreciative comments. Women are said to have no sense of humour; but the young ladies with the complexions did liberal justice to the pleasantry of the scene. Toward the last indeed their attention rather flagged; for even the best joke suffers by reiteration, and when you have seen a stupefied young man, infinitely bedusted, slip out of the embrace of a couple of clumsy roughs for the twentieth time, you may very properly suppose that you have arrived at the furthest limits of the ludicrous.

After the great race had been run I quitted my perch and spent the rest of the afternoon in wandering about the grassy concave I have mentioned. It was amusing and picturesque; it was just a huge Bohemian encampment. Here also a great number of carriages were stationed, freighted in like manner with free-handed youths and young ladies with gilded hair. These young ladies were almost the only representatives of their sex with pretensions to elegance; they were often pretty and always exhilarated. Gentlemen in pairs, mounted on stools, habited in fantastic sporting garments and offering bets to whomsoever listed, were a conspicuous feature of the scene. It was equally striking that they were not preaching in the desert and that they found plenty of patrons among the baser sort. I returned to my place in time to assist at the rather complicated operation of starting for the drive back to London. Putting in horses and getting vehicles into line seemed in the midst of the general crush and entanglement a process not to be facilitated even by the most liberal swearing on the part of those engaged in it. But little by little we came to the end of it; and as by this time a kind of mellow cheerfulness pervaded the upper atmosphere – the region of the perpendicular whip – even those interruptions most trying to patience were somehow made to minister to jollity. It was for people below not to get trampled to death or crunched between opposing wheel-hubs, but it was all for *them* to manage it. Above, the carnival of 'chaff' had set in, and it deepened as the lock of vehicles grew denser. As they were all locked together (with a comfortable padding of pedestrians at points of acutest contact), they contrived somehow to move together; so that we gradually got away and into the road. The four or five hours consumed on the road were simply an exchange of repartee, the profusely good-humoured savour of which, on the whole, was certainly striking. The chaff was not brilliant nor subtle nor especially graceful; and here and there it was quite too tipsy to be even articulate. But as an expression of that un-buttoning of the popular straight-jacket of which I spoke a while since, it had its wholesome and even innocent side. It took indeed frequently an importunate physical form; it sought emphasis in the use of pea-shooters and water-squirts. At its best, too, it was extremely low and rowdyish. But a stranger even of the most refined tastes might be glad to have a glimpse of this popular revel, for it would make him feel that he was learning something more about the English people. It would give a meaning to the old description of England as merry. It would remind him that the natives of that country are subject to some of the lighter of the human impulses, and that the decent, dusky vistas of the London residential streets – those discreet creations of which Thackeray's Baker Street is the type – are not a complete symbol of the complicated race that erected them.

## II

It seemed to me such a piece of good fortune to have been asked down to Oxford at Commemoration by a gentleman implicated in the re-markable ceremony which goes on under that name, who kindly offered me the hospitality of his college, that I scarcely stayed even to thank him – I simply went and awaited him, I had had a glimpse of Oxford in former years,[3] but I had never slept in a low-browed room looking out on a grassy quadrangle and opposite a medieval clock-tower. This satisfaction was vouchsafed me on the night of my arrival; I was made free of the rooms of an absent undergraduate. I sat in his deep armchairs; I turned his candles and read his books, and I hereby thank him as effusively as possible. Before going to bed I took a turn through the streets and renewed in the silent darkness that impression of the charm imparted to them by the quiet college fronts which I had gathered in former years. The college fronts were now quieter than ever, the streets were empty, and the old scholastic city was sleeping in the warm starlight. The undergraduates had retired in large numbers, encouraged in this impulse by the collegiate authorities, who deprecate their presence at Commemoration. However many young gownsmen may be sent away, there yet always remain a collection sufficient to represent the sound of many voices. There can be no better indication of the resources of Oxford in a spectacular way than this fact that the first step toward preparing an impressive ceremony is to get rid of as many as possible of the actors.

In the morning I breakfasted with a young American who, in common with a number of his countrymen, had come hither to seek stimulus for a finer strain of study. I know not whether he would have reckoned as such stimulus the conversation of a couple of those ingenuous youths, sons of the soil, whose society I always find charming; but it added, from my own point of view, in respect to the place, to the element of intensity of character. After the entertainment was over I repaired, in company with a crowd of ladies and elderly people, interspersed with gownsmen, to the hoary rotunda of the Sheldonian theatre, which every visitor to Oxford will remember from its curious cincture of clumsily carven heads of warriors and sages perched upon stone posts. The interior of this edifice is the scene of the classic hooting, stamping, and cat-calling by which the undergraduates confer the last consecration upon the distinguished gentlemen who come up for the honorary degree of D.C.L. It is with the design of attenuating as much as possible this volume of sound that the heads of colleges, on the close of the term, a few days before Commemoration, speed their too demonstrative disciples upon the homeward way. As I have already hinted, however, the contingent of irreverence was on this occasion quite large enough to preserve the type of the racket. This made the scene a very singular one. An American of course, with his fondness for antiquity, his relish for picturesqueness, his 'emotional' attitude at historic shrines, takes Oxford much more seriously than its sometimes unwilling familiars can be expected to do. These people are not always upon the high horse; they are not always in a state of fine vibration. Nevertheless, there is a certain maximum of disaccord with their beautiful circumstances which the ecstatic outsider vaguely expects them not to transcend. No effort of the intellect beforehand would enable him to imagine one of those silver-grey temples of learning converted into a semblance of the Bowery Theatre when the Bowery Theatre is being trifled with.

The Sheldonian edifice, like everything at Oxford, is more or less monumental. There is a double tier of galleries, with sculptured pulpits protruding from them; there are full-length portraits of kings and

*spires of Oxford and the Radcliffe Camera seen from the interior of Queen's College* worthies; there is a general air of antiquity and dignity, which, on the occasion of which I speak, was enhanced by the presence of certain ancient scholars seated in crimson robes in high-backed chairs. Formerly, I believe, the undergraduates were placed apart – packed together in a corner of one of the galleries. But now they are scattered among the general spectators, a large number of whom are ladies. They muster in especial force, however, on the floor of the theatre, which has been cleared of its benches. Here the dense mass is at last severed in twain by the entrance of the prospective D.C.L.'s walking in single file, clad in crimson gowns, preceded by mace-bearers and accompanied by the Regius Professor of Civil Law, who presents them individually to the Vice-Chancellor of the University, in a Latin speech which is of course a glowing eulogy. The five gentlemen to whom this distinction had been offered in 1877 were not among those whom fame has trumpeted most loudly; but there was something 'as pretty as a picture' in their standing in their honourable robes, with heads modestly bent, while the orator, as effectively draped, recited their titles sonorously to the venerable dignitary in the high-backed chair. Each of them, when the little speech is ended, ascends the steps leading to the chair; the Vice-Chancellor bends forward and shakes his hand, and the new D.C.L. goes and sits in the blushing row of his fellow doctors. The impressiveness of all this is much diminished by the boisterous conduct of the 'students', who superabound in extravagant applause, in impertinent interrogation and in lively disparagement of the orator's Latinity. Of the scene that precedes the episode I have just described I have given no account; vivid portrayal of it is not easy. Like the return from the Derby it is a carnival of 'chaff'; and it is a singular fact that the scholastic festival should have forcibly reminded me of the great popular 'lark'. In each case it is the same race enjoying a certain definitely chartered licence; in the young votaries of a liberal education and the London rabble on the Epsom road it is the same perfect good-humour, the same muscular jocosity.

After the presentation of the doctors came a series of those collegiate exercises which have a generic resemblance all the world over: a reading of Latin verses and English essays, a spouting of prize poems and Greek paraphrases. The prize poem alone was somewhat attentively listened

*The Sheldonian Theatre, Oxford*

to; the other things were received with an infinite variety of critical ejaculation. But after all, I reflected as the ceremony drew to a close, the romping element is more characteristic than it seems; it is at bottom only another expression of the venerable and historic side of Oxford. It is tolerated because it is traditional; it is possible because it is classical. Looked at it in this light it became romantically continuous with the human past that everything else referred to.

I was not obliged to find ingenious pretexts for thinking well of another ceremony of which I was witness after we adjourned from the

Sheldonian theatre. This was a lunch-party at the particular college in which I should find it the highest privilege to reside and which I may not further specify. Perhaps indeed I may go so far as to say that the reason for my dreaming of this privilege is that it is deemed by persons of a reforming turn the best-appointed abuse in a nest of abuses. A commission for the expurgation of the universities has lately been appointed by Parliament to look into it – a commission armed with a gigantic broom, which is to sweep away all the fine old ivied and cobwebbed improprieties. Pending these righteous changes, one would like while one is about it – about, that is, this business of admiring Oxford – to attach one's self to the abuse, to bury one's nostrils in the rose before it is plucked. At the college in question there are no undergraduates. I found it agreeable to reflect that those grey-green cloisters had sent no delegates to the slangy congregation I had just quitted. This delightful spot exists for the satisfaction of a small society of Fellows who, having no dreary instruction to administer, no noisy hobbledehoys to govern, no obligations but toward their own culture, no care save for learning as learning and truth as truth, are presumably the happiest and most charming people in the world. The party invited to lunch assembled first in the library of the college, a cool, grey hall, of very great length and height, with vast wall-spaces of rich-looking book titles and statues of noble scholars set in the midst. Had the charming Fellows ever anything more disagreeable to do than to finger these precious volumes and then to stroll about together in the grassy courts, in learned comradeship, discussing their precious contents? Nothing, apparently, unless it were to give a lunch at Commemoration in the dining-hall of the college. When lunch was ready there was a very pretty procession to go to it. Learned gentlemen in crimson gowns, ladies in bright finery, paired slowly off and marched in a stately diagonal across the fine, smooth lawn of the quadrangle, in a corner of which they passed through a hospitable door. But here we cross the threshold of privacy; I remained on the further side of it during the rest of the day. But I brought back with me certain memories of which, if I were not at the end of my space, I should attempt a discreet adumbration: memories of a *fête champêtre* in the beautiful gardens of one of the other colleges – charming lawns and spreading trees, music of Grenadier Guards, ices in striped marquees, mild flirtation of youthful gownsmen and bemuslined maidens: memories, too, of quiet dinner in common-room, a decorous, excellent repast; old portraits on the walls and great windows open upon the ancient court, where the afternoon light was fading in the stillness; superior talk upon current topics, and over all the peculiar air of Oxford – the air of liberty to care for the things of the mind assured and secured by machinery which is in itself a satisfaction to sense.[4]

First published as 'Three Excursions' in *The Galaxy*, XXIV (September 1877), 346–56; revised and shortened for reprinting in *Portraits of Places* (1883), and *English Hours* (1905).

# In Warwickshire

There is no better way to plunge *in medias res*, for the stranger who wishes to know something of England, than to spend a fortnight in Warwickshire. It is the core and centre of the English world; midmost England, unmitigated England. The place has taught me a great many English secrets; I have been interviewing the genius of pastoral Britain. From a charming lawn – a lawn delicious to one's sentient boot-sole – I looked without obstruction at a sombre, soft, romantic mass whose outline was blurred by mantling ivy. It made a perfect picture, and in the foreground the great trees overarched their boughs, from right and left, so as to give it a majestic frame. This interesting object was the castle of Kenilworth.[1] It was within distance of an easy walk, but one hardly thought of walking to it, any more than one would have thought of walking to a purple-shadowed tower in the background of a Berghem or a Claude. Here were purple shadows and slowly shifting lights, with a soft-hued, bosky country for the middle distance.

Of course, however, I did walk over to the castle; and of course the walk led me through leafy lanes and beside the hedgerows that make a tangled screen for large lawn-like meadows. Of course too, I am bound to add, there was a row of ancient pedlars outside the castle wall, hawking twopenny pamphlets and photographs. Of course, equally, at the foot of the grassy mound on which the ruin stands were half a dozen public-houses and, always of course, half a dozen beery vagrants sprawling on the grass in the moist sunshine. There was the usual respectable young woman to open the castle gate and to receive the usual sixpenny fee. There were the usual squares of printed cardboard, suspended upon venerable surfaces, with further enumeration of twopence, threepence, fourpence. I do not allude to these things querulously, for Kenilworth is a very tame lion – a lion that, in former years, I had stroked more than

*Kenilworth*

once. I remember perfectly my first visit to this romantic spot; how I chanced upon a picnic; how I stumbled over beer bottles; how the very echoes of the beautiful ruin seemed to have dropped all their *h*'s. That was a sultry afternoon; I allowed my spirits to sink and I came away hanging my head. This was a beautiful fresh morning, and in the interval I had grown philosophic. I had learned that, with regard to most romantic sites in England, there is a constant cockneyfication with which you must make your account. There are always people on the field before you, and there is generally something being drunk on the premises.

I hoped, on the occasion of which I am now speaking, that the attack would not be acute, and indeed for the first five minutes I flattered myself that this was the case. In the beautiful grassy court of the castle, on my entrance, there were not more than eight or ten fellow intruders. There were a couple of old ladies on a bench, eating something out of a newspaper; there was a dissenting minister, also on a bench, reading the guide-book aloud to his wife and sister-in-law; there were three or four children pushing each other up and down the turfy hillocks. This was sweet seclusion indeed; and I got a capital start with the various noble square-windowed fragments of the stately pile. They are extremely majestic, with their even, pale-red colour, their deep-green drapery, their princely vastness of scale. But presently the tranquil ruin began to swarm like a startled hive. There were plenty of people, if they chose to show themselves. They emerged from crumbling doorways and gaping chambers with the best conscience in the world; but I know not, after all, why I should bear them a grudge, for they gave me a pretext for wandering about in search of a quiet point of view. I cannot say that I found my point of view, but in looking for it I saw the castle, which is certainly an admirable ruin. And when the respectable young woman had let me out of the gate again, and I had shaken my head at the civil-spoken pedlars who form a little avenue for the arriving and departing visitor, I found it in my good-nature to linger a moment on the trodden, grassy slope, and to think that in spite of the hawkers, the paupers and the beer shops, there was still a good deal of old England in the scene. I say in spite of these things, but it may have been, in some degree, because of them. Who shall resolve into its component parts any impression of this richly complex English world, where the present is always seen, as it were, in profile, and the past presents a full face? At all events the solid red castle rose behind me, towering above its small old ladies and its in-vestigating parsons; before me, across the patch of common, was a row of ancient cottages, black-timbered, red-gabled, pictorial, which evidently had a memory of the castle in its better days. A quaintish village straggled away on the right, and on the left the dark, fat meadows were lighted up with misty sun-spots and browsing sheep. I looked about for the village stocks; I was ready to take the modern vagrants for Shake-spearean clowns; and I was on the point of going into one of the ale-houses to ask Mrs Quickly for a cup of sack.

I began these remarks, however, with no intention of talking about the celebrated curiosities in which this region abounds, but with a design rather of noting a few impressions of some of the shyer and more elusive ornaments of the show. Stratford of course is a very sacred place, but I prefer to say a word, for instance, about a charming old rectory a good many miles distant, and to mention the pleasant picture it made, of a summer afternoon, during a domestic festival. These are the happiest of a stranger's memories of English life, and he feels that he need make no apology for lifting the corner of the curtain. I drove through the leafy lanes I spoke of just now, and peeped over the hedges into fields where the yellow harvest stood waiting. In some places they were already shorn, and, while the light began to redden in the west and to make a horizontal glow behind the dense wayside foliage, the gleaners here and there came brushing through gaps in the hedges with enormous sheaves upon their shoulders. The rectory was an ancient, gabled building, of pale red brick, with facings of white stone and creepers that wrapped it up. It dates, I imagine, from the early Hanoverian time; and as it stood there upon its cushiony lawn and among its ordered gardens, cheek to cheek with its little Norman church, it seemed to me the model of a quiet, spacious, easy English home. The cushiony lawn, as I have called it, stretched away to the edge of a brook, and afforded to a number of very amiable people an opportunity of playing lawn tennis. There were half a dozen games going forward at once, and at each of them a great many 'nice girls', as they say in England, were distinguishing themselves. These young ladies kept the ball going with an agility worthy of the sisters and sweethearts of a race of cricketers, and gave me a chance to admire their flexibility of figure and their freedom of action. When they came back to the house, after the games, flushed a little and a little dishevelled, they might have passed for the attendant nymphs of Diana flocking in from the chase. There had, indeed, been a chance for them to wear the quiver, a target for archery being erected on the lawn. I remembered George Eliot's Gwendolen,[2] and waited to see her step out of the muslin group; but she was not forthcoming, and it was plain that if lawn tennis had been invented in Gwendolen's day this young lady would have captivated Mr Grandcourt by her exploits with the racket. She certainly would have been a mistress of the game; and, if the suggestion be not too gross, the alertness she would have learned from it might have proved an inducement to her boxing the ears of the insupportable Deronda.

After a while it grew too dark for lawn tennis; but while the twilight was still mildly brilliant I wandered away, out of the grounds of the charming parsonage, and turned into the little churchyard beside it. The small weather-worn, rust-coloured church had an appearance of high antiquity; there were some curious Norman windows in the apse. Unfortunately I could not get inside; I could only glance into the open door across the interval of an old-timbered, heavy-hooded, padlocked porch. But the sweetest evening stillness hung over the place, and the sunset was red behind a dark row of rook-haunted elms. The stillness seemed the greater because three or four rustic children were playing, with little soft cries, among the crooked, deep-buried grave-stones. One poor little girl, who seemed deformed, had climbed some steps that served as a pedestal for a tall, medieval-looking cross. She sat perched there and stared at me through the gloaming. This was the heart of England, unmistakably; it might have been the very pivot of the wheel on which her fortune revolves. One need not be a rabid Anglican to be extremely sensible of the charm of an English country church – and indeed of some of the features of an English rural Sunday. In London there is a certain flatness in the observance of this festival; but in the country some of the ceremonies that accompany it have an indefinable harmony with an ancient, pastoral landscape. I made this reflection on an occasion that is still very fresh in my memory. I said to myself that the walk to church from a beautiful country house, of a lovely summer afternoon, may be the prettiest possible adventure. The house stands perched upon a pedestal of rock and looks down from its windows and terraces upon a shadier spot in the wooded meadows, of which the blunted tip of a spire explains the character. A little company of people, whose costume denotes the highest pitch of civilisation, winds down through the blooming gardens, passes out of a couple of small gates and reaches the footpath in the fields. This is especially what takes the fancy of the sympathetic stranger; the level, deep-green meadows, studded here and there with a sturdy oak; the denser grassiness of the footpath, the lily-sheeted pool beside which it passes, the rustic stiles, where he stops and looks back at the great house and its wooded background. It is in the highest degree probable that he has the privilege of walking with a pretty girl, and it is morally certain that he thinks a pretty English girl the very type of the maddening magic of youth. He knows that she doesn't know how lovely is this walk of theirs; she has been taking it – or taking another quite as good – any time these twenty years. But her want of immediate intelligence only makes her the more a part of his delicate entertainment. The latter continues unbroken while they reach the little churchyard and pass up to the ancient porch, round which the rosy rustics are standing, decently and deferentially, to watch the arrival of the smarter contingent. This party takes its place in a great square pew, as large as a small room, and with seats all round, and while he listens to the respectable intonings the sympathetic stranger reads over the inscriptions on the mural tablets before him, all to the honour of the earlier bearers of a name which is, for himself, a symbol of hospitality.

When I came back to the parsonage the entertainment had been transferred to the interior, and I had occasion to admire the maidenly vigour of all the nice girls who, after playing lawn tennis all the afternoon, were modestly expecting to dance all the evening. And in regard to this it is not impertinent to say that from almost any group of young English creatures of this order – though preferably from such as have passed their lives in quiet country homes – an American receives a delightful impression of something that he may describe as an intimate salubrity. He notices face after face in which this rosy absence of a morbid strain – this simple, natural, affectionate development – amounts to positive beauty. If the young lady have no other beauty the air I speak of is a charm in itself; but when it is united, as it so often is, to real perfection of feature and colour the result is the most delightful thing in nature. It makes the highest type of English beauty, and to my sense there is nothing so satisfyingly high as that. Not long since I heard a clever foreigner indulge, in conversation with an English lady – a very wise and liberal woman – in a little lightly restrictive criticism of her countrywomen. 'It is possible,' she answered, in regard to one of his objections; 'but such as they are, they are inexpressibly dear to their husbands.' This is doubtless true of good wives all over the world; but I felt, as I listened to these words of my friend, that there is often something in an English girl-face which gives it an extra touch of *justesse*. Such as the woman is, she has here, more than elsewhere, the look of being completely and profoundly, without reservations for other uses, at the service of the man she loves. This look, after one has been a while in England, comes to seem so much a proper and indispensable part of a 'nice' face, that the absence of it appears a sign of irritability or of shallowness. Latent responsiveness to the manly appeal – that is what it means; which one must take as a very comfortable meaning.

As for the prettiness, I cannot forbear, in the face of a fresh reminiscence, to give it another word. And yet in regard to prettiness what do words avail? This was what I asked myself the other day as I looked at a young girl who stood in an old oaken parlour, the rugged panels of which made a background for her lovely head, in simple conversation with a handsome lad. I said to myself that the faces of the English young have often a perfect charm, but that this same charm is too soft and shy a thing to talk about. The face of this fair creature had a pure oval, and her clear brown eyes a quiet warmth. Her complexion was as bright as a sunbeam after rain, and she smiled in a way that made any other way of smiling than that seem a shallow grimace – a mere creaking of the facial muscles. The young man stood facing her, slowly scratching his thigh and shifting from one foot to the other. He was tall and straight, and so sun-burned that his fair hair was lighter than his complexion. He had honest, stupid blue eyes, and a simple smile that showed handsome teeth. He had the look of a gentleman. Presently I heard what they were saying. 'I suppose it's pretty big,' said the beautiful young girl. 'Yes; it's pretty big,' said the handsome young man. 'It's nicer when they are big,' said his interlocutress. The young man looked at her, and at everything in general, with his slowly apprehending blue eye, and for some time no further remark was made. 'It draws ten feet of water,' he at last went on. 'How much water is there?' said the young girl. She spoke in a charming voice. 'There are thirty feet of water,' said the young man. 'Oh, that's enough,' rejoined the damsel. I had had an idea they were flirting, and perhaps indeed that is the way it is done. It was an ancient room and extremely delightful; everything was polished over with the brownness of centuries. The chimney-piece was carved a foot thick, and the windows bore, in coloured glass, the quarterings of ancestral couples. These had stopped two hundred years before; there was nothing newer than that date. Outside the windows was a deep, broad moat, which washed the base of grey walls – grey walls spotted over with the most delicate yellow lichens.

In such a region as this mellow conservative Warwickshire an appreciative American finds the small things quite as suggestive as the great. Everything indeed is suggestive, and impressions are constantly melting into each other and doing their work before he has had time to ask them whence they came. He can scarce go into a cottage muffled in plants, to see a genial gentlewoman and a 'nice girl', without being reminded forsooth of 'The Small House at Allington'. Why of 'The Small House at Allington'? There is a larger house to which the ladies come up to dine; but that is surely an insufficient reason. That the ladies are charming – even that is not reason enough; for there have been other nice girls in the world than Lily Dale and other mild matrons than her mamma. Reminded, however, he is – especially when he goes out upon the lawn. Of course there is lawn tennis, and it seems all ready for Mr Crosbie to come and take a racket. This is a small example of the way in which in the presence of English life the imagination must be constantly at play on the part of members of a race in whom it has necessarily been trained to do extra service. In driving and walking, in looking and listening, everything affected one as in some degree or other characteristic of a rich, powerful, old-fashioned society. One had no need of being told that this is a conservative county; the fact seemed written in the hedgerows and in the verdant acres behind them. Of course the owners of these things were conservative; of course they were stubbornly unwilling to see the harmonious edifice of their constituted, convenient world the least bit shaken. I had a feeling, as I went about, that I should find some very ancient and curious opinions still comfortably domiciled in the fine old houses whose clustered gables and chimneys appeared here and there, at a distance, above their ornamental woods. Imperturbable British Toryism, viewed in this vague and conjectural fashion – across the fields and behind the oaks and beeches – is by no means a thing the irresponsible stranger would wish away; it deepens the very colour of the air; it may be said to be the style of the landscape. I got a sort of constructive sense of its presence in the picturesque old towns of Coventry and Warwick, which appear to be filled with those institutions – chiefly of an eleemosynary order – that make the undoubting more undoubting still. There are ancient charities in these places – hospitals, almshouses, asylums, infant schools – so quaint and venerable that they almost make the existence of respectful dependence a delectable and satisfying thought. In Coventry in especial, I believe, these pious foundations are so numerous as fairly to place a premium upon personal woe. Invidious reflections apart, however, there are few things that speak more quaintly and suggestively of the old England that an American loves than these clumsy little monuments of ancient benevolence. Such an institution as Leicester's Hospital at Warwick seems indeed to exist primarily for the sake of its spectacular effect upon the American tourists, who, with the dozen rheumatic old soldiers maintained in affluence there, constitute its principal *clientèle*.[3]

The American tourist usually comes straight to this quarter of England – chiefly for the purpose of paying his respects to the birthplace of Shakespeare.[4] Being here, he comes to Warwick to see the castle; and being at Warwick, he comes to see the odd little theatrical-looking refuge for superannuated warriors which lurks in the shadow of one of the old gate-towers. Every one will remember Hawthorne's account of the place,[5] which has left no touch of charming taste to be added to any reference to it. The hospital struck me as a little museum kept up for the amusement and confusion of those inquiring Occidentals who are used to seeing charity more dryly and practically administered. The old hospitallers – I am not sure, after all, whether they are necessarily soldiers, but some of them happen to be – are at once the curiosities and the keepers. They sit on benches outside of their door, at the receipt of custom, all neatly brushed and darned and ready to do you the honours, They are only twelve in number, but their picturesque dwelling, perched upon the old city rampart and full of dusky little courts, cross-timbered gable-ends and deeply sunken lattices, seems a wonderfully elaborate piece of machinery for its humble purpose. Each of the old gentlemen must be provided with a wife or 'housekeeper'; each of them has a dusky parlour of his own; and they pass their latter days in their scoured and polished little refuge as softly and honourably as a company of retired lawgivers or pensioned soothsayers.

At Coventry I went to see a couple of old charities of a similar pattern – places with black-timbered fronts, little clean-swept courts and Elizabethan windows. One of them was a romantic residence for a handful of old women, who sat, each of them, in a cosy little bower, in a sort of mediaeval darkness; the other was a school for little boys of humble origin, and this last establishment was charming. I found the little boys playing at 'top' in a gravelled court, in front of the prettiest old building of tender-coloured stucco and painted timber, ornamented with two delicate little galleries and a fantastic porch. They were dressed in small blue tunics and odd caps, like those worn by sailors, but, if I remember rightly, with little yellow tags affixed. I was able to wander at my pleasure all over the establishment; there was no sign of pastor or master anywhere; nothing but the little yellow-headed boys playing before the ancient house and practising most correctly the Warwickshire accent. I went indoors and looked at a fine old oaken staircase; I even ascended it and walked along a gallery and peeped into a dormitory at a row of very short beds; and then I came down and sat for five minutes on a bench hardly wider than the top rail of a fence, in a little, cold, dim refectory where there was not a crumb to be seen, nor any lingering odour of bygone repasts to be perceived. And yet I wondered how it was that the sense of many generations of boyish feeders seemed to abide there. It came, I suppose, from the very bareness and, if I may be allowed the expression, the clean-licked aspect of the place, which wore the appearance of the famous platter of Jack Sprat and his wife.

Inevitably, of course, the sentimental tourist has a great deal to say to himself about this being Shakespeare's county – about these densely grassed meadows and parks having been, to his musing eyes, the normal landscape, the green picture of the world. In Shakespeare's day, doubtless, the coat of nature was far from being so prettily trimmed as it is now; but there is one place, nevertheless, which, as he passes it in the summer twilight, the traveller does his best to believe unaltered. I allude, of course, to Charlecote Park,[6] whose venerable verdure seems a survival from an earlier England and whose innumerable acres, stretching away, in the early evening, to vaguely seen Tudor walls, lie there like the backward years receding to the age of Elizabeth. It was, however, no part of my design in these remarks to pause before so thickly besieged a shrine as this; and if I were to allude to Stratford it would not be in connection with the fact that Shakespeare planted there, to grow for ever, the torment of his unguessed riddle. It would be rather to speak of a delightful old house, near the Avon, which struck me as the ideal home for a Shakespearean scholar, or indeed for any passionate lover of the poet. Here, with books and memories and the recurring reflection that he had taken his daily walk across the bridge at which you look from your windows straight down an avenue of fine old trees, with an ever-closed gate at the end of them and a carpet of turf stretched over the decent drive – here, I say, with old brown wainscotted chambers to live in, old polished doorsteps to lead you from one to the other, deep window-seats to sit in, with a play in your lap, here a person for whom the cares of life should have resolved themselves into a care for the greatest genius who has represented and ornamented life might find a very congruous asylum. Or, speaking a little wider of the mark, the charming, rambling, low-gabled, many-staired, much-panelled mansion would be a very agreeable home for any person of taste who should prefer an old house to a new. I find I am talking about it quite like an auctioneer; but what I chiefly had at heart was to commemorate the fact that I had lunched there and, while I lunched, kept saying to myself that there is nothing in the world so delightful as the happy accidents of old English houses.

And yet that same day, on the edge of the Avon, I found it in me to say that a new house too may be a very charming affair. But I must add that the new house I speak of had really such exceptional advantages that it could not fairly be placed in the scale. Besides, was it new after all? It must have been, and yet one's impression there was all of a kind of silvered antiquity. The place stood upon a decent Stratford road, from which it looked usual enough; but when, after sitting a while in a charming modern drawing-room, one stepped thoughtlessly through an open window upon a verandah, one found that the horizon of the morning call had been wonderfully widened. I will not pretend to detail all I saw after I stepped off the verandah; suffice it that the spire and chancel of the beautiful old church in which Shakespeare is buried, with the Avon sweeping its base, were one of the elements of the vision. Then there were the smoothest lawns in the world stretching down to the edge of this liquid slowness and making, where the water touched them, a line as even as the rim of a champagne glass – a verge near which you inevitably lingered to see the spire and the chancel (the church was close at hand) among the well-grouped trees, and look for their reflection in the river. The place was a garden of delight; it was a stage set for one of Shakespeare's comedies – for *Twelfth Night* or *Much Ado*. Just across the river was a level meadow, which rivalled the lawn on which I stood, and this meadow seemed only the more essentially a part of the scene by reason of the voluminous sheep that were grazing on it. These sheep were by no means mere edible mutton; they were poetic, historic, romantic sheep; they were not there for their weight or their wool, they were there for their presence and their compositional value, and they visibly knew it. And yet, knowing as they were, I doubt whether the wisest old ram of the flock could have told me how to explain why it was that this happy mixture of lawn and river and mirrored spire and blooming garden seemed to me for a quarter of an hour the richest corner of England.

If Warwickshire is Shakespeare's country, I found myself not dodging the consciousness that it is also George Eliot's. The author of *Adam Bede* and *Middlemarch* has called the rural background of those admirable fictions by another name, but I believe it long ago ceased to be a secret that her native Warwickshire had been in her intention. The stranger who treads its eternal stretched velvet recognises at every turn the elements of George Eliot's novels – especially when he carries himself back in imagination to the Warwickshire of forty years ago. He says to himself that it would be impossible to conceive anything – anything equally rural – more sturdily central, more densely definite. It was in one of the old nestling farmhouses, beyond a hundred hedgerows, that Hetty Sorrel[7] smiled into her milk-pans as if she were looking for a reflection of her pretty face; it was at the end of one of the leafy-pillared avenues that poor Mrs Casaubon paced up and down with her many questions. The country suggests in especial both the social and the natural scenery of *Middlemarch*. There must be many a genially perverse old Mr Brooke there yet, and whether there are many Dorotheas or not, there must be many a well-featured and well-acred young country gentleman, of the pattern of Sir James Chettam, who, as he rides along the leafy lanes, softly cudgels his brain to know why a clever girl shouldn't wish to marry him. But I doubt whether there be many Dorotheas, and I suspect that the Sir James Chettams of the county are not often pushed to that intensity of meditation. You feel, however, that George Eliot could not have placed her heroine in a local medium better fitted to throw her fine impatience into relief – a community more likely to be startled and perplexed by a questioning attitude on the part of a well-housed and well-fed young gentlewoman.

Among the edifying days that I spent in these neighbourhoods there is one in especial of which I should like to give a detailed account. But I find on consulting my memory that the details have melted away into the single deep impression of a perfect ripeness of civilisation. It was a long excursion, by rail and by carriage, for the purpose of seeing three extremely interesting old country-houses. Our errand led us, in the first place, into Oxfordshire, through the ancient market town of Banbury, where of course we made a point of looking out for the Cross referred to in the famous nursery rhyme. It stood there in the most natural manner – though I am afraid it has been 'done up' – with various antique gables around it, from one of whose exiguous windows the young person appealed to in the rhyme may have looked at the old woman as she rode and heard the music of her bells. The houses we went to see have not a national reputation; they are simply interwoven figures in the rich pattern of the Midlands. They have indeed a local renown but they are not thought of as unexampled, still less as abnormal, and the stranger has a feeling that his surprises and ecstasies are held to betray the existence, on his part, of a blank background. Such places, to a Warwickshire mind of good habits, must appear the pillars and props of a heaven-appointed order of things; and accordingly, in a land on which heaven smiles, they are as natural as the geology of the county or the supply of mutton. But nothing could well give a stranger a stronger impression of the wealth of England in such matters – of the interminable list of her territorial homes – than this fact that the so eminent specimens I speak of should have but a limited fame, should not be lions of the first magnitude. Of one of them,

*Broughton Castle, near Banbury*

the finest in the group, one of my companions, who lived but twenty miles away, had never even heard. Such a place was not thought a subject for local swagger. Its peers and mates are scattered all over the country; half of them are not even mentioned in the county guide-books. You stumble upon them in a drive or a walk. You catch a glimpse of an ivied front at some midmost point of wide acres, and taking your way, by leave of a serious old woman at a lodge-gate, along an over-arching avenue, you find yourself introduced to an edifice so human-looking in its beauty that it seems for the occasion fairly to reconcile art and morality.

To Broughton Castle,[8] the first seen in this beautiful group, I must do no more than allude; but this is not because I failed to think it, as I think every house I see, the most delightful habitation in England. It lies rather low, and its woods and pastures slope down to it; it has a deep, clear moat all round it, spanned by a bridge that passes under a charming old gate-tower, and nothing can be sweeter than to see its clustered walls of yellow-brown stone so sharply islanded while its gardens bloom on the other side of the water. Like several other houses in this part of the country, Broughton Castle played a part (on the Parliamentary side) in the civil wars, and not the least interesting features of its beautiful interior are the several mementoes of Cromwell's station there. It was within a moderate drive of this place that in 1642 the battle of Edgehill was fought – the first great battle of the war – and gained by neither party. We went to see the battlefield, where an ancient tower and an artificial ruin (of all things in the world) have been erected for the entertainment of convivial visitors. These ornaments are perched upon the edge of a slope which commands a view of the exact scene of the contest, upwards of a mile away. I looked in the direction indicated and saw misty meadows a little greener perhaps than usual and colonnades of elms a trifle denser. After this we paid our respects to another old house which is full of memories and suggestions of that most dramatic period of English history. But of Compton Wyniates[9] (the name of this seat of enchantment) I despair of giving any coherent or adequate account. It belongs to the Marquis of Northampton, and it stands empty all the year round. It sits on the grass at the bottom of a wooded hollow, and the glades of a superb old park go wandering upward away from it. When I came out in front of the house from a short and steep but stately avenue I said to myself that here surely we had arrived at the farthest limits of what ivy-smothered brick-work and weather-beaten gables, conscious old windows and clustered mossy roofs can accomplish for the eye. It is impossible to imagine a more finished picture. And its air of solitude and delicate decay – of having been dropped into its grassy hollow as an ancient jewel is deposited upon a cushion, and being shut in from the world and back into the past by its circling woods – all this drives the impression well home. The house is not large, as great houses go, and it sits, as I have said, upon the grass, without even a flagging or a footpath to conduct you from the point where the avenue stops to the beautiful sculptured doorway which admits you into the small, quaint inner court. From this court you are at liberty to pass through the crookedest series of oaken halls and chambers, adorned with treasures of old wainscotting and elaborate doors and chimenypieces. Outside, you may walk all round the house on a grassy bank, which is raised above the level on which it stands, and find it from every point of view a more charming composition. I should not omit to mention that Compton Wyniates is supposed to have been in Scott's eye when he described the dwelling of the old royalist knight in *Woodstock*. In this case he simply transferred the house to the other side of the county. He has indeed given several of the features of the place, but he has not given what one may call its colour. I must add that if Sir Walter could not give the colour of Compton Wyniates, it is useless for any other writer to try. It is a matter for the brush and not for the pen.

And what shall I say of the colour of Wroxton Abbey,[10] which we visited last in order and which in the thickening twilight, as we approached its great ivy-muffled face, laid on the mind the burden of its felicity? Wroxton Abbey, as it stands, is a house of about the same period as Compton Wyniates – the latter years, I suppose, of the sixteenth century. But it is quite another affair. The place is inhabited, 'kept up', full of the most interesting and most splendid detail. Its happy occupants, however, were fortunately not in the act of staying there (happy occupants, in England, are almost always absent), and the house was exhibited with a civility worthy of its merit. Everything that in the material line can render life noble and charming has been gathered into it with a profusion which makes the whole place a monument to past opportunity. As I wandered from one rich room to another and looked at these things that intimate appeal to the romantic sense which I just mentioned was mercilessly emphasised. But who can tell the story of the romantic sense when that adventurer really rises to the occasion – takes its ease in an old English country house while the twilight darkens the corners of expressive rooms and the victim of the scene, pausing at the window, turns his glance from the observing portrait of a handsome ancestral face and sees the great soft billows of the lawn melt away into the park?

First published in *The Galaxy*, XXIV (November 1877), 671–80; reprinted in *Portraits of Places* (1883), and *English Hours* (1905).

# Abbeys and Castles

It is a frequent perception with the stranger in England that the beauty and interest of the country are private property and that to get access to them a key is always needed. The key may be large or it may be small, but it must be something that will turn a lock. Of the things that contribute to the happiness of an American observer in these tantalising conditions, I can think of very few that do not come under this definition of private property. When I have mentioned the hedgerows and the churches I have almost exhausted the list. You can enjoy a hedgerow from the public road, and I suppose that even if you are a Dissenter you may enjoy a Norman abbey from the street. If therefore you talk of anything beautiful in England, the presumption will be that it is private; and indeed such is my admiration of this delightful country that I feel inclined to say that if you talk of anything private the presumption will be that it is beautiful. This is something of a dilemma. When the observer permits himself to commemorate charming impressions he is in danger of giving to the world the fruits of friendship and hospitality. When on the other hand he withholds his impression he lets something admirable slip away without having marked its passage, without having done it proper honour. He ends by mingling discretion with enthusiasm, and he says to himself that it is not treating a country ill to talk of its treasures when the mention of each has tacit reference to some kindness conferred.

The impressions I have in mind in writing these lines were gathered in a part of England of which I had not before had even a traveller's glimpse; but as to which, after a day or two, I found myself quite ready to agree with a friend who lived there and who knew and loved it well, when he said very frankly 'I do believe it is the loveliest corner of the world!' This was not a dictum to quarrel about, and while I was in the neighbourhood I was quite of his opinion. I felt I might easily come to care for it very much as he cared for it; I had a glimpse of the kind of romantic passion such a country may inspire. It is a capital example of that density of feature which is the great characteristic of English scenery. There are no waste details; everything in the landscape is something particular – has a history, has played a part, has a value to the imagination. It is a region of hills and blue undulations, and, though none of the hills are high, all of them are interesting – interesting as such things are interesting in an old, small country, by a kind of exquisite modulation, something suggesting that outline and colouring have been retouched and refined by the hand of time. Independently of its castles and abbeys, the definite relics of the ages, such a landscape seems charged and interfused. It has, has always had, human relations and is intimately conscious of them. That little speech about the loveliness of his county, or of his own part of his county, was made to me by my companion as we walked up the grassy slope of a hill, or 'edge', as it is called there, from the crest of which we seemed in an instant to look away over most of the remainder of England. Certainly one would have grown to love such a view as that quite in the same way as to love some magnificent yet sensitive friend. The 'edge' plunged down suddenly, as if the corresponding slope on the other side had been excavated, and you might follow the long ridge for the space of an afternoon's walk with this vast, charming prospect before your eyes. Looking across an English county into the next but one is a very pretty entertainment, the county seeming by no means so small as might be supposed. How can a county seem small in which, from such a vantage-point as the one I speak of, you see, as a darker patch across the lighter green, the great territory of one of the greatest representatives of territorial greatness? These things constitute immensities, and beyond them are blue undulations of varying tone, and then another bosky province which furnishes forth, as you are told, the residential and other umbrage of another magnate. And to right and left of these, in wooded expanses, lie other domains of equal consequence. It was therefore not the smallness but the vastness of the country that struck me, and I was not at all in the mood of a certain American who once, in my hearing, burst out laughing at an English answer to my inquiry as to whether my interlocutor often saw Mr

B——. 'Oh no,' the answer had been, 'we never see him: he lives away off in the West.' It was the western part of his county our friend meant, and my American humorist found matter for infinite jest in his meaning. 'I should as soon think,' he remarked, 'of talking of my own west or east foot.'

I do not think, even, that my sensibility to the charm of this delightful region – for its hillside prospect of old red farmhouses lighting up the dark-green bottoms, of gables and chimney-tops of great houses peeping above miles of woodland, and, in the vague places of the horizon, of far away towns and sites that one had always heard of – was conditioned upon having 'property' in the neighbourhood, so that the little girls in the town should suddenly drop curtsies to me in the street; though that too would certainly have been pleasant. At the same time having a little property would without doubt have made the attachment stronger. People who wander about the world without money in their pockets indulge in dreams – dreams of the things they would buy if their pockets were workable. These dreams are very apt to have relation to a good estate in any neighbourhood in which the wanderer may happen to find himself. For myself, I have never been in a country so unattractive that I didn't find myself 'drawn' to its most exemplary mansion. In New England and other portions of the United States I have felt my heart go out to the Greek temple, the small Parthenon, in white-painted wood; in Italy I have made imaginary proposals for the yellow-walled villa with statues on the roof. My fancy, in England, has seldom fluttered so high as the very best house, but it has again and again hovered about one of the quiet places, unknown to fame, which are locally spoken of as merely 'good'. There was one in especial, in the neighbourhood I allude to, as to which the dream of having impossibly acquired it from an embarrassed owner kept melting into the vision of 'moving in' on the morrow. I saw this place, unfortunately, to small advantage; I saw it in the rain, but I am glad fine weather didn't meddle with the affair, for the irritation of envy might in this case have poisoned the impression. It was a long, wet Sunday, and the waters were deep. I had been in the house all day, for the weather can best be described by my saying that it had been deemed to exonerate us from church. But in the afternoon, the pro-

spective interval between lunch and tea assuming formidable proportions, my host took me a walk, and in the course of our walk he led
me into a park which he described as 'the paradise of a small English
country-gentleman'. It was indeed a modern Eden, and the trees might
have been trees of knowledge. They were of high antiquity and magnificent girth and stature; they were strewn over the grassy levels in
extraordinary profusion, and scattered upon and down the slopes in a
fashion than which I have seen nothing more felicitous since I last looked
at the chestnuts above the Lake of Como. The point was that the property was small, but that one could perceive nowhere any limit. Shortly
before we turned into the park the rain had renewed itself, so that we
were awkwardly wet and muddy; but, being near the house, my companion proposed to leave his card in a neighbourly way. The house was
most agreeable: it stood on a kind of terrace, in the middle of a lawn and
garden, and the terrace overhung one of the most copious rivers in
England, as well as looking across to those blue undulations of which I
have already spoken. On the terrace also was a piece of ornamental
water, and there was a small iron paling to divide the lawn from the
park. All this I beheld in the rain. My companion gave his card to the
butler with the remark that we were too much bespattered to come in,
and we turned away to complete our circuit. As we turned away I
became acutely conscious of what I should have been tempted to call the
cruelty of this proceeding. My imagination gauged the whole position.
It was a blank, a blighted Sunday afternoon – no one could come. The
house was charming, the terrace delightful, the oaks magnificent, the
view most interesting. But the whole thing confessed to the blankness if
not to the dullness. In the house was a drawing-room, and in the drawing-room was – by which I meant *must be* – an English lady, a perfectly
harmonious figure. There was nothing fatuous in believing that on this
rainy Sunday afternoon it would not please her to be told that two
gentlemen had walked across the country to her door only to go
through the ceremony of leaving a card. Therefore, when, before we
had gone many yards, I heard the butler hurrying after us, I felt how just
my sentiment of the situation had been. Of course we went back, and I
carried my muddy boots into the drawing-room – just the drawing-

room I had imagined – where I found – I will not say just the lady I had imagined, but a lady even more in keeping .Indeed there were two ladies, one of whom was staying in the house. In whatever company you find yourself in England, you may always be sure that some one present is 'staying', and you come in due time to feel the abysses within the word. The large windows of the drawing-room I speak of looked away over the river to the blurred and blotted hills, where the rain was drizzling and drifting. It was very quiet, as I say; there was an air of large leisure. If one wanted to do anything here, there was evidently plenty of time – and indeed of every other appliance – to do it. The two ladies talked about 'town': that is what people talk about in the country. If I were disposed I might represent them as talking with a positive pathos of yearning. At all events I asked myself how it could be that one should live in this charming place and trouble one's head about what was going on in London in July. Then we had fine strong tea and bread and butter.

I returned to the habitation of my friend – for I too was guilty of 'staying' – through an old Norman portal, massively arched and quaintly sculptured, across whose hollow threshold the eye of fancy might see the ghosts of monks and the shadows of abbots pass noiselessly to and fro. This aperture admits you to a beautiful ambulatory of the thirteenth century – a long stone gallery or cloister, repeated in two stories, with the interstices of its traceries now glazed, but with its long, low, narrow, charming vista still perfect and picturesque, with its flags worn away by monkish sandals and with huge round-arched doorways opening from its inner side into great rooms roofed like cathedrals. These rooms are furnished with narrow windows, of almost defensive aspect, set in embrasures three feet deep and ornamented with little grotesque medieval faces. To see one of the small monkish masks grinning at you while you dress and undress, or while you look up in the intervals of inspiration from your letter-writing, is a mere detail in the entertainment of living in a *ci-devant* priory. This entertainment is inexhaustible; for every step you take in such a house confronts you in one way or another with the remote past. You devour the documentary, you inhale the historic. Adjoining the house is a beautiful ruin, part of the walls and windows and bases of the piers of the magnificent church administered by the prececessor of your host, the mitred abbot. These relics are very desultory, but they are still abundant, and they testify to the great scale and the stately beauty of the abbey. You may lie upon the grass at the base of an ivied fragment, measure the girth of the great stumps of the central columns, half smothered in soft creepers, and think how strange it is that in this quiet hollow, in the midst of lonely hills, so exquisite and elaborate a work of art should have risen. It is but an hour's walk to another great ruin, which has held together more completely. There the central tower stands erect to half its altitude and the round arches and massive pillars of the nave make a perfect vista on the unencumbered turf. You get an impression that when catholic England was in her prime great abbeys were as thick as milestones. By native amateurs even now the region is called 'wild', though to American eyes it seems almost suburban in its smoothness and finish. There is a noiseless little railway running through the valley, and there is an ancient little town at the abbey gates – a town indeed with no great din of vehicles, but with goodly brick houses, with a dozen 'publics', with tidy, white-washed cottages, and with little girls, as I have said, bobbing curtsies in the street. Yet even now, if one had wound one's way into the valley by the railroad, it would be rather a surprise to find a great architectural display in a setting so peaceful and pastoral. How impressive then must the beautiful church have been in the days of its prosperity, when the pilgrim came down to it from the grassy hillside and its bells made the stillness sensible! The abbey was in those days a great affair; it sprawled, as my companion said, all over the place. As you walk away from it you think you have got to the end of its geography, but you encounter it still in the shape of a rugged outhouse enriched with an early-English arch, of an ancient well hidden in a kind of sculptured cavern. It is noticeable that even if you are a traveller from a land where there are no early English – and indeed few late-English – arches, and where the well-covers are, at their hoariest, of fresh-looking shingles, you grow used with little delay to all this antiquity. Anything very old seems extremely natural; there is nothing we suffer to get so near us as the tokens of the remote. It is not too much to say that after spending twenty-four hours in a house that is six hundred years old you seem yourself to have lived in it six hundred years. You seem yourself to have hollowed the flags with your tread and to have polished the oak with your touch. You walk along the little stone gallery where the monks used to pace, looking out of the Gothic window places at their beautiful church, and you pause at the big, round, rugged doorway that admits you to what is now the drawing-room. The massive step by which you ascend to the threshold is a trifle crooked, as it should be; the lintels are cracked and worn by the myriad-fingered years. This strikes your casual glance. You look up and down the miniature cloister before you pass in; it seems wonderfully old and queer. Then you turn into the drawing-room, where you find modern conversation and late publications and the prospect of dinner. The new life and the old have melted together; there is no dividing line. In the drawing-room wall is a queer funnel-shaped hole, with the broad end inward, like a small casemate. You ask what it is, but people have forgotten. It is something of the monks; it is a mere detail. After dinner you are told that there is of course a ghost – a grey friar who is seen in the dusky hours at the end of passages. Sometimes the servants see him; they afterwards go surreptitiously to sleep in the village. Then, when you take your chamber-candle and go wandering bedward by a short cut through empty rooms, you are conscious of an attitude toward the grey friar which you hardly know whether to read as a fond hope or as a great fear.

A friend of mine, an American, who knew this country, had told me not to fail, while I was in the neighbourhood, to go to Stokesay and two or three other places. 'Edward IV and Elizabeth,' he said, 'are still hanging about there.' So admonished, I made a point of going at least to Stokesay, and I saw quite what my friend meant. Edward IV and Elizabeth indeed are still to be met almost anywhere in the county; as regards domestic architecture few parts of England are still more vividly old-English. I have rarely had, for a couple of hours, the sensation of dropping back personally into the past so straight as while I lay on the grass beside the well in the little sunny court of this small castle and lazily appreciated the still definite details of medieval life.[1] The place is a capital example of a small *gentilhommière* of the thirteenth century. It has a good deep moat, now filled with wild verdure, and a curious gatehouse of a much later period – the period when the defensive attitude had been well-nigh abandoned. This gatehouse, which is not in the least in the style of the habitation, but gabled and heavily timbered, with quaint cross-beams protruding from surfaces of coarse white plaster, is a very effective anomaly in regard to the little grey fortress on the other side of the court. I call this a fortress, but it is a fortress which might easily have been taken, and it must have assumed its present shape at a time when people had ceased to peer through narrow slits at possible besiegers. There are slits in the outer walls for such peering, but they are noticeably broad and not particularly oblique, and might easily have been applied to the uses of a peaceful parley. This is part of the charm of the place; human life there must have lost an earlier grimness; it was lived in by people who were beginning to believe in good intentions. They must have lived very much together; that is one of the most obvious reflections in the court of a medieval dwelling. The court was not always grassy and empty, as it is now, with only a couple of gentlemen in search of impressions lying at their length, one of them handling a wine flask that colours the clear water drawn from the well into a couple of tumblers by a decent, rosy, smiling, talking old woman who has come bustling out of the gatehouse and who has a large, dropsical, innocent husband standing about on crutches in the sun and making no sign when you ask after his health. This poor man has reached that ultimate depth of human simplicity at which even a chance to talk about one's ailments is not appreciated. But the civil old woman talks for every one, even for an artist who has come out of one of the rooms, where I see him afterward reproducing its mouldering repose. The rooms are all unoccupied and in a state of extreme decay, though the castle is, as yet, far from being a ruin. From one of the windows I see a young lady sitting under a tree, across a meadow, with her knees up, dripping something into her mouth. It is indubitably a camel's hair paint-brush; the young lady is inevitably sketching. These are the only besiegers to which the place is exposed now, and they can do no great harm, as I doubt whether the young lady's aim is very good. We wandered about the empty interior, thinking it a pity such things should fall to pieces. There is a beautiful great hall – great, that is, for a small castle (it would be extremely handsome in a modern house) – with tall, ecclesiastical-looking windows and a long staircase at one end, which climbs against the wall into a spacious bedroom. You may still apprehend very well the main lines of that simpler life; and it must be said that, simpler though it was, it was apparently by no means destitute of many of our own conveniences. The chamber at the top of the staircase ascending from the hall is charming still, with its irregular shape, its low-browed ceiling, its cupboards in the walls, its deep bay window formed of a series of small lattices. You can fancy people stepping out from it upon the platform of the staircase, whose rugged wooden logs, by way of steps, and solid, deeply-guttered hand rail, still remain. They looked down into the hall, where, I take it, there was always a congregation of retainers, much lounging and waiting and passing to and fro, with a door open into the court. The court, as I said just now, was not the grassy, æsthetic spot which you may find it at present of a summer's day; there were beasts tethered in it, and hustling men at arms, and the earth was trampled into puddles. But my lord or my lady, looking down from the chamber-door, commanded the position and, no doubt, issued their orders accordingly. The sight of the groups on the floor beneath, the calling up and down, the oaken tables spread and the brazier in the middle – all this seemed present again; and it was not difficult to pursue the historic vision through the rest of the building – through the portion which connected the great hall with the tower (where the confederate of the sketching young lady without had set up the peaceful three-legged engine of his craft); through the dusky, roughly circular rooms of the tower itself, and up the corkscrew staircase of the same to that most charming part of every old castle, where visions must leap away off the battlements to elude you – the bright, dizzy platform at the tower-top, the place where the castle standard hung and the vigilant inmates surveyed the approaches. Here, always, you really overtake the impression of the place – here, in the sunny stillness, it seems to pause, panting a little, and give itself up.

It was not only at Stokesay that I lingered a while on the summit of the keep to enjoy the complete impression so overtaken. I spent such another half-hour at Ludlow,[2] which is a much grander and more famous monument. Ludlow, however, is a ruin – the most impressive and magnificent of ruins. The charming old town and the admirable castle form a capital object of pilgrimage. Ludlow is an excellent example of a small English provincial town that has not been soiled and disfigured by industry; it exhibits no tall chimneys and smoke-streamers, no attendant purlieus and slums. The little city is perched upon a hill near which the goodly Severn wanders, and it has a remarkable air of civic dignity. Its streets are wide and clean, empty and a little grass-grown, and bordered with spacious, midly ornamental brick houses which look as if there had been more going on in them in the first decade of the century than there is in the present, but which can still nevertheless hold up their heads and keep their window-panes clear, their knockers brilliant and their door-steps whitened. The place seems to say that some hundred years ago it was the centre of a large provincial society and that this society was very 'good' of its kind. It must have transported itself to Ludlow for the season – in rumbling coaches and heavy curricles – and there entertained itself in decent emulation of that more majestic capital which a choice of railway lines had not as yet placed within its immediate reach. It had balls at the assembly rooms; it had Mrs Siddons[3] to play; it had Catalani to sing. Miss Burney's and Miss Austen's heroines might perfectly well have had their first love affair there; a journey to Ludlow would certainly have been a great event to Fanny Price or Emma Woodhouse,[4] or even to those more romantically connected young ladies Evelina and Cecilia.[5] It is a place on which a provincial aristocracy has left so sensible a stamp as to enable you to measure both the grand manners and the small ways. It is a very interesting array of houses of the period after the poetry of domestic architecture had begun to wane and before the vulgarity had come – a fine familiar classic prose. Such places, such houses, such relics and intimations, carry us back to the near antiquity of that pre-Victorian England which it is still easy for a stranger to picture with a certain vividness, thanks to the partial survival of many of its characteristics. It is still easier for a stranger who has dwelt a time in England to form an idea of the tone, the habits, the aspect of the social life before its classic insularity had begun to wane, as all observers agree that it did about thirty years ago. It is true that the mental operation in this matter reduces itself to our imaging some of the things which form the peculiar national notes as infinitely exaggerated: the rigidly aristocratic constitution of society, the unæsthetic temper of the people, the small public fund of convenience, of elegance. Let an old gentleman of conservative tastes, who can remember the century's youth, talk to you at a club *temporis acti* – tell you wherein it is that from his own point of view London, as a residence for a gentleman, has done nothing but fall off for the last forty years. You will listen, of course, with an air of decent sympathy, but privately you will say to yourself how difficult a place of sojourn London must have been in those days for the traveller from other countries – how little cosmopolitan, how bound, in a thousand ways, with narrowness of custom. What was true of the great city at that time was of course doubly true of the provinces; and a community of the type of Ludlow must have been a kind of focus of insular propriety. Even then, however, the irritated alien would have had the magnificent ruins of the castle to dream himself back into good humour in. They would effectually have transported him beyond all waning or waxing Philistinisms.

First published in *Lippincott's Magazine*, XX (October 1877), 434–42; reprinted in *Portraits of Places* (1883), and *English Hours* (1905).

# English Vignettes

## I

Toward the last of April, in Monmouthshire, the primroses were as big as your fist. I say in Monmouthshire, because I believe that a certain grassy mountain which I gave myself the pleasure of climbing and to which I took my way across the charming country, through lanes where the hedges were perched upon blooming banks, lay within the borders of this ancient province. It was the festive Eastertide, and a pretext for leaving London had not been wanting. Of course it rained – it rained a good deal – for man and the weather are usually at cross-purposes. But there were intervals of light and warmth, and in England a couple of hours of brightness islanded in moisture assert their independence and leave an uncompromised memory. These reprieves were even of longer duration; that whole morning for instance on which, with a companion, I scrambled up the little Skirrid. One had a feeling that one was very far from London; as in fact one was, after six or seven hours in a swift, straight train. In England this is a long span; it seemed to justify the half-reluctant confession, which I heard constantly made, that the country was extremely 'wild'. There is wildness and wildness, I thought; and though I had not been a great explorer I compared this rough district with several neighbourhoods in another part of the world that passed for tame. I went even so far as to wish that some of its ruder features might be transplanted to that relatively unregulated landscape and commingled with its suburban savagery. We were close to the Welsh border, and a dozen little mountains in the distance were peeping over each other's shoulders, but nature was open to the charge of no worse disorder than this. The Skirrid (I like to repeat the name) wore, it is true, at a distance, the aspect of a magnified extinguisher; but when, after a bright, breezy walk through lane and meadow, we had scrambled over the last of the thickly flowering hedges which lay around its shoulders like loosened strings of coral and begun to ascend the grassy cone (very much in the attitude of Nebuchadnezzar), it proved as smooth-faced as a garden mound. Hard by, on the flanks of other hills, were troops of browsing sheep, and the only thing that confessed in the least to a point or an edge was the strong, damp wind. But even the high breeze was good-humoured and only wanted something to play with, blowing about the pearly morning mists that were airing themselves upon neighbouring ridges and shaking the vaporous veil that fluttered down in the valley over the picturesque little town of Abergavenny. A breezy, grassy English hill-top, looking down on a country full of suggestive names and ancient memories and implied stories (especially if you are exhilarated by a beautiful walk and have a flask in your pocket), shows you the world as a very smooth place, fairly rubbed so by human use.

I was warned away from church, on Sunday, by my mistrust of its medieval chill – lumbago there was so clearly catching. In the still hours, when the roads and lanes were empty, I simply walked to the church-yard and sat upon one of the sun-warmed gravestones. I say the roads were empty, but they were peopled with the big primroses I just now spoke of – primroses of the size of ripe apples and yet, in spite of their rank growth, of as pale and tender a yellow as if their gold had been diluted with silver. It was indeed a mixture of gold and silver, for there was a wealth of the white wood-anemone as well, and these delicate flowers, each of so perfect a coinage, were tumbled along the green wayside as if a prince had been scattering largess. The outside of an old English country church in service time is a very pleasant place; and this is as near as I often dare approach the celebration of the Anglican mysteries. A just sufficient sense of their august character may be gathered from that vague sound of village music which makes its way out into the still-ness and from the perusal of those portions of the Prayer Book which are inscribed upon mouldering slabs and dislocated headstones. The church I speak of was a beautiful specimen of its kind – intensely aged, variously patched, but still solid and useful and with no touch of restoration. It was very big and massive and, hidden away in the fields, had a kind of lonely grandeur; there was nothing in particular near it but its out-of-the-world little parsonage. It was only one of ten thousand; I had seen a hundred such before. But I watched the watery sunshine upon the rugosities of its ancient masonry; I stood a while in the shade of two or three spreading yews which stretched their black arms over graves decorated for Easter, according to the custom of that country, with garlands of primrose and dog violet; and I reflected that in a 'wild' region it was a blessing to have so quiet a place of refuge as that.

Later I chanced upon a couple of other asylums which were more spacious and no less tranquil. Both of them were old country houses, and each in its way was charming. One was a half-modernised feudal dwelling, lying in a wooded hollow – a large concavity filled with a delightful old park. The house had a long grey façade and half a dozen towers, and the usual supply of ivy and of clustered chimneys relieved against a background of rook-haunted elms. But the windows were all closed and the avenue was untrodden; the house was the property of a lady who could not afford to live in it in becoming state and who had let it, furnished, to a rich young man, 'for the shooting'. The rich young man occupied it but for three weeks in the year and for the rest of the time left it a prey to the hungry gaze of the passing stranger, the would-be redresser of æsthetic wrongs. It seemed a great æsthetic wrong that so charming a place should not be a conscious, sentient home. In England all this is very common. It takes a great many plain people to keep a 'perfect' gentleman going; it takes a great deal of wasted sweetness to make up a saved property. It is true that, in the other case I speak of, the sweetness, which here was even greater, was less sensibly squandered. If there was no one else in the house at least there were ghosts. It had a dark red front and grim-looking gables; it was perched upon a vague terrace, quite high in the air, which was reached by steep, crooked, mossy steps. Beneath these steps was an ancient bit of garden, and from the hither side of the garden stretched a great expanse of turf. Out of the midst of the turf sprang a magnificent avenue of Scotch firs – a perfect imitation of the Italian stone pine. It looked like the Villa Borghese transplanted to the Welsh hills. The huge, smooth stems, in their double row, were crowned with dark parasols. In the Scotch fir or the Italian pine there is always an element of oddity; the open umbrella in a rainy country is not a poetical analogy, and the case is not better if you compare the tree to a colossal mushroom. But, without analogies, there was something very striking in the effect of this enormous, rigid vista, and in the grassy carpet of the avenue, with the dusky, lonely, high-featured house looking down upon it. There was something solemn and tragical; the place was made to the hand of a story-seeker, who might have found his characters within, as, the leaden lattices being open, the actors seemed ready for the stage.

## II

The Isle of Wight is at first disappointing. I wondered why it should be, and then I found the reason in the influence of the detestable little railway. There can be no doubt that a railway in the Isle of Wight is a gross impertinence, is in evident contravention to the natural style of the place. The place is pure picture or is nothing at all. It is ornamental only – it exists for exclamation and the water-colour brush. It is separated by nature from the dense railway system of the less diminutive island, and is the corner of the world where a good carriage road is most in keeping. Never was a clearer opportunity for sacrificing to prettiness; never was a better chance for not making a railway. But now there are twenty trains a day, so that the prettiness is twenty times less. The island is so small that the hideous embankments and tunnels are obtrusive; the sight of them is as painful as it would be to see a pedlar's pack on the shoulders of a lovely woman. This is your first impression as you travel (naturally by the objectionable conveyance) from Ryde to Ventnor; and the fact that the train rumbles along very smoothly and stops at half a dozen little stations, where the groups on the platform enable you to perceive that the population consists almost exclusively of gentlemen in costumes suggestive of unlimited leisure for attention to cravats and trousers (an immensely large class in England), of old ladies of the species denominated in France *rentières*, of young ladies of the highly educated and sketching variety, this circumstance fails to reconcile you to the chartered cicatrix which forms your course. At Ventnor, however, face to face with the sea, and with the blooming shoulder of the Undercliff close behind you, you lose sight to a certain extent of the superfluities of civilisation. Not indeed that Ventnor has not been diligently civilised. It is a formed and finished watering place, it has been reduced to a due degree of cockneyfication. But the glittering ocean remains, shimmering at moments with blue and silver, and the large gorse-covered downs rise superbly above it. Ventnor hangs upon the side of a steep hill, and here and there it clings and scrambles, is propped up and terraced, like one of the bright-faced little towns that look down upon the Mediterranean. To add to the Italian effect the houses are all denominated villas, though it must be added that nothing is less like an Italian villa than an English. Those which ornament the successive ledges at Ventnor are for the most part small semi-detached boxes, predestined, even before they have fairly come into the world, to the entertainment of lodgers. They stand in serried rows all over the place, with the finest names in the Peerage painted upon their gate-posts. Their severe similarity of aspect, how-ever, is such that even the difference between Plantagenet and Percival, between Montgomery and Montmorency, is hardly sufficient to en-lighten the puzzled visitor. An English place of recreation is more com-fortable than an American; in a Plantagenet villa the art of receiving 'summer guests' has usually been brought to a higher perfection than in an American rural hotel. But what strikes an American, with regard to even so charmingly nestled a little town as Ventnor, is that it is far less natural, less pastoral and bosky than his own fond image of a summer retreat. There is too much brick and mortar; there are too many smoking chimneys and shops and public houses; there are no woods nor brooks nor lonely headlands; there is none of the virginal stillness of Nature. Instead of these things there is an esplanade mostly paved with asphalt, bordered with benches and little shops and provided with a German band. To be just to Ventnor, however, I must hasten to add that once you get away from the asphalt there is a great deal of vegetation. The little village of Bonchurch, which closely adjoins it, is buried in the most elaborate verdure, muffled in the smoothest lawns and the densest shrubbery. Bonchurch is simply delicious and indeed in a manner quite absurd. It is like a model village in imitative substances, kept in a big glass case; the turf might be of green velvet and the foliage of cut paper. The villagers are all happy gentlefolk, the cottages have plate-glass windows, and the rose trees on their walls looked as if tied up with ribbon 'to match'. Passing from Ventnor through the elegant umbrage of Bonchurch, and keeping along the coast toward Shanklin, you come to the prettiest part of the Undercliff, or in other words to the prettiest place in the world. The immense grassy cliffs which form the coast of the island make what the French would call a 'false descent' to the sea. At a certain point the descent is broken, so that a wide natural terrace, all overtangled with wild shrubs and flowers, hangs there in mid-air, halfway above salt water. It is impossible to imagine anything more charming than this long, blooming platform, protected from the north by huge green bluffs and plunging on the other side into the murmuring tides. This delightful arrangement constitutes for a distance of some fifteen miles the south shore of the Isle of Wight; but the best of it, as I have said, is to be found in the four or five that separate Ventnor from Shanklin. Of a lovely afternoon in April these four or five miles are an admirable walk.

Of course you must first catch your lovely afternoon. I caught one; in fact I caught two. On the second I climbed up the downs and perceived that it was possible to put their gorse-covered stretches to still other than pedestrian uses – to devote them to sedentary pleasures. A long lounge in the lee of a stone wall, the lingering, fading afternoon light, the reddening sky, the band of blue sea above the level-topped bunches of gorse – these things, enjoyed as an undertone to the conversation of an amiable compatriot, seemed indeed a very sufficient substitute for that primitive stillness of the absence of which I ventured just now to complain.

## III

It was probably a mistake to stop at Portsmouth. I had done so, however, in obedience to a familiar theory that seaport towns abound in local colour, in curious types, in the quaint and the strange. But these charms, it must be confessed, were signally wanting to Portsmouth, along whose sordid streets I strolled for an hour, vainly glancing about me for an overhanging façade or a group of Maltese sailors. I was distressed to perceive that a famous seaport could be at once untidy and prosaic. Portsmouth is dirty, but it is also dull. It may be roughly divided into the dockyard and the public houses. The dockyard, into which I was unable to penetrate, is a colossal enclosure, signalised externally by a grim brick wall, as featureless as an empty blackboard. The dockyard eats up the town, as it were, and there is nothing left over but the gin shops, which the town drinks up. There is not even a crooked old quay of any consequence, with brightly-patched houses looking out upon a forest of masts. To begin with, there are no masts; and then there are no polyglot sign-boards, no overhanging upper stories, no outlandish parrots and macaws perched in open lattices. I had another hour or so before my train departed, and it would have gone hard with me if I had not bethought myself of hiring a boat and being pulled about in the harbour. Here a certain amount of entertainment was to be found. There were great ironclads and white troopships that looked vague and spectral, like the floating home of the flying Dutchman, and small, devilish vessels whose mission was to project the infernal torpedo. I coasted about these metallic islets, and then, to eke out my entertainment, I boarded the *Victory*. The *Victory* is an ancient frigate of enormous size, which in the days of her glory carried I know not how many hundred guns, but whose only function now is to stand year after year in Portsmouth waters and exhibit herself to the festive cockney. Bank holiday is now her great date; once upon a time it was Trafalgar. The *Victory*, in short, was Nelson's ship; it was on her huge deck that he was struck, and in her deep bowels he breathed his last. The venerable shell is provided with a company of ushers, like the Tower of London or Westminster Abbey, and is hardly less solid and spacious than either of the land vessels. A good man in uniform did me the honours of the ship with a terrible displacement of *h*'s, and there seemed something strange in the way it had lapsed from its heroic part. It had carried two hundred guns and a mighty warrior, and boomed against the enemies of England; it had been the scene of one of the most thrilling and touching events in English history. Now, it was hardly more than a mere source of income to the Portsmouth watermen an objective point for Whitsuntide excursionists, a thing a pilgrim from afar must allude to very casually, for fear of seeming vulgar or even quite serious.

## IV

But I recouped myself, as they say, by stopping afterwards at Chichester. In this dense and various old England two places may be very near together and yet strike a very different note. I knew in a general way that this one had for its main sign a cathedral, and indeed had caught the sign, in the form of a beautiful spire, from the window of the train. I had always regarded an afternoon in a small cathedral town as a high order of entertainment, and a morning at Portsmouth had left me in the mood for not missing such an exhibition. The spire of Chichester at a little distance greatly resembles that of Salisbury.[1] It is on a small scale, but it tapers upward with a delicate slimness which, like that of its famous rival, makes a picture of the level landscape in which it stands. Unlike the spire of Salisbury, however, it has not at present the charm of antiquity. A few years ago the old steeple collapsed and tumbled into the church, and the present structure is but a modern facsimile.[2] The cathedral is not of the highest interest; it is rather inexpressive, and except for a curious old detached bell-tower which stands beside it, has no particular element of unexpectedness. But an English cathedral of restricted grandeur may yet be a very charming affair; and I spent an hour or so circling round this highly respectable edifice, with the spell of contemplation unbroken by satiety. I approached it, from the station, by the usual quiet red-brick street of the usual cathedral town – a street of small, excellent shops, before which, here and there, one of the vehicles of the neighbouring gentry was drawn up beside the curbstone while the grocer or the bookseller, who had hurried out obsequiously, was waiting upon the comfortable occupant. I went into a bookseller's to buy a Chichester guide,[3] which I perceived in the window; I found the shopkeeper talking to a young curate in a soft hat. The guide seemed very desirable, though it appeared to have been but scantily desired; it had been published in the year 1841, and a very large remnant of the edition, with a muslin back and a little white label and paper-covered boards, was piled up on the counter. It was dedicated, with terrible humility, to the Duke of Richmond, and ornamented with primitive wood-cuts and steel plates; the ink had turned brown and the page musty; and the style itself – that of a provincial antiquary of upwards of forty years ago penetrated with the grandeur of the aristocracy – had grown rather sallow and stale. Nothing could have been more mellifluous and urbane than the young curate: he was arranging to have *The Times* newspaper sent him every morning for perusal. 'So it will be a penny if it is fetched away at noon?' he said, smiling very sweetly and with the most gentlemanly voice possible; 'and it will be three halfpence if it is fetched away at four o'clock?' At the top of the street, into which, with my guide-book, I relapsed, was an old market-cross of the fifteenth century – a florid, romantic little structure. It consists of a stone pavilion, with open sides and a number of pinnacles and crockets and buttresses, besides a goodly medallion of the high-nosed visage of Charles I, which was placed above one of the arches, at the Restoration, in compensation for the violent havoc wrought upon the little town by the Parliamentary soldiers, who had wrested the place from the Royalists and who amused themselves, in their grim fashion, with infinite hacking and hewing in the cathedral. Here, to the left, the cathedral discloses itself, lifting its smart grey steeple out of a pleasant garden. Opposite to the garden was the Dolphin or the Dragon – in fine the most eligible inn. I must confess that for a time it divided my attention with the cathedral, in virtue of an ancient, musty parlour on the second floor, with hunting pictures hung above hair-cloth sofas; of a red-faced waiter, in evening dress; of a big round of cold beef and a tankard of ale. The prettiest thing at Chichester is a charming little three-sided cloister, attached to the cathedral, where, as is usual in such places, you may sit upon a gravestone amid the deep grass in the middle and measure the great central mass of the church – the large grey sides, the high foundations of the spire, the parting of the nave and transept. From this point the greatness of a cathedral seems more complex and impressive. You watch the big shadows slowly change their relations; you listen to the cawing of rooks, and the twittering of swallows; you hear a slow footstep echoing in the cloisters.

*Magdalen College, Oxford*

## V

If Oxford were not the finest thing in England the case would be clearer for Cambridge. It was clear enough there, for that matter, to my imagination, for thirty-six hours. To the barbaric mind, ambitious of culture, Oxford is the usual image of the happy reconciliation between research and acceptance. It typifies to an American the union of science and sense – of aspiration and ease. A German university gives a greater impression of science and an English country house or an Italian villa a greater impression of idle enjoyment; but in these cases, on one side, knowledge is too rugged, and on the other satisfaction is too trivial.

Oxford lends sweetness to labour and dignity to leisure. When I say Oxford I mean Cambridge, for a stray savage is not the least obliged to know the difference, and it suddenly strikes me as being both very pedantic and very good-natured in him to pretend to know it. What institution is more majestic than Trinity College? what can affect more a stray savage than the hospitality of such an institution? The first quadrangle is of immense extent, and the buildings that surround it, with their long, rich fronts of time-deepened grey, are the stateliest in the world. In the centre of the court are two or three acres of close-shaven lawn, out of the midst of which rises a grand Gothic fountain, where the serving men fill up their buckets. There are towers and battlements and statues, and besides these things there are cloisters and gardens and bridges. There are charming rooms in a kind of stately gate-tower, and the rooms, occupying the thickness of the building, have windows looking out on one side over the magnificent quadrangle, with half a mile or so of Decorated architecture, and on the other into deep-bosomed trees. And in the rooms is the best company conceivable – distinguished men who are thoroughly conversible, intimately affable. I spent a beautiful Sunday morning walking about the place with one of these gentlemen and attempting to *débrouiller* its charms. These are a very complicated tangle, and I do not pretend, in memory, to keep the colleges apart. There are none the less half a dozen points that make ineffaceable pictures. Six or eight of the colleges stand in a row, turning their backs to the river; and hereupon ensues the loveliest confusion of Gothic windows and ancient trees, of grassy banks and mossy balustrades of sun-chequered avenues and groves, of lawns and gardens and terraces, of single-arched bridges spanning the little stream, which is small and shallow and looks as if it had been turned on for ornamental purposes. The thin-flowing Cam appears to exist simply as an occasion for these brave little bridges – the beautiful covered gallery of John's or the slightly collapsing arch of Clare. In the way of college courts and quiet scholastic porticoes, of grey-walled gardens and ivied nooks of study, in all the pictorial accidents of a great English university, Cambridge is delightfully and inexhaustibly rich. I looked at these one by one and said to myself always that the last was the best. If I were called upon, however, to mention the

King's College

*Of course the single object at Cambridge that makes the most abiding
impression is the famous chapel of King's College – the most beautiful chapel
in England. The effect it attempts to produce within is all in the sphere of the
sublime. The attempt succeeds, and the success is attained by a design so light
and elegant that at first it almost defeats itself. The sublime usually has more
of a frown and straddle, and it is not until after you have looked about you for*

Chapel

ten minutes that you perceive the chapel to be saved from being the prettiest church in England by the accident of its being one of the noblest. It is a cathedral without aisles or columns or transepts, but (as a compensation) with such a beautiful slimness of clustered tracery soaring along the walls and spreading, bending and commingling in the roof, that its simplicity seems only a richness the more.

prettiest corner of the world, I should draw out a thoughtful sigh and point the way to the garden of Trinity Hall. My companion, who was very competent to judge (but who spoke indeed with the partiality of a son of the house), declared, as he ushered me into it, that it was, to his

*King's College, Cambridge from the Backs*

mind, the most beautiful *small* garden in Europe. I freely accepted, and I promptly repeat, an affirmation so magnanimously conditioned. The little garden at Trinity Hall is narrow and crooked; it leans upon the river, from which a low parapet, all muffled in ivy, divides it; it has an ancient wall adorned with a thousand matted creepers on one side, and on the other a group of extraordinary horse-chestnuts. The trees are of prodigious size; they occupy half the garden, and are remarkable for the fact that their giant limbs strike down into the earth, take root again and emulate, as they rise, the majesty of the parent stem. The manner in which this magnificent group of horse-chestnuts sprawls about over the grass, out into the middle of the lawn, is one of the most heart-shaking features of the garden of Trinity Hall. Of course the single object at Cambridge that makes the most abiding impression is the famous chapel of King's College – the most beautiful chapel in England.[4] The effect it attempts to produce within is all in the sphere of the sublime. The attempt succeeds, and the success is attained by a design so light and elegant that at first it almost defeats itself. The sublime usually has more of a frown and straddle, and it is not until after you have looked about you for ten minutes that you perceive the chapel to be saved from being the prettiest church in England by the accident of its being one of the noblest. It is a cathedral without aisles or columns or transepts, but (as a compensation) with such a beautiful slimness of clustered tracery soaring along the walls and spreading, bending and commingling in the roof, that its simplicity seems only a richness the more. I stood there for a quarter of an hour on a Sunday morning; there was no service, but in the choir behind the great screen which divides the chapel in half the young choristers were rehearsing for the afternoon. The beautiful boy-voices rose together and touched the splendid vault; they hung there, expanding and resounding, and then, like a rocket that spends itself, they faded and melted toward the end of the building. It was positively a choir of angels.

## VI

Cambridgeshire is one of the so-called ugly counties; which means that it is observedly flat. It is for this reason that the absence of terrestrial accent which culminates at Newmarket constitutes so perfect a means to an end. The country is like a board of green cloth; the turf presents itself as a friendly provision of nature. Nature offers her gentle bosom as a gaming-table; card-tables, billiard-tables are but a humble imitation of Newmarket Heath. It was odd to think that amid so much of the appearance of the humility of real virtue, there is more profane betting than anywhere else in the world. The large, neat English meadows roll away to a humid-looking sky, the young partridges jump about in the hedges, and nature looks not in the least as if she were offering you odds. The gentlemen look it, though, the gentlemen whom you meet on the roads and in the railway carriage; they have that marked air – it pervades a man from the cut of his whisker to the shape of his boot-toe – as of the sublimated stable. It is brought home to you that to an immense number of people in England the events in the *Racing Calendar* constitute the most important portion of contemporary history. The very breeze has an equine snort, if it doesn't breathe as hard as a hostler; the blue and white of the sky, dappled and spotty, recalls the figure of the necktie of 'spring meetings'; and the landscape is coloured as a sporting print is coloured – with the same gloss, the same that seems to say a thousand grooms have rubbed it down.

The destruction of partridges is, if an equally classical, a less licentious pursuit, for which, I believe, Cambridgeshire offers peculiar facilities. Among these is a particular shooting-box which is a triumph of the familiar, the accidental style and a temple of clear hospitality. The shooting belongs to the autumn, not to this vernal period; but as I have spoken of echoes I suppose that if I had listened attentively I might have heard the ghostly crack of some of the famous shots that have been discharged there. The air, notedly, had vibrated to several august rifles, but all that I happened to hear by listening was some excellent talk.

In England, at any rate, as I said just now, a couple of places may be very near together and yet have what the philosophers call a connotation strangely different. Only a few miles beyond Newmarket lies Bury St Edmunds, a town whose tranquil antiquity[5] turns its broad grey back straight upon the sporting papers. I confess that I went to Bury simply on the strength of its name, which I had often encountered and which had always seemed to me to have a high value for the picture-seeker. I knew that St Edmund[6] had been an Anglo-Saxon worthy, but my conviction that the little town that bore his name would move me to rapture between trains had nothing definite to rest upon.[7] The event, however, rewarded my faith – rewarded it with the sight of a magnificent old gate-house of the thirteenth century, the most substantial of many relics of the great abbey which once flourished there. There are many others; they are scattered about the old precinct of the abbey, a large portion of which has been converted into a rambling botanic garden, the resort at Whitsuntide of a thousand very modern merry-makers. The monument I speak of has the proportions of a triumphal arch; it is at once a gateway and a fortress; it is covered with beautiful ornament, and is altogether the lion of Bury.

First published in *Lippincott's Magazine*, XXIII (April 1879), 407–18, with illustrations by C. P. Nichols and J. Sachs; reprinted without illustrations in *Portraits of Places* (1883), but in *English Hours* (1905) the essay had 'the benefit' of twelve drawings by Joseph Pennell.

# An English New Year

It will hardly be pretended this year that the English Christmas has been a merry one, or that the New Year has the promise of being particularly happy. The winter is proving very cold and vicious – as if Nature herself were loath to be left out of the general conspiracy against the comfort and self-complacency of man. The country at large has a sense of embarrassment and depression, which is brought home more or less to every class in the closely graduated social hierarchy, and the light of Christmas firesides has by no means dispelled the gloom. Not that I mean to overstate the gloom. It is difficult to imagine any combination of adverse circumstances powerful enough to infringe very sensibly upon the appearance of activity and prosperity, social stability and luxury, which English life must always present to a stranger. Nevertheless the times are distinctly of the kind synthetically spoken of as hard – there is plenty of evidence of it – and the spirits of the public are not high. The depression of business is extreme and universal; I am ignorant whether it has reached so calamitous a point as that almost hopeless prostration of every industry which it is assured us you have lately witnessed in America, and I believe the sound of lamentation is by no means so loud as it has been on two or three occasions within the present century. The possibility of distress among the lower classes has been minimised by the gigantic poor-relief system which is so characteristic a feature of English civilisation and which, under especial stress, is supplemented (as is the case at present) by private charity proportionately huge. I notice too that in some parts of the country discriminating groups of workpeople have selected these dismal days as a happy time for striking. When the labouring classes rise to the recreation of a strike I suppose the situation may be said to have its cheerful side. There is, however, great distress in the North, and there is a general feeling of scant money to play with throughout the country. The *Daily News* has sent a correspondent to the great industrial regions, and almost every morning for the last three weeks a very cleverly executed picture of the misery of certain parts of Yorkshire and Lancashire has been served up with the matutinal tea and toast. The work is a good one, and, I take it, eminently worth doing, as it appears to have had a visible effect upon the purse-strings of the well-to-do. There is nothing more striking in England than the success with which an 'appeal' is always made. Whatever the season or whatever the cause, there always appears to be enough money and enough benevolence in the country to respond to it in sufficient measure – a remarkable fact when one remembers that there is never a moment of the year when the custom of 'appealing' intermits. Equally striking perhaps is the perfection to which the science of distributing charity has been raised – the way it has been analysed and organised and made one of the exact sciences. You perceive that it has occupied for a long time a foremost place among administrative questions, and has received all the light that experience and practice can throw upon it. Is there in this perception more of a lightened or more of an added weight for the brooding consciousness? Truly there are aspects of England at which one can but darkly stare.

I left town a short time before Christmas and went to spend the festive season in the North, in a part of the country with which I was unacquainted. It was quite possible to absent one's self from London without a sense of sacrifice, for the charms of the capital during the last several weeks have been obscured by peculiarly vile weather. It is of course a very old story that London is foggy, and this simple statement raises no blush on the face of Nature as we see it here. But there are fogs and fogs, and the folds of the black mantle have been during the present winter intolerably thick. The thickness that draws down and absorbs the smoke of the house-tops, causes it to hang about the streets in impenetrable density, forces it into one's eyes and down one's throat, so that one is half blinded and quite sickened – this form of the particular plague has been much more frequent than usual. Just before Christmas, too, there was a heavy snowstorm, and even a tolerably light fall of snow has London quite at its mercy. The emblem of purity is almost immediately converted into a sticky, lead-coloured mush, the cabs sulk out of sight or take up their stations before the lurid windows of a public house, which glares through the sleety darkness at the desperate wayfarer with an air of vulgar bravado. For recovery of one's nervous balance the only course was flight – flight to the country and the confinement of one's vision to the large area of one of those admirable homes which at this season overflow with hospitality and good cheer. By this means the readjustment is effectually brought about – these are conditions that you cordially appreciate. Of all the great things that the English have invented and made a part of the credit of the national character, the most perfect, the most characteristic, the one they have mastered most completely in all its details, so that it has become a compendious illustration of their social genius and their manners, is the well-appointed, well-administered, well-filled country house. The grateful stranger makes these reflections –and others besides – as he wanders about in the beautiful library of such a dwelling, of an inclement winter afternoon, just at the hour when six o'clock tea is impending. Such a place and such a time abound in agreeable episodes; but I suspect that the episode from which, a fortnight ago, I received the most ineffaceable impression was but indirectly connected with the charms of a luxurious fireside. The country I speak of was a populous manufacturing region, full of tall chimneys and of an air that is grey and gritty. A lady had made a present of a Christmas tree to the children of a workhouse, and she invited me to go with her and assist at the distribution of the toys. There was a drive through the early dusk of a very cold Christmas eve, followed by the drawing up of a lamp-lit brougham in the snowy quadrangle of a grim-looking charitable institution. I had never been in an English workhouse before, and this one transported me, with the aid of memory, to the early pages of *Oliver Twist*. We passed through cold, bleak passages, to which an odour of suet pudding, the aroma of Christmas cheer, failed to impart an air of hospitality; and then, after waiting a while in a little parlour appertaining to the superintendent, where the remainder of a dinner of by no means eleemosynary simplicity and the attitude of a gentleman asleep with a flushed face on the sofa seemed to effect a tacit exchange of references, we were ushered into a large frigid refectory, chiefly illumined by the twinkling tapers of the Christmas tree. Here entered to us some hundred and fifty little children of charity, who had been making a copious dinner and who brought with them an atmosphere of hunger memorably satisfied – together with other traces of the occasion upon their pinafores and their small red faces. I have said that the place reminded me of *Oliver Twist*, and I glanced through this little herd for an infant figure that should look as if it were cut out for romantic adventures. But they were all very prosaic little mortals. They were made of very common clay indeed, and a certain number of them were idiotic. They filed up and received their little offerings, and then they compressed themselves into a tight infantine bunch and, lifting up their small hoarse voices, directed a melancholy hymn toward their benefactress. The scene was a picture I shall not forget, with its curious mixture of poetry and sordid prose – the dying wintry light in the big bare, stale room; the beautiful Lady Bountiful, standing in the twinkling glory of the Christmas tree; the little multitude of staring and wondering, yet perfectly expressionless, faces.

First published unsigned in *The Nation*, XXVIII (23 January 1879), 65–6, as 'The New Year in England'; reprinted in *Portraits of Places* (1883); shortened and revised in *English Hours* (1905).

# An English Winter Watering-place

I have just been spending a couple of days at a well-known resort upon the Kentish coast, and though such an exploit is by no means unprecedented, yet, as to the truly observing mind no opportunity is altogether void and no impressions are wholly valueless, I have it on my conscience to make a note of my excursion. Superficially speaking, it was wanting in originality; but I am afraid that it afforded me as much entertainment as if the idea of paying a visit to Hastings had been an invention of my own. This is so far from being the case that the most striking feature of the town in question is the immense provision made there for the entertainment of visitors. Hastings and St Leonards, standing side by side, present a united sea-front of more miles in length than I shall venture to compute. It is sufficient that in going from one end of the place to the other I had a greater sense of having taken a long, straight walk through street scenery than I had done since I last measured the populated length of Broadway. This is not an image that evokes any one of the graces, and it must be confessed that the beauty of Hastings does not reside in a soft irregularity or a rural exuberance. Like all the larger English watering-places it is simply a little London *super mare*. The graceful, or at least the pictorial, is always to be found in England if one will take the trouble of looking for it; but it must be conceded that at Hastings this element is less obtrusive than it might be. I had heard it described as a 'dull Brighton', and this description had been intended to dispose of the place. In fact, however – such is the perversity of the inquiring mind – it had rather quickened than quenched my interest. It occurred to me that it might be as entertaining to follow out the variations of Brighton, the possible embroideries of the theme, as it is often found to listen to those with which some expressed musical idea is over-scored by another composer. Four or five miles of lodging-houses and hotels staring at the sea across a 'parade adorned with iron benches, with hand-organs and German bands, with nursemaids and British babies, with ladies and gentlemen of leisure – looking rather embarrassed with it and trying rather unsuccessfully to get rid of it – this is the great feature which Brighton and Hastings have in common. At Brighton there is a certain variety and gaiety of colour – something suggesting crookedness and yellow paint – which gives the scene a kind of cheerful, easy, more or less vulgar, foreign air. But Hastings is very grey and sober and English, and indeed it is because it seemed to me so English that I gave my best attention to it. If one is attempting to gather impressions of a people and to learn to know them, everything is interesting that is characteristic, quite apart from its being beautiful. English manners are made up of such a multitude of small details that the portrait a stranger has privately sketched in is always liable to receive new touches. And this indeed is the explanation of his noting a great many small points, on the spot, with a degree of relish and appreciation which must often, to persons who are not in his position, appear exaggerated, if not absurd. He has formed a mental picture of the civilisation of the people he lives among, and whom, when he has a great deal of courage, he makes bold to say he is studying; he has drawn up a kind of tabular view of their manners and customs, their idiosyncrasies, their social institutions, their general features and properties;[1] and when once he has suspended this rough cartoon in the chambers of his imagination he finds a great deal of occupation in touching it up and filling it in. Wherever he goes, whatever he sees, he adds a few strokes. That is how I spent my time at Hastings.

I found it, for instance, a question more interesting than it might superficially appear to choose between the inns – between the Royal Hotel upon the Parade and an ancient hostel, a survival of the posting days, in a side street. A friend had described the latter establishment to me as 'mellow', and this epithet complicated the problem. The term mellow, as applied to an inn, is the comparative degree of a state of things of which (say) 'musty' would be the superlative. If you can seize this tendency in its comparative stage you may do very well indeed; the trouble is that, like all tendencies, it contains, even in its earlier phases, the germs of excess. I thought it very possible that the Swan would be over-ripe; but I thought it equally probable that the Royal would be crude. I could claim a certain acquaintance with 'royal' hotels – I knew just how they were consituted. I foresaw the superior young woman sitting at a ledger, in a kind of glass cage, at the bottom of the stairs, and expressing by refined intonations her contempt for a gentleman who should decline to 'require' a sitting-room. The functionary whom in America we know and dread as an hotel clerk belongs in England to the sex which, at need, is able to look over your head to a still further point. Large hotels here are almost always owned and carried on by companies, and the company is represented by a well-shaped female figure belonging to the class whose members are more particularly known as 'persons'.[2] The chambermaid is a young woman, and the female tourist is a lady; but the occupant of the glass cage, who hands you your key and assigns you your apartment, is designated in the manner I have mentioned. The 'person' has various methods of revenging herself for her shadowy position in the social scale, and I think it was from a vague recollection of having on former occasions felt the weight of her embittered spirit that I determined to seek the hospitality of the humbler inn, where it was probable that one who was himself humble would enjoy a certain consideration. In the event, I was rather oppressed by the feather-bed quality of the welcome extended to me at the Swan. Once established there, in a sitting-room (after all), the whole affair had all the local colour I could desire.

I have sometimes had occasion to repine at the meagreness and mustiness of the old-fashioned English inn, and to feel that in poetry and in fiction these defects had been culpably glossed over. But I said to myself the other evening that there is a kind of venerable decency even in some of its dingiest consistencies, and that in an age in which the conception of good manners is losing most of its ancient firmness one should do justice to an institution that is still more or less of a stronghold of the faded amenities. It is a satisfaction in moving about the world to be treated as a gentleman, and this gratification appears to be more than, in the light of modern science, a Company can profitably undertake to bestow. I have an old friend, a person of admirably conservative instincts, from whom, a short time since, I borrowed a hint of this kind. This lady had been staying at a small inn in the country with her daughter; the daughter, whom we shall call Mrs B., had left the house a few days before the mother. 'Did you like the place?' I asked of my friend; 'was it comfortable?' 'No, it was not comfortable; but I liked it. It was shabby, and I was much overcharged; but it pleased me.' 'What was the mysterious charm?' 'Well, when I was coming away, the landlady – she had cheated me horribly – came to my carriage, and dropped a curtsey, and said: "My duty to Mrs B., ma'am." Que voulez-vous? That pleased me.' There was an old waiter at Hastings who would have been capable of that – an old waiter who had been in the house for forty years and who was not so much an individual waiter as the very spirit and genius, the incarnation and tradition of waiterhood. He was faded and weary and rheumatic, but he had a sort of mixture of the paternal and the deferential, the philosophic and the punctilious, which seemed but grossly requited by a present of a small coin. I am not fond of jugged hare for dinner, either as a light *entrée* or as a *pièce de résistance*; but this accomplished attendant had the art of presenting you such a dish in a manner that persuaded you, for the time, that it was worthy of your serious consideration. The hare, by the way, before being subjected to the mysterious operation of jugging, might have been seen dangling from a hook in the bar of the inn, together with a choice collection of other viands. You might peruse the bill of fare in an elementary form as you passed in and out of the house, and make up your *menu* for the day by poking with your stick at a juicy-looking steak or a promising fowl. The landlord and his spouse were always on the threshold of the bar, polishing a brass candlestick and paying you their respects; the place was pervaded by an aroma of rum-and-water and of commercial travellers' jokes.

This description, however, is lacking in the element of gentility, and I will not pursue it farther, for I should give a very false impression of Hastings if I were to omit so characteristic a feature. It was, I think, the element of gentility that most impressed me. I know that the word I have just ventured to use is under the ban of contemporary taste; so I may as well say outright that I regard it as indispensable in almost any attempt at portraiture of English manners. It is vain for an observer of such things to

*Fishing-boats in Hastings harbour*

pretend to get on without it. One may talk of foreign life indefinitely –
of the manners and customs of France, Germany, and Italy – and never
feel the need of this suggestive, yet mysteriously discredited, epithet.
One may survey the remarkable face of American civilisation without
finding occasion to strike this particular note. But in England no cir-
cumlocution will serve – the note must be definitely struck. To attempt
to speak of an English watering-place in winter and yet pass it over in
silence would be to forfeit all claims to the analytic spirit. For a stranger,
at any rate, the term is invaluable – it is more convenient than I should find
easy to say. It is instantly evoked in my mind by long rows of smuttily
plastered houses, with a card inscribed 'Apartments' suspended in the
window of the ground-floor sitting-room – that portion of the dwelling
which is known in lodging-house parlance as 'the parlours'. Everything,
indeed, suggests it – the bath-chairs, drawn up for hire in a melancholy
row; the innumerable and excellent shops, adorned with the latest
photographs of the royal family and of Mrs Langtry;[3] the little reading-
room and circulating library on the Parade, where the daily papers,
neatly arranged, may be perused for a trifling fee, and the novels of the
season are stacked away like the honeycombs in an apiary; the long pier,

stretching out into the sea, to which you are admitted by the payment of a penny at a wicket, and where you may enjoy the music of an indefatigable band, the enticements of several little stalls for the sale of fancy work, and the personal presence of good local society. It is only the winking, twinkling, easily rippling sea that is not genteel. But, really, I was disposed to say at Hastings that if the sea was not genteel, so much the worse for Neptune; for it was the favourable aspect of the great British proprieties and solemnities that struck me. Hastings and St Leonards, with their long, warm sea-front and their multitude of small, cheap comforts and conveniences, offer a kind of *résumé* of middle-class English civilisation and of advantages of which it would ill become an American to make light. I don't suppose that life at Hastings is the most exciting or the most gratifying in the world, but it must certainly have its advantages, If I were a quiet old lady of modest income and nice habits – or even a quiet old gentleman of the same pattern – I should certainly go to Hastings. There, amid the little shops and the little libraries, the bath-chairs and the German bands, the Parade and the long Pier, with a mild climate, a moderate scale of prices and the consciousness of a high civilisation, I should enjoy a seclusion which would have nothing primitive or crude.

First published unsigned in *The Nation*, XXVIII (3 April 1879), 228–9; reprinted in *Portraits of Places* (1883), and *English Hours* (1905).

# Winchelsea, Rye, and 'Denis Duval'

I have recently had a literary adventure which, though not followed by the prostration that sometimes ensues on adventures, has nevertheless induced meditation. The adventure itself indeed was not astounding, and I mention it, to be frank, only in the interest of its sequel. It consisted merely, on taking up an old book again for the sake of a certain desired and particular light, of my having found that the light was in fact not there to shine, but was, on the contrary, directly projected *upon* the book from the very subject itself as to which I had invoked assistance. The case, in short, to put it simply, was that Thackeray's charming fragment of *Denis Duval* proved to have much less than I had supposed to say about the two little old towns with which the few chapters left to us are mainly concerned, but that the two little old towns, on the other hand, unexpectedly quickened reflection on *Denis Duval*. Reading over Thackeray to help me further to Winchelsea, I became conscious, of a sudden, that Winchelsea – which I already in a manner knew – was only helping me further to Thackeray. Reinforced in this service by its little sister-city of Rye, it caused a whole question to open, and the question, in turn, added a savour to a sense already, by good fortune, sharp. Winchelsea and Rye form together a very curious small corner, and the measure, candidly undertaken, of what the unfinished book had done with them, brought me to a nearer view of them – perhaps even to a more jealous one; as well as to some consideration of what books in general, even when finished, may do with curious small corners.

I dare say I speak of *Denis Duval* as 'old' mainly to make an impression on readers whose age is less. I remember, after all, perfectly, the poetry of its original appearance – there was such a thrill, in those days, even after *Lovel the Widower* and *Philip*, at any new Thackeray – in the cherished *Cornhill*[1] of the early time, with a drawing of Frederick

Walker[2] to its every number and a possibility of its being like *Esmond* in its embroidered breast. If, moreover, it after a few months broke short off, that really gave it something as well as took something away. It might have been as true of works of art as of men and women, that if the gods loved them they died young. *Denis Duval* was at any rate beautiful, and was beautiful again on reperusal at a later time. It is all beautiful once more to a final reading, only it is remarkably different: and this is precisely where my story lies. The beauty is particularly the beauty of its being its author's – which is very much, with book after book, what we find ourselves coming to in general, I think, at fifty years. Our appreciation changes – how in the world, with experience always battering away, shouldn't it? – but our feeling, more happily, doesn't. There *are* books, of course, that criticism, when we are fit for it, only consecrates, and then, with association fiddling for the dance, we are in possession of a literary pleasure that is the highest of raptures. But in many a case we drag along a fond indifference, an element of condonation, which is by no means of necessity without its strain of esteem, but which, obviously, is not founded on one of our deeper satisfactions. Each can but speak, at all events, on such a matter, for himself. It is a matter also, doubtless, that belongs to the age of the loss – so far as they quite depart – of illusions at large. The reason for liking a particular book becomes thus a better, or at least a more generous, one than the particular book seems in a position itself at last to supply. Woe to the mere official critic, the critic who has never felt the *man*. You go on liking *The Antiquary* because it is Scott. You go on liking *David Copperfield* – I don't say you go on reading it, which is a very different matter – because it is Dickens. So you go on liking *Denis Duval* because it is Thackeray – which, in this last case, is the logic of the charm I alluded to.

The recital here, as every one remembers, is autobiographic; the old battered, but considerably enriched, world-worn, but finely sharpened Denis looks back upon a troubled life from the winter fireside and places you, in his talkative and contagious way – he is a practised literary artist – in possession of the story. We see him in a placid port after many voyages, and have that amount of evidence – the most, after all, that the most artless reader needs – as to the 'happy' side of the business. The evidence indeed is, for curiosity, almost excessive, or at least premature; as he again and again puts it before us that the companion of his later time, the admirable wife seated there beside him, is nobody else at all, any hopes of a more tangled skein notwithstanding, than the object of his infant passion, the little French orphan, slightly younger than himself, who is brought so promptly on the scene. The way in which this affects us as undermining the 'love-interest' bears remarkably on the specific question of the subject of the book as the author would have expressed this subject to his own mind. We get, to the moment the work drops, not a glimpse of his central idea; nothing, if such had been his intention, was in fact ever more triumphantly concealed. The darkness therefore is intensified by our seeming to gather that, like the love-interest, at all events, the 'female interest' was not to have been largely invoked. The narrator is in general, from the first, full of friendly hints, in Thackeray's way, of what is to come; but the chapters completed deal only with his childish years, his wondrous boy-life at Winchelsea and Rye, the public and private conditions of which – practically, in the last century, the same for the two places – form the background for this exposition. The south-eastern counties, comparatively at hand, were enriched at that period by a considerable French immigration, the accession of Huguenot fugitives too firm in their faith to have bent their necks to the dire rigours with which the revocation of the Edict of Nantes was followed up. This corner of Sussex received – as it had received in previous centuries – its forlorn contingent; to the interesting origin of which many Sussex family names – losing, as it were, their drawing but not their colour – still sufficiently testify. Portions of the stranger race suffered, struggled, sank; other portions resisted, took root and put forth branches, and Thackeray, clearly, had found his rough material in some sketchy vision of one of these obscure cases of troubled adjustment, which must often have been, for difficulty and complexity, of the stuff of dramas. Such a case, for the informed fancy, might indeed overflow with possibilities of character, character reinforced, in especial, by the impression, gathered and matured on the spot, of the two small ghosts of the Cinque Ports family, the pair of blighted hill-towns that were once sea-towns and that now draw out their days in the dim after-sense of a mere indulged and encouraged picturesqueness. *Denis Duval* could only, it would seem, have been conceived as a 'picturesque' affair; but that may serve exactly as a reason for the attempt to refigure it.

Little hilltop communities sensibly even yet, with the memory of their tight walls and stiff gates not wholly extinct, Rye and Winchelsea hold fast to the faint identity which remains their least fragile support, their estate as 'Antient Towns' involved (with the distincter Five and raising the number of seven), in that nominal, though still occasionally pompous, Wardenship the image – for our time – of the most famous assignment of which is preserved in Longfellow's fine verses on the death of the Duke of Wellington. The sea, in previous times half friend half foe, began long since to fight, in each character, shy of them, and now, in wrinkled wistfulness, they look across at the straight blue band, two miles or so away, that tells of the services they rendered, the illusions they cherished – illusions in the case of poor Winchelsea especially absurd – and the extreme inconvenience they repeatedly suffered. They were again and again harried and hacked by the French, and might have had, it would seem, small appetite for the company, however reduced and disarmed, of these immemorial neighbours. The retreating waters, however, had even two centuries ago already placed such dangers on a very different footing, and the recovery and evocation of some of the old processes of actual absorption may well have presented themselves to Thackeray as a problem of the sort that tempts the lover of human histories. Happy and enviable always the first trepidation of the artist who lights on a setting that 'meets' his subject or on a subject that meets his setting. The editorial notes to *Denis Duval* yield unfortunately no indication of whether Winchelsea put into his head the idea of this study, or of whether he carried it about till he happened judiciously to drop it there. Appearances point, in truth, to a connection of the latter kind, for the fragment itself contains no positive evidence that Thackeray ever, with the mere eye of sense, beheld the place; which is precisely one of the ambiguities that challenge the critic and an item in the unexpectedness that I spoke of at the beginning of these remarks. What – in the light, at least, of later fashions – the place has to offer the actual observer is the effect of an object seen, a thing of aspect and suggestion, situation and colour; but what had it to offer Thackeray – or the taste of forty years ago – that he so oddly forbore to give us a tangled clue to? The impression of today's reader is that the chapters we possess might really have been written without the author's having stood on the spot; and that is just why they have, as I began by saying, so much less to contribute to our personal vision than this influence, for its part, has to suggest in respect to the book itself.

Evidently, none the less, the setting, little as it has got itself 'rendered', did somehow come into the painter's ken; we know this, moreover, independently, and we make out that he had his inner mysteries and his reasons. The little house of Duval, faring forth from the stress of the Alsatian fatherland, seeks safety and finds business in the shrunken city, scarce at last more than a hamlet, of Edward the First's defeated design, where, in three generations, well on into the century, it grinds and sleeps, smuggles and spends, according to the fashions of the place and time. These communities appear to have had, in their long decline, little industry but their clandestine traffic with other coasts, in the course of which they quite mastered the art of going, as we say, 'one better' than the officers of the revenue. It is to this hour a part of the small romance of Rye that you may fondly fancy such scant opulence as rears its head to have had its roots in the malpractice of forefathers not too rude for much cunning – in nightly plots and snares and flurries, a hurrying, shuffling hiding, that might at any time have put a noose about most necks. Some of those of the small gentry who were not smugglers were recorded highwaymen, flourishing about in masks and with pistols; and indeed in the general scene, as rendered by the supposed chronicler, these appear the principal features. The only others are those of his personal and private situation, which in fact, however, strikes me as best expressed in the fact that the extremely talkative, discursive, ejaculatory and moralising Denis was possessed in perfection of his master's maturest style. He writes, almost to the life, the language of 'The Roundabout Papers'; so that if the third person had been exchanged, throughout, for his first, and his occasional present tense been superseded by the past, the rest of the text would have needed little rearrangement. This imperfect unity was more or less inevitable – the difficulty of projecting yourself as somebody else is never so great as when you retain the *form* of being yourself; but another of the many reflections suggested by reperusal is as to whether the speaker is not guilty of a slight abuse. Of course it may be said that what really has happened was that Thackeray had, on his side, anticipated his hero in the use of his hero's natural idiom. It may thus have been less that Denis had come to write highly 'evolved' nineteenth-century English than that his creator had arrived, in 'The Roundabout Papers' and elsewhere, at writing excellent reconstructed eighteenth. It would not, however, were the inquiry to be pushed, be only on the autobiographer's personal and grammatical, but on his moral and sentimental accent, as it were, that criticism would probably most bear. His manner of thinking and feeling is quite as 'Roundabout' as his manner of saying.

A dozen wonderments rise here, and a dozen curiosities and speculations; as to which, in truth, I am painfully divided between the attraction of such appeals and a certain other aspect of my subject to which I shall attempt presently to do justice. The superior stroke, I remind myself – possibly not in vain – would be to deal handsomely with both solicitations. The almost irresistible fascination, critically speaking, of the questions thus abruptly, after long years, thrust forth by the book, lies in their having reference to this very opposition of times and tastes. The thing is not forty years old, but it points already – and that is above all the amusement of it – to a general *poetic* that, both on its positive and its negative sides, we have left well behind. Can the author perhaps have had in mind, misguidedly, some idea of what his public 'wanted' or didn't want? The public is really, to a straight vision, I think, not a capacity for wanting, at all, but only an unlimited capacity for *taking* – taking that (whatever it is) which will, in effect, make it open its mouth. It goes to the expense of few preconceptions, and even on the question of opening its mouth has a consciousness limited to the suspicion that in a given case this orifice *has* – or has not – gaped. We are therefore to imagine Thackeray as perfectly conscious that he himself, working by his own fine light, constituted the public he had most to reckon with. On the other hand, his time, in its degree, had helped to shape him, and a part of the consequence of this shaping, apparently, was his extraordinary avoidance of picture. This is the mystery that drives us to the hypothesis of his having tried to pay, in some uncanny quarter, some deluded deference. Was he under the fear that, even as *he* could do it, 'description' would not, in the early sixties, be welcome? It is impossible to stand to-day in the high, loose, sunny, haunted square of Winchelsea without wondering what he could have been thinking of. There are ladies in view with easels, sun-bonnets, and white umbrellas – often perceptibly, too, with nothing else that makes for successful representation; but I doubt if it were these apparitions that took the bloom from his vision, for they were much less frequent in those looser days, and moreover would have formed much more a reason for not touching the place at all than for taking it up indifferently. Of any impulse to make the reader see it with seeing eyes his page, at all events, gives no sign. We must presently look at it for ourselves, even at the cost, or with the consequence, of a certain loyal resentment. For Winchelsea is strange, individual, charming. What *could* he – yes – have been thinking of? We are wound up saying that he has given his subject away, until we suddenly remember that, to this hour, we have never really made out what his subject was to have been.

Never was a secret more impenetrably kept. Read over the fragment itself – which reaches, after all, to some two hundred and fifty pages; read over, at the end of the volume, the interesting editorial notes; address yourself, above all, in the charming series of introductions lately prepared by Mrs Richmond Ritchie for a new and, so far as possible, biographical edition of her father's works, to the reminiscences briefly bearing on Denis, and you will remain in each case equally distant from a clue. It is the most puzzling thing in the world, but there *is* no clue. There are indications, in respect to the book, from Thackeray's hand, memoranda on matters of detail, and there is in especial a highly curious letter to his publisher; yet the clue that his own mind must have held never shows the tip of its tail. The letter to his publisher, in which, according to the editor of the fragment, he 'sketches his plot for the information of' that gentleman, reads like a mystification by which the gentleman was to be temporarily kept quiet. With an air of telling him a good deal, Thackeray really tells him nothing – nothing, I mean, by which he himself would have been committed to (any more than deterred from) any idea kept up his sleeve. If he were holding this card back, to be played at his own time, he could not have proceeded in the least differently; and one can construct today, with a free hand, one's picture of his private amusement at the success of his diplomacy. All the while, what *was* the card? The production of a novel finds perhaps its nearest analogy in the ride across country; the competent novelist – that is, the novelist with the real seat – presses his subject, in spite of hedges and ditches, as hard as the keen fox-hunter presses the game that has been started for his day with the hounds. The fox is the novelist's idea, and when he rides straight he rides, regardless of danger, in whatever direction that animal takes. As we lay down *Denis Duval*, however, we feel not only that we are off the scent, but that we never really have been, with the author, on it. The fox has got quite away. For it carries us no further, surely, to say – as may possibly be objected – that the author's subject was to have been neither more or less than the adventures of his hero; inasmuch as, turn the thing as we will, these 'adventures' could at the best have constituted nothing more than its *form*. It is an affront to the memory of a great writer to pretend that they were to have been arbitrary and unselected, that there was nothing in his mind to determine them. The book was, obviously, to have been, as boys say, 'about' them. But what were *they* to have been about? Thackeray carried the mystery to his grave.

## II

If I spoke just now of Winchelsea as haunted, let this somewhat over-worked word stand as an ineffectual tribute to the small, sad, civic history that the place appeals to us to reconstruct as we gaze vaguely about. I have a little ancient and most decorative map of Sussex – testifying remarkably to the changes of relation between sea and land in this corner of the coast – in which 'Old Winchelsey Drowned' figures as the melancholy indication of a small circular spot quite out at sea. If new Winchelsea is old, the earlier town is today but the dim ghost of a tradition, with its very site – distant several miles from that of its successor – rendered uncertain by the endless mutation of the shore. After suffering, all through the thirteenth century, much stress of wind and weather, it was practically destroyed in 1287 by a great storm which cast up masses of beach, altered the course of a river and roughly handled the face of many things, The reconstruction of the town in another place was thereupon decreed by a great English king, and we need but a little fuller chronicle to help us to assist at one of those migrations of a whole city of which antiquity so often gives us the picture. The survivors of Winchelsea were colonised, and colonised in much state. The 'new' community, whose life was also to be so brief, sits on the pleasant table of a great cliff-like hill which, in the days of the Plantagenets, was an admirable promontory washed by the waves. The sea surrounded its base, came up past it to the east and north in a long inlet, and stretched away, across the level where the sheep now graze, to stout little neighbouring Rye, perched – in doubtless not quite equal pride – on an eminence more humble, but which must have counted then even for more than today in the pretty figure made, as you stand off, by the small, compact, pyramidal port. The 'Antient Towns' looked at each other then across the water, which made almost an island of the rock of huddled, church-crowned[3] Rye – which had too much to say to them alike, on evil days, at their best time, but which was too soon to begin to have too little. If the early Winchelsea was to suffer by 'drowning', its successor was to bear the stroke of remaining high and dry. The haven on the hill-top – a bold and extraordinary conception – had hardly had time to get, as we should now say, 'started', before it began to see its days numbered. The sea and the shore were never at peace together, and it was, most remarkably, not the sea that got the best of it. Winchelsea had only time to dream a great dream – the dream of a scant pair of centuries – before its hopes were turned to bitterness and its boasts to lamentation. It had literally, during its short career, put in a claim to rivalship with the port of London. The irony of fate now sits in its empty lap; but the port of London has never suggested even a frustrate *Denis Duval*.

While Winchelsea dreamed, at any rate, she worked, and the noble fragment of her great church, rising solid from the abortive symmetry of her great square, helps us to put our hand on her deep good faith. She built at least as she believed – she planned as she fondly imagined. The huge ivy-covered choir and transepts of St Thomas of Canterbury – to whom the structure was addressed – represent to us a great intention. They are not so mighty, but they are almost as brave, as the wondrous fragment of Beauvais. Walled and closed on their unfinished side, they form at present all the church, and, with its grand lines of arch and window, its beautiful Gothic tombs and general hugeness and height, the church – mercifully exempt as yet from restoration – is wonderful for the place. You may at this hour – if you are given to such emotions – feel a mild thrill, not be unaware even of the approach of tears, as you measure the scale on which the building had been planned and the ground that the nave and aisles would have covered. You murmur, in the summer twilight, a soft 'Bravo!' across the ages – to the ears of heaven knows what poor nameless ghosts. The square – apparently one of many – was to have been worthy of New York or of Turin; for the queerest, quaintest, most touching thing of all is that the reinstated city was to have been laid out on the most approved modern lines. Nothing is more interesting – to the mooning, sketching spectator – than this evidence that the great Edward had anticipated us all in the convenient chess-board pattern. It is true – attention has been called to the fact – that Pompeii had anticipated *him*; but I doubt if he knew much about Pompeii. His abstract avenues and cross-streets straggle away, through the summer twilight, into mere legend and mystery. In speaking awhile since of the gates of these shattered strongholds as 'stiff', I also spoke of their walls as 'tight'; but the scheme of Winchelsea must have involved, after all, a certain looseness of cincture. The old vague girdle is lost today in the fields where the sheep browse, in the parkish acres where the great trees cluster. The Sussex oak is mighty – it was of the Sussex oak that, in the old time, the king's ships were built; it was, in particular, to her command of this material that Rye owed the burdensome honour of supplying vessels, on constant call, to the royal navy. Strange is this record, in Holloway's History of that town, and in presence of the small things of today; so perpetual, under stress, appears to have been the demand and so free the supply and the service.

Rye continued indeed, under her old brown south cliff, to build big boats till this industry was smitten by the adoption of iron. That was the last stroke; though even now you may see things as you stand on the edge of the cliff: best of all on the open, sunny terrace of a dear little old garden – a garden brown-walled, red-walled, rose-covered on its other sides, divided by the width of a quiet street of grass-grown cobbles from the house of its master, and possessed of a little old glass-fronted, panelled pavilion which I hold to be the special spot in the world where Thackeray might most fitly have figured out his story. There is not much room in the pavilion, but there is room for the hard-pressed table and the tilted chair – there is room for a novelist and his friends. The panels have a queer paint and a venerable slant; the small chimney-place is at your back; the south window is perfect, the privacy bright and open. How can I tell what old – what young – visions of visions and memories of images come back to me under the influence of this quaint receptacle, into which, by kind permission, I occasionally peep, and still more under the charm of the air and the view that, as I just said, you may enjoy, close at hand, from the small terrace? How can I tell why I always keep remembering and losing there the particular passages of some far-away foolish fiction, absorbed in extreme youth, which haunt me, yet escape me, like the echo of an old premonition? I seem to myself to have lain on the grass somewhere, as a boy, poring over an English novel of the period, presumably quite bad – for they were pretty bad then too – and losing myself in the idea of just such another scene as this. But even could I rediscover the novel I wouldn't go back to it. It couldn't have been so good as this; for this – all concrete and doomed and minimised as it is – is the real thing. The other little gardens, other little odds and ends of crooked brown wall and supported terrace and glazed winter sun-trap, lean over the cliff that still, after centuries, keeps its rude drop; they have beneath them the river, a tide that comes and goes, and the mile or more of grudging desert level, beyond it, which now throws the sea to the near horizon, where, on summer days, with a depth of blue and a scattered gleam of sails, it looks forgiving and resigned. The little old shipyard at the base of the rock is for the most part quite empty, with only vague piles of brown timber and the deposit of generations of chips; yet a fishing-boat or two are still on the stocks – an 'output' of three or four a year! – and the ring of the hammer on the wood, a sound, in such places, rare to the contemporary ear, comes up, through the sunny stillness, to your meditative perch.

The tidal river, on the left, wanders away to Rye Harbour and its bar, where the black fishing-boats, half the time at lop-sided rest in the mud, make a cluster of slanting spears against the sky. When the river is full we are proud of its wide light and many curves; when it is empty we call it, for vague reasons, 'rather Dutch'; and empty or full we sketch it in the fine weather as hard as ever we can. When I say 'we' I mean *they* do – it is to speak with hospitality. They mostly wear, as I have hinted, large sun-bonnets, and they crouch on low camp-stools; they put in, as they would say, a bit of white, in places often the least likely. Rye is in truth a rudimentary drawing-lesson, and you quite embrace the questions when you have fairly seized the formula. Nothing so 'quaint' was ever so easy – nothing so easy was ever so quaint. Much more to be loved than feared, she has not, alas, a scrap of 'style', and she may be effectively rendered without the obligation of subtlety. At favoured seasons there appear within her precinct sundry slouch-hatted gentlemen who study her humble charms through a small telescope formed by their curved fingers and thumb, and who are not unliable to define themselves as French artists leading a train of English and American lady pupils. They distribute their disciples over the place, at selected points where the master, going his round from hour to hour, reminds you of nothing so much as a busy *chef* with many saucepans on the stove and periodically lifting their covers for a sniff and a stir. There are ancient doorsteps that are fairly haunted, for their convenience of view, by the 'class', and where the fond proprietor, going and coming, has to pick his way among paraphernalia or to take flying leaps over genius and industry. If Winchelsea is, as I gather, less beset, it is simply that Winchelsea enjoys the immunity of her greater distinction. She is full of that and must be even more difficult than she at first appears. But I forsook her and her distinction, just now, and I must return to them; though the right moment would quite have been as we stood, at Rye, on the terrace of the little old south-garden, to which she presents herself, beyond two or three miles of flat Dutch-looking interval, from the extreme right, her few red roofs almost lost on her wooded hill and her general presence masking, for this view, the headland of Hastings, ten miles, by the coast, westward.

It was about her spacious solitude that we had already begun to stroll; for the purpose, however, mainly, of measuring the stretch, south and north, to the two more crumbled of her three old gates. They are very far gone, each but the ruin of a ruin; but it is their actual countrified state that speaks of the circuit – one hundred and fifty acres – they were supposed to defend. Under one of them you may pass, much round about, by high-seated villages and in constant sight of the sea, toward Hastings; from the other, slightly the less dilapidated, you may gather, if much so minded, the suggestion of some illustration or tail-piece in a volume of Italian travel. The steep white road plunges crookedly down to where the poor arches that once were massive straddle across it, while a spreading chestnut, beside them, plays exactly the part desired – prepares you, that is, for the crack of the whip of the *vetturino* trudging up beside his travelling carriage. With a bare-legged urchin and a browsing goat the whole thing would be there. But we turn, at that point, to mount again and cross the idle square and come back to the east gate, which is the aspect of Winchelsea that presents itself most – and in fact quite admirably – as the front. Yet by what is it that, at the end of summer afternoons, my sense of an obliterated history is fed? There is little but the church really to testify, for the extraordinary groined vaults and crypts that are part of the actual pride of the place – treasure houses of old merchants, foundations of upper solidities that now are dust – count for nothing, naturally, in the immediate effect. The early houses passed away long ago, and the present ones speak, in broken accents and scant and shabby signs, but of the last hundred, the last couple of hundred, years. Everything that ever happened is gone, and, for that matter, nothing very eminent, only a dim mediocrity of life, ever did happen. Rye has Fletcher the dramatist, the Fletcher of Beaumont,[4] whom it brought to birth; but Winchelsea has only the last preachment, under a tree still shown, of John Wesley.[5] The third Edward and the Black Prince, in 1350, overcame the Spaniards in a stout sea fight within sight of the walls; but I am bound to confess that I do not at all focus that performance, am unable, in the changed conditions, to 'place' anything so

pompous. In the same way I fail to 'visualise', thank goodness, either of
the several French inroads that left their mark of massacre and ruin.
What I do see, on the other hand, very comfortably, is the little un-
distinguished picture of a nearer antiquity, the antiquity for a glimpse of
which I reopened *Denis Duval*. Where, please, was the barber's shop of
the family of that hero, and where the apartments, where the preferred
resorts, the particular scenes of occupation and diversion of the dark
Chevalier de la Motte? Where did this subtle son of another civilisation,
with whom Madame de Saverne had eloped from France, *en plein
ancien régime*, without the occurrence between them of the least im-
propriety, spend his time for so long a period; where had he his little
habits and his numerous indispensable conveniences? What was the
general geography, to express it synthetically, of the state of life of the
orphaned Clarisse, quartered with a family of which one of the sons,
furiously desirous of the girl, was, at his lost moments, a highwayman
stopping coaches in the dead of night? Over nothing in the whole fragment does such vagueness hover as over the domestic situation, in her
tender years, of the future Madame Denis. Yet these are just the things I
should have liked to know – the things, above all, I should have liked
most to tell. Into a vision of *them*, at least, we can work ourselves; it is
exactly the sort of vision into which Rye and Winchelsea, and all the land
about, full of lurking hints and modest memories, most throw us back.
I should, in truth, have liked to lock up our novelist in our little pavilion
of inspiration, the gazebo at Rye, not letting him out till he should quite
have satisfied us.

Close beside the east gate, so close that one of its battered towers leans
heavily on the little garden, is a wonderfully perched cottage, of which
the mistress is a very celebrated lady who resorts to the place in the
intervals of an exacting profession – the scene of her renown, I may go so
far as to mention, is the theatre – for refreshment and rest. The small
grounds of this refuge, supported by the old town-wall and the steep
plunge of the great hill, have a rare position and view. The narrow garden
stretches away in the manner of a terrace to which the top of the wall
forms a low parapet; and here it is that, when the summer days are long,
the sweet old soul of all the land seems most to hang in the air. It is almost

a question indeed whether this fine Winchelsea front, all silver-grey and ivy-green, is not even better when making a picture itself from below than when giving you one, with much immensity, from its brow. This picture is always your great effect, artfully prepared by an absence of prediction, when you take a friend over from Rye; and it would appear quite to settle the small discussion – that may be said to come up among us so often – of which is the happier abode. The great thing is that if you live at Rye you have Winchelsea to show; whereas if you live at Winchelsea you have nothing but Rye. This latter privilege I should be sorry to cry down; but nothing can alter the fact that, to begin with, the pedestal of Winchelsea has twice the height, by a rough measure, of that of its neighbour; and we all know the value of an inch at the end of a nose. Almost directly under the Winchelsea hill, crossing the little bridge of the Brede, you pass beyond a screen of trees and take in, at the top of the ascent, the two round towers and arch, ivied and mutilated, but still erect, of the old main gate. The road either way is long and abrupt, so that people kind to their beasts alight at the foot, and cyclists careful of their necks alight at the head. The brooding spectator, more-over, who forms a class by himself, pauses infallibly, as he goes, to admire the way the great trees cluster and compose on the high slope, always striking, for him, as day gathers in and the whole thing melts together, a classic academic note, the note of Turner and Claude. From the garden of the distinguished cottage, at any rate, it is a large, melan-choly view – a view that an occasional perverse person whom it fails to touch finds easy, I admit, to speak of as dreary; so that those who love it and are well advised will ever, at the outset, carry the war into the enemy's country by announcing it, with glee, as sad. Just this it must be that nourishes the sense of obliterated history as to which I a moment ago wondered. The air is like that of a room through which something has been carried that you are aware of without having seen it. There is a vast deal of level in the prospect, but, though much depends on the day and still more on the hour, it is, at the worst, all too delicate to be ugly. The best hour is that at which the compact little pyramid of Rye, crowned with its big but stunted church and quite covered by the westering sun, gives out the full measure of its old browns that turn to

*Rye from the marshes beneath Winchelsea*

red and its old reds that turn to purple. These tones of evening are now pretty much all that Rye has left to give, but there are truly, sometimes, conditions of atmosphere in which I have seen the effect as fantastic. I sigh when I think, however, what it might have been if, perfectly placed as it is, the church tower[6] – which in its more perverse moods only resembles a big central button, a knob on a pin-cushion – had had the grace of a few more feet of stature. But that way depression lies, and the humiliation of those moments at which the brooding spectator says to himself that both tower and hill *would* have been higher if the place had only been French or Italian. Its whole pleasant little pathos, in point of fact, is just that it is homely English. And even with this, after all, the imagination can play. The wide, ambiguous flat that stretches eastward from Winchelsea hill, and on the monotone of whose bosom, seen at sunset from a friendly eminence that stands nearer, Rye takes the form of a huge floating boat, its water-line sharp and its bulk defined from stem to stern – this dim expanse is the great Romney Marsh, no longer a marsh today, but, at the end of long years, drained and ordered, a wide pastoral of grazing, with 'new' Romney town, a Port no more – not the least of the shrunken Five – mellowed to mere russet at the far end, and other obscure charms, revealed best to the slow cyclist, scattered over its breast; little old 'bits' that are not to be described, yet are known, with a small thrill, when seen; little lonely farms, red and grey; little mouse-

193

coloured churches; little villages that seem made only for long shadows and summer afternoons. Brookland, Old Romney, Ivychurch, Dymchurch, Lydd – they have positively the prettiest names. But the point to be made is that, comparing small things with great – which may always be done when the small things are amiable – if Rye and its rock and its church are a miniature Mont-Saint-Michel, so, when the summer deepens, the shadows fall, and the mounted shepherds and their dogs pass before you in the grassy desert, you find in the mild English 'marsh' a recall of the Roman Campagna.[7]

First published in *Scribner's Magazine*, XXIX (January 1901), 44–53, with illustrations by E. C. Peixotto; the essay was not reprinted until it appeared in *English Hours* (1905).

# Old Suffolk

I am not sure that before entering the county of Suffolk in the early part of August, I had been conscious of any personal relation to it save my share in what we all inevitably feel for a province enshrining the birth-place of a Copperfield. The opening lines of David's history offered in this particular an easy perch to my young imagination; and to recall them today, though with a memory long unrefreshed, is to wonder once more at the depth to which early impressions strike down.[1] This one in especial indeed has been the privilege of those millions of readers who owe to Dickens the glow of the prime response to the romantic, that first bite of the apple of knowledge which leaves a taste for ever on the tongue. The great initiators give such a colour to mere names that the things they represent have often, before contact, been a lively part of experience. It is hard therefore for an undefended victim of this kind of emotion to measure, when contact arrives, the quantity of picture already stored up, to point to the nucleus of the gallery or trace the history of the acquaint-ance. It is true that for the divine plant of sensibility in youth the water-ing need never have been lavish. It flowered, at all events, at the right moment, in a certain case, into the branching image of Blunderstone – which, by the way, I am sorry to see figure as 'Blunderston' in gazetteers of recent date and more than questionable tact. Dickens took his Rookery exactly where he found it, and simply fixed it for ever; he left the cradle of the Copperfields the benefit of its delightful name; or I should say better, perhaps, left the delightful name and the obscure nook the benefit of an association ineffaceable: all of which makes me the more ashamed not as yet to have found the right afternoon – it would have in truth to be abnormally long – for a pious pilgrimage to the distracting little church where, on David's sleepy Sundays, one used to lose one's self with the sketchy Phiz. One of the reasons of this omission, so profane on a prior view, is doubtless that everything, in England, in old-time corners, has the connecting touch and the quality of illustration, and that, in a particularly golden August, with an impression in every bush, the immediate vision, wherever one meets it, easily attaches and suffices. Another must have been, I confess, the somewhat depressed memory of a visit paid a few years since to the ancient home of the Peggottys, supposedly so 'sympathetic', but with little left, today, as the event then proved, of the glamour it had worn to the fancy. Great Yarmouth, it will be remembered, was a convenient drive from Blunderstone; but Great Yarmouth, with its mile of cockneyfied sea-front and its overflow of nigger minstrelsy, now strikes the wrong note so continuously that I, for my part, became conscious, on the spot, of a chill to the spirit of research.

This time, therefore, I have allowed that spirit its ease; and I may perhaps intelligibly make the point I desire if I contrive to express somehow that I have found myself, most of the month, none the less abundantly occupied in reading a fuller sense into the lingering sound given out, for a candid mind, by my superscription and watching whatever it may stand for gradually flush with a stronger infusion. It takes, in England, for that matter, no wonderful corner of the land to make the fiddle-string vibrate. The old usual rural things do this enough, and a part of the charm of one's exposure to them is that they ask one to rise to no heroics. What is the charm, after all, but just the abyss of the familiar? The peopled fancy, the haunted memory are themselves what pay the bill. The game can accordingly be played with delightful economy, a thrift involving the cost of little more than a good bicycle.[2] The bicycle indeed, since I fall back on that admission, may perhaps, without difficulty, be too good for the roads. Those of the more devious kind often engender hereabouts, like the Aristotelian tragedy, pity and terror; but almost equally with others they lead, on many a chance, to the ruddiest, greenest hamlets. What this comes to is saying that I have had, for many a day, the sweet sense of living, æsthetically, at really high pressure without, as it were, drawing on the great fund. By the great fund I mean the public show, the show for admission to which you are charged and overcharged, made to taste of the tree of possible disappointment. The beauty of old Suffolk in general, and above all of the desperate depth of it from which I write, is that these things whisk you straight out of conceivable relation to that last danger.

I defy any one, at desolate, exquisite Dunwich, to be disappointed in anything. The minor key is struck here with a felicity that leaves no sigh to be breathed, no loss to be suffered; a month of the place is a real education to the patient, the inner vision. The explanation of this is, appreciably, that the conditions give you to deal with not, in the manner of some quiet countries, what is meagre and thin, but what has literally, in a large degree, ceased to be at all. Dunwich is not even the ghost of its dead self; almost all you can say of it is that it consists of the mere letters of its old name. The coast, up and down, for miles, has been, for more centuries than I presume to count, gnawed away by the sea. All the grossness of its positive life is now at the bottom of the German Ocean, which moves for ever, like a ruminating beast, an insatiable, indefatigable lip. Few things are so melancholy – and so redeemed from mere ugliness by sadness – as this long, artificial straightness that the monster has impartially maintained. If at low tide you walk on the shore, the cliffs, of little height, show you a defence picked as bare as a bone; and you can say nothing kinder of the general humility and general sweetness of the land than that this sawlike action gives it, for the fancy, an interest, a sort of mystery, that more than makes up for what it may have surrendered. It stretched, within historic times, out into towns and promontories for which there is now no more to show than the empty eye-holes of a skull; and half the effect of the whole thing, half the secret of the impression, and what I may really call, I think, the source of the distinction, is this very visibility of the mutilation. Such at any rate is the case for a mind that can properly brood. There is a presence in what is missing – there is history in there being so little. It is so little, today, that every item of the handful counts.

The biggest items are of course the two ruins, the great church and its tall tower, now quite on the verge of the cliff, and the crumbled, ivied wall of the immense cincture of the Priory. These things have parted with almost every grace, but they still keep up the work that they have been engaged in for centuries and that cannot better be described than as the adding of mystery to mystery. This accumulation, at present prodigious, is, to the brooding mind, unconscious as the shrunken little Dunwich of today may be of it, the beginning and the end of the matter. I hasten to add that it is to the brooding mind only, and from it, that I speak. The mystery sounds for ever in the hard, straight tide, and hangs, through the long, still summer days and over the low, diked fields, in the soft, thick light. We play with it as with the answerless question, the question of the spirit and attitude, never again to be recovered, of the little city submerged. For it *was* a city, the main port of Suffolk, as even its poor relics show; with a fleet of its own on the North Sea, and a big religious house on the hill. We wonder what were then the apparent conditions of security, and on what rough calculation a community could so build itself out to meet its fate. It keeps one easy company here today to think of the whole business as a magnificent mistake. But Mr Swinburne, in verses of an extraordinary poetic eloquence, quite brave enough for whatever there may have been, glances in the right direction much further than I can do. Read moreover, for other glances, the 'Letters of Edward Fitzgerald',[3] Suffolk worthy and whimsical subject, who, living hard by at Woodbridge, haunted these regions during most of his life, and has left, in delightful pages, at the service of the emulous visitor, the echo of every odd, quaint air they could draw from his cracked, sweet instrument. He has paid his tribute, I seem to remember, to the particular delicate flower – the pale Dunwich rose – that blooms on the walls of the Priory. The emulous visitor, only yesterday, on the most vulgar of vehicles – which, however, he is quite aware he must choose between using and abusing – followed, in the mellow afternoon, one of these faint hints across the land and as far as the old, old town of Aldeburgh, the birthplace and the commemorated 'Borough' of the poet Crabbe.

Fitzgerald, devoted to Crabbe, was apparently not less so to this small break in the wide, low, heathery bareness that brings the sweet Suffolk commons – rare purple and gold when I arrived – nearly to the edge of the sea. We don't, none the less, always gather the particular impression we bravely go forth to seek. We doubtless gather another indeed that will serve as well any such turn as here may wait for it; so that if it was somehow not easy to work Fitzgerald into the small gentility of the sea-front, the little 'marina', as of a fourth-rate watering-place, that has elbowed away, evidently in recent years, the old handful of character, one could at least, to make up for that, fall back either on the general sense of the happy trickery of genius or on the special beauty of the mixture, in the singer of Omar Kháyyám, that, giving him such a place for a setting, could yet feed his fancy so full. Crabbe, at Aldeburgh, for that matter, is perhaps even more wonderful – in the light, I mean, of what is left of the place by one's conjuring away the little modern vulgar accumulation. What is left is just the stony beach and the big gales and the cluster of fishermen's huts and the small, wide, short street of decent, homely, shoppy houses. These are the private emotions of the historic sense – glimpses in which we recover for an hour, or rather perhaps, with an intensity, but for the glimmer of a minute, the conditions that, grimly enough, could engender masterpieces, or at all events classics. What a mere pinch of manners and customs in the midst of winds and waves! Yet if it was a feature of these to return a member to Parliament, what wonder that, up to the Reform Bill, dead Dunwich should have returned two?

The glimpses I speak of are, in all directions, the constant company of the afternoon 'spin'. Beginning, modestly enough, at Dunwich itself, they end, for intensity, as far inland as you have time to go; far enough – this is the great point – to have shown you, in their quiet vividness of type, a placid series of the things into which you may most read the old story of what is softest in the English complexity. I scarce know what murmur has been for weeks in my ears if it be not that of the constant word that, as a recall of the story, may serve to be put under the vignette. And yet this word is in its last form nothing more eloquent than the mere admonition to be pleased. Well, so you are, even as I was yesterday at Wesselton with the characteristic 'value' that expressed itself, how-ever shyly, in the dear old red inn at which I halted for the queer restora-tive – I thus discharge my debt to it – of a bottle of lemonade with a 'dash'. The dash was only of beer, but the refreshment was immense. So even was that of the sight of a dim, draped, sphinx-like figure that loomed, at the end of a polished passage, out of a little dusky back parlour which

had a windowful of the choked light of a small green garden – a figure
proving to be an old woman desirous to dilate on all the years she had
sat there with rheumatism 'most cruel'. So, inveterately – and in these
cases without the after-taste – is that of the pretty little park gates you
pass to skirt the walls and hedges beyond which the great affair, the
greatest of all, the deep, still home, sits in the midst of its acres and strikes
you all the more for being, precisely, so unrenowned. It is the charming
repeated lesson that the amenity of the famous seats in this country is
nothing to that of the lost and buried ones. This impression in particular
may bring you round again harmoniously to Dunwich and above all
perhaps to where the Priory, laid, as I may say, flat on its back, rests its
large outline on what was once the high ground, with the inevitable
'big' house, beyond and a little above, folded, for privacy, in a neat,
impenetrable wood. Here as elsewhere the cluster offers without complication just the signs of the type. At the base of the hill are the dozen
cottages to which the village has been reduced, and one of which
contains, to my hearing, though by no means, alas, to his own, a very
ancient man who will count for you on his fingers, till they fail, the
grand acres that, in his day, he has seen go the way of the rest. He likes
to figure that he ploughed of old where only the sea ploughs now.
Dunwich, however, will still last his time; and that of as many other as
– to repeat my hint – may yet be drawn here (though not, I hope, on the
instance of these prudent lines) to judge for themselves into how many
meanings a few elements can compose. One never need be bored, after
all, when 'composition' really rules. It rules in the way the brown
hamlet disposes itself, and the grey square tower of the church, in just
the right relation, peeps out of trees that remind me exactly of those
which, in the frontispieces of Birket Foster,[4] offered to my childish
credulity the very essence of England. Let me put it directly for old
Suffolk that this credulity finds itself here, at the end of time, more than
ever justified. Let me put it perhaps also that the very essence of England
has a way of presenting itself with completeness in almost any fortuitous
combination of rural objects at all, so that, wherever you may be, you
get, reduced and simplified, the whole of the scale. The big house and its
woods are always at hand; with a 'party' always, in the intervals of

shooting, to bring down to the rustic sports that keep up the tradition of the village green. The russet, low-browed inn, the 'ale-house' of Shakespeare, the immemorial fountain of beer, looking over that expanse, swings, with an old-time story-telling creak, the sign of the Marquis of Carabas. The pretty girls, within sight of it, alight from the Marquis's wagonette; the young men with the one eye-glass and the new hat sit beside them on the benches supplied for their sole accommodation, and thanks to which the meditator on manners has, a little, the image, gathered from faded fictions by female hands, of the company brought over, for the triumph of the heroine, to the hunt or the county ball. And it is always Hodge and Gaffer that, at bottom, *font les frais* – always the mild children of the glebe on whom, in the last resort, the complex superstructure rests.

The discovery, in the twilight of time, of the merits, as a building-site, of Hodge's broad bent back remains surely one of the most sagacious strokes of the race from which the squire and the parson were to be evolved. He is there in force – at the rustic sports – in force or in feebleness, with Mrs Hodge and the Miss Hodges, who participate with a silent glee in the chase, over fields where their shadows are long, of a pig with a greased tail. He pulls his forelock in the tent in which, after the pig is caught, the rewards of valour are dispensed by the squire's lady, and if he be in favour for respectability and not behind with rent, he penetrates later to the lawn within the wood, where he is awaited by a band of music and a collation of beer, buns, and tobacco.

I mention these things as some of the light notes, but the picture is never too empty for a stronger one not to sound. The strongest, at Dunwich, is indeed one that, without in the least falsifying the scale, counts immensely for filling in. The pail in the rustic sports is for the bluejackets; as, in England, of course, nothing is easier than for the village green to alternate with the element that Britannia still more admirably rules. I had often dreamed that the ideal refuge for a man of letters was a cottage so placed on the coast as to be circled, as it were, by the protecting arm of the Admiralty. I remember to have heard it said in the old country – in New York and Boston – that the best place to live in is next to an engine-house, and it is on this analogy that, at

Dunwich, I have looked for ministering peace in near neighbourhood to one of those stations of the coastguard that, round all the edge of England, at short intervals, on rock and sand and heath, make, with shining whitewash and tar, clean as a great State is at least theoretically clean, each its own little image of the reach of the empire It is in each case an image that, for one reason and another, you respond to with a sort of thrill; and the thing becomes as concrete as you can wish on your discovering in the three or four individual members of the simple staff of the establishment all sorts of educated decency and many sorts of beguilement to intercourse. Prime among the latter, in truth, is the great yarn-spinning gift. It differs from man to man, but here and there it glows like a cut ruby. May the last darkness close before I cease to care for sea-folk! – though this, I hasten to add, is not the private predilection at which, in these incoherent notes, I proposed most to glance. Let me have mentioned it merely as a sign that the fault is all my own, if this summer the arm of the Admiralty has not, in the full measure of my theory, represented the protection under which the long literary morning may know – abyss of delusion! – nothing but itself.

First published in *Harper's Weekly*, XLI (25 September 1897), 946; not reprinted until it appeared in *English Hours* (1905) where it was incorrectly dated 1879.

# Notes

## I. 'A NOTE ON THE TEXT'

1 The essays had originally appeared in various periodicals, and all but two ('Winchelsea, Rye and "Denis Duval"', and 'Old Suffolk') had appeared earlier in *Transatlantic Sketches* (1875), *Portraits of Places* (1883), *Foreign Parts* (1883), or *Essays in London and Elsewhere* (1893).

2 James's respect for the art of illustration and his admiration for his illustrator-friends is evident in *Picture and Text* (1893).

3 However, the sketches 'at the last moment . . . had suddenly to begin to live their little life without assistance'. It was not until 1900 that Pennell's illustrations gave them the benefit they 'always lacked', and *A Little Tour in France* became 'the picture-book it was designed to be' (Preface, vi).

4 A letter to Pennell dated 6 January 1888; reprinted in *Selected Letters of Henry James*, edited with an introduction by Leon Edel (1956), 121.

5 Pennell considered *Italian Hours* the best travel book on Italy; he had also illustrated others, among them Howell's *Italian Journeys*. He considered *A Little Tour in France* the best travel book of that country as well (*Adventures of an Illustrator*, 1925, 260–5).

6 Preface to *The Golden Bowl* in *The Art of the Novel: Critical Prefaces by Henry James*, edited by Richard P. Blackmur (1947), 332.

7 *Ibid.*, 333; statement regarding Alvin Langdon Coburn's photographic illustrations for the New York edition of *The Novels and Tales of Henry James*, 1907–09.

8 The first statement was made by Mr Eisenhower (then President-elect of the United States) at the time the English-Speaking Union announced its King George VI Memorial Fund, October 1952; the second statement was made at London Airport, 2 September 1959.

9 Quoted in 'The King George VI Memorial Fund Brochure' published by the English-Speaking Union of the United States, 1957, 1. Ralph Waldo Emerson made a similar remark in 1856: 'The stability of England is the security of the modern world' (*English Traits*, 143).

10 Morton Dauwen Zabel, *Henry James: The Art of Travel* (1958). George Alvin Finch also reprinted several of the essays in *Portraits of Places* (1948).

II. INTRODUCTION (The quotation is from James's *Notebooks*, 36)
PART I

1 *The Letters of Henry James*, selected and edited by Percy Lubbock (1920), II, 509. In both deed and word James spoke for the Allied cause: 'To all who listened to him in those days it must have seemed that he gave us what we lacked – a voice; there was a trumpet note in it that was heard nowhere else and that alone rose to the height of the truth,' wrote Percy Lubbock. 'If he had lived to see America join the Allies he would have had the deepest joy of his life' (*Letters*, II, 393;5).
Leon Edel also says that the letters James wrote during 1914–15 'are among the most eloquent of all his utterances' (*Selected Letters of Henry James*, 249).

2 In a letter to his nephew, James set forth the reasons for his action (*Letters*, II, 494–7).
James moved from Rye to London in order that he might do what he could for the war effort, both with his time and his fluent pen. Like Walt Whitman, he spent much of his time visiting wounded soldiers. He was a constant visitor, as well as a contributor, to the Chelsea centre for Belgian refugees; he became chairman of the American Volunteer Motor Ambulance Corps; and he wrote a series of essays in support of these causes (*Within the Rim and Other Essays*, 1914–15, 1919 ).
For a fuller account of these war years see: Leon Edel, 'Henry James: the War Chapter, 1914–1916', *The University of Toronto Quarterly*, X (January 1941), 125–38.

3 James's letters indicate that the emotional and physical strain were too much for him: 'My aged nerves can scarcely stand it, and I bear up but as I can. I dip my nose, or try to, into the inkpot as often as I can; but it's as if there were no ink there, and I take it out smelling gunpowder, smelling blood...' (*Letters*, II, 402).
Stephen Spender says that it was James's realisation of the meaning of the war that affected his health. On 4 August 1914, James wrote to Howard Sturgis: 'The plunge of civilisation into this abyss of blood and darkness by the wanton feat of those two infamous autocrats is a thing that so gives away the whole long age during which we have supposed the world to be, with whatever abatement, gradually bettering, that to have to take it all now for what the treacherous years were all the while really making for

and *meaning* is too tragic for any words' (*Letters*, II, 398; also Stephen Spender, 'The School of Experience in the Early Novels', *Hound & Horn*, VII, April-June 1934, 424).

4 *Letters*, I, 143.
Emerson phrased it this way: 'The American is only the continuation of the English genius into new conditions, more or less propitious' (*English Traits*, 42).

5 From childhood James had loved France. His friends, his tutors, his relatives – who were always 'there' – his travels and his reading all served to drive in 'the golden nail'. As a youth he had been an avid reader of French literature (he found every page of the *Revue des Deux Mondes* a delight), and in 1875 he went to France in order to learn what he could from the great French masters. He cherished to the end of his days his friendship with some of them. Cf. Mervyn Jones-Evans, 'Henry James's Year in France', *Horizon*, XIV (July 1946), 52–60; W. C. D. Pacey, 'Henry James & His French Contemporaries', *American Literature*, XIII (November 1941), 240–56; and I. D. McFarlane, 'A Literary Friendship: Henry James and Paul Bourget', *Cambridge Journal*, IV (1951), 144–61.

6 *Italian Hours* (1909), 502. James's love for Italy was a matter of the heart as well as the head; she was indeed his mistress. He had fallen in love with her as a youth; and when he visited the country for the last time, he found Venice still so lovely that it was 'a great pleasure to write the word'. And as he took leave of Rome, he remarked: 'No one who has ever loved Rome as Rome could be loved in youth . . . wants to stop loving her' *Ibid.*, 3, 304).

7 Emerson considered London to be 'the epitome of our times, and the Rome of today' (*English Traits*, 298).

8 *English Hours*, 10.

9 *Letters*, I, 143.

10 Mr Zabel has a longer list in *The Art of Travel*, 12–19; 25, 31. See also: Orie Long, *Literary Pioneers: Early American Explorers of European Culture* (1935); R. B. Mowat, *Americans in England* (1935); and R. E. Spiller, *The American in England* (1926).

11 *English Traits*, 298.

12 Randall Stewart, *Nathaniel Hawthorne: A Biography* (1948), 175.

13 Quoted in Oliver Wendell Holmes, *Our Hundred Days in Europe* (1892), 203.

14 *Ibid.*, 205.

15 Albert Bigelow Paine, *Mark Twain: A Biography* (1912), II, 470. Twain

had intended to write a book about England, but the project was never completed (*Ibid.*, II, 465–72).

16  *The Autobiography of Mark Twain*, edited with an introduction by Charles Neider (1959), 349.

17  Thomas G. Appleton spoke for many Americans when he said: 'Good Americans, when they die, go to Paris' (quoted in Van Wyck Brooks, *New England: Indian Summer*, 1940, 286 fn.). Howells also spoke for many of his compatriots when he remarked: 'The citizen of every free country loves Italy next to his own land, and feels her prosperous fortune to be the advantage of civilisation' (quoted in James L. Woodress, Jr., *Howells & Italy*, 1952, frontispiece).

18  Unless it be Hawthorne. Julian wrote of the Hawthornes' first visit to England: 'Few Americans ever journeyed thither better equipped than they for appreciating and enjoying what lay before them'; and of Hawthorne in London: 'No American better qualified than he to appreciate its sights, its historic and literary associations, its antiquities and its immensity had ever before lost himself in its streets' (Julian Hawthorne, *Nathaniel Hawthorne and His Wife: A Biography*, 1884, II, 3; 70–1).

19  *Partial Portraits*, (1888), 327–8.

20  *A Small Boy and Others*, (1913), 80–1 passim.
James later explained: 'In those days, in America, the manufacture of children's picture-books was an undeveloped industry; the best things came from London, and brought with them the aroma of a richer civilisation' (*Partial Portraits*, 330).

21  *A Small Boy and Others*, 276 James was to remember all his life two other rides: one through the streets of Paris at the age of two; and another, at the age of twelve, from Lyon to Geneva. The latter gave him his first view of a ruined castle and a peasant. 'It made a bridge over to more things than I then knew,' he remarked later (*Ibid*, 53–4; 281–5).

22  *Ibid.*, 261; 309–10.

23  *Partial Portraits*, 329. This observation is repeated in 'A London Life', 93; and in *English Hours*, 29–30.

24  Scattered throughout the travel essays there is also a great deal of incidental criticism of works of art (particularly in *Transatlantic Sketches* and *Italian Hours*) which should be compared with James's formal essays on the pictorial arts. Most of the latter have been reprinted in *The Painter's Eye*, edited with an introduction by John L. Sweeney (1956).

25  Perry was a devoted friend of the James family as his letters testify. Cf.

Virginia Harlow, *Thomas Sergeant Perry: A Biography, and Letters to Perry from William, Henry, and Garth Wilkinson James* (1950).

The warm friendship which existed between James and La Farge is made clear in: *Notes of a Son and Brother* (1914), 85–108; 'Henry James's Letters to the La Farges', edited with replies from the La Farges by John La Farge, S. J., *New England Quarterly*, XXII (June 1949), 173–92; Leon Edel, *Henry James: The Untried Years*, 1843–1870, 142–4; 159–66; and Robert Charles Le Clair, *Young Henry James*, 1843–1870, 286–9, 341–3.

26  That James had been writing stories before this we know from the family letters. On 15 October 1857, the father wrote from Boulogne: 'Harry is ... a devourer of libraries, and an immense writer of novels and dramas. He has considerable talent as a writer, but I am at a loss to know whether he will ever accomplish much' (Ralph Barton Perry, *The Thought and Character of William James*, 1935, I, 184). While young Wilkie was away in the army, he wrote to his father asking him to tell Harry that 'I am anxiously waiting for his "next". I can find a large sale for any blood and thunder tale among the darks' (Letter dated 31 December 1864, in *Alice James: Her Brothers, Her Journal*, edited with an introduction by Anna Robeson Burr, 1934, 36).

27  James published his first short story, 'A Tragedy of Error', in *The Continental Monthly*, V (February 1864), 204–16, unsigned. Mr Edel, who discovered the story, has reprinted it with a prefatory note in the *New England Quarterly*, XXIX (September 1956), 291–317. James's first review also appeared in 1864 unsigned.

28  *Notes of a Son and Brother*, 294; 405.

29  Robert Cantwell believes that prior to 1865 James 'had evidently written ten stories which he did not preserve' ('A Little Reality', *Hound & Horn*, VII, April–June, 1934, 494).

30  Cf. *A Bibliography of Henry James*, edited by Leon Edel and Dan H. Laurence (1957), Section D.

31  William also felt that Henry's talents demanded a richer background than America had to offer during the latter part of the nineteenth century. In a letter to Wilkie, written in 1873, he explained Harry's dilemma: 'his temperament is so exclusively artistic that the vacuous, simple atmosphere of America ends by tiring him to death' (Perry, *op. cit.*, I, 351).

In the famous essay on Hawthorne, James himself listed 'the items of high civilisation' that were 'absent from the texture of American life' during the nineteenth century (*Hawthorne*, 1879, 43).

32 E.g., *Letters*, I, 15–21; 'A Passionate Pilgrim', 1–30; the essay 'London', 1–7; and *The Middle Years*, 3–15, as well as in numerous other passages scattered throughout the novels and tales.

Mr Le Clair points out that ramifications of James's impressions and conclusions of 1869–70 'extend from *Travelling Companions* to *The Golden Bowl*' (*Young Henry James*, 434).

33 *Letters*, I, 17–18; 28.

34 *The Middle Years*, 6–7, 10.

PART II

1 These essays show James to be a master of the metaphor and simile, and they serve as a prologue to his later observations in *The American Scene* (1907). Of American men on vacation at Saratoga, James remarked: 'They are hard nuts, which have grown and ripened as they could. When they talk among themselves, I seem to hear the cracking of the shells.' He was equally gifted with the simile: Niagara Falls was like the sound of 'millions of bass-voices'; yet it was 'as gentle as the pouring of wine from a flagon – of melody from the lip of a singer' (*Portraits of Places*, 1883, 328–9, 371).

2 It was with much pride that the family showed Henry's letters to their literary friends, who enjoyed them with 'unfeigned delight'. His father and William agreed that the letters ought to be published. 'Your letters from Italy are beyond praise,' wrote William. 'It is a great pity that they should be born to blush unseen by the general public and that just the matter that they contain, in a little less rambling style, should not appear in the columns of *The Nation*' (Perry, *op. cit.*, I, 309).

Henry certainly hoped to make use of his letters later on for he wrote to William: 'You mustn't let my letters bore you. Don't read them if you don't feel like it – but keep them nevertheless. They will serve me in the future as a series of notes or observations – the only ones I shall have written' (Manuscript letter from Henry to William, 8 April 1869, in the Houghton Library, Harvard University; quoted in *Young Henry James*, 431).

3 Mr Le Clair has demonstrated that a study of the travel essays of Lowell, Adams and James, 'three of the most outstanding American travellers and residents in England' between 1850–85, reveals characteristics of these writers not otherwise apparent (*Three American Travellers in England: James Russell Lowell, Henry Adams, Henry James*, 1945, Preface, v).

4 *Transatlantic Sketches*, 230–1.

James was embarrassed that some of the American travellers who were 'swarming' over Europe had an 'unhappy poverty of voice' and an 'incredible lack of *culture*'; he added with evident pride that they had at least '*character* . . . energy, capacity and intellectual stuff in ample measure' (*Letters*, I, 22, 23). James pursued this subject in such articles as 'Americans Abroad', *The Nation*, XXVII (3 October 1878), 208–9. Later, while visiting in America, he discussed the speech and manners of American women: 'The Speech of American Women', *Harper's Bazar*, XL (November-December 1906), 979–82, 1103–6; XLI (January-February 1907), 17–21, 113–17; and 'The Manners of American Women', *Harper's Bazar*, XLI (April-July 1907), 355–9, 453–8, 537–41, 646–51.

5 *Transatlantic Sketches*, 248.

6 In James's fiction the members of his own society hold the centre of the stage; but in his travel writings it is the shepherds, farmers, beggars, waiters, gondoliers, washerwomen and peasants who are the dramatis personae. It is the poor, young and old, an artist's model or an old woman trudging under her burden of faggots who capture James's attention.

7 In Italy, on one occasion, James 'wedged' himself into a 'tightly packed third-class car' in order to journey with the populace to the Grotta Ferrata; and in spite of his discomfort, he enjoyed the jollity of 'the blessed Italian temperament' (*Transatlantic Sketches*, 173–4).

8 As James talked with the young man, he 'presently acknowledged himself a brooding young radical and a communist, filled with hatred of the present Italian government, raging with discontent and crude political passion, professing a ridiculous hope that Italy would soon have, as France had had, her " '89", and declaring that he for his part would willingly lend a hand to chop off the heads of the king and the royal family' (*Italian Hours*, 166).

9 The idea for *The Princess Casamassima* came to James while he was 'walking the streets' of London (Preface, in *The Art of the Novel: Critical Prefaces by Henry James*, 59). In his letters, notebooks and autobiographical writings James explains what his walking meant to his art.

10 *English Hours*, 24.

11 *Italian Hours*, 461.
James was not perturbed when, at Narbonne, he was forced to sleep in a *maison bourgeoise* with 'an entrance like a stable' and 'an odour compared with which that of a stable would have been delicious' (*A Little Tour in France*, 1900, 165).

12 *Letters*, I, 26–7.

13 *Transatlantic Sketches*, 232.
James had endured the odours at Anacapri with more concern for St

Anthony than for himself. He 'squeezed' himself into the church with as many worshippers 'as the robust odour mainly prevailing there allowed room for' and then remarked: 'It was surely the smell, thick and resisting, that was least successfully to be elbowed. Meanwhile the good saint, before he could move into the air, had, among the tapers and the tinsel, the opera-music and the pulpit poundings, bravely to snuff it up' (*Italian Hours*, 488).

14 For James's use of these houses and gardens as symbols in his fiction see: R. W. Stallman, 'The Houses that James Built – *The Portrait of a Lady*', *The Texas Quarterly*, I (Winter 1958), 176–96.
The beauty of the gardens at Oxford prompted James to indulge 'in the happy belief the world is all an English garden and time a fine old English afternoon' (quoted in *The Untried Years*, 291).

15 Class barriers were particularly repugnant to James; but he also thought other customs 'harsh' and distasteful, such as putting a widow out of her home in order that her son might inherit the estate (e.g. 'A London Life' and *The Spoils of Poynton*).

16 *Transatlantic Sketches*, 245–6.


PART III

1 James drew upon his travels in France for his first short story, 'A Tragedy of Error' (1864), and later for 'Gabrielle de Bergerac' (1869). The latter, a story of pre-Revolutionary France, incorporates his own youthful experiences with castles, tutors, servants, etc. 'Travelling Companions' (1870) not only echoes his first adult tour of Italy, but it also forecasts his later concern with the 'international theme'. 'A Passionate Pilgrim' (1871) is scarcely more than a fictionalised travelogue of his own tour of England in 1869–70; and 'At Isella', written in the same year, reflects his first-hand knowledge of Switzerland. Mr Zabel says of James's travel essays: 'Delightful, charming, amusing, and instructive as his essays are . . . the greater value and profit of his explorings shows itself in his fiction.' James's travel experiences 'constitute the appropriate imagery of his subject matter, are part and substance of the theme he made basic to his lifework, and so become the matrix of the moral and historical drama his fiction unfolds' (*The Art of Travel*, 34, 8).

2 James wrote his travel sketches specifically for American periodicals, and it was not until 1883 that a selected group of the sketches was published in London as *Portraits of Places* (1883). James's 'travel and art sketches were highly praised' by American critics, who considered James 'a nearly perfect traveller-reporter' (Richard Nicholas Foley, *Criticism in American Periodicals*

*of the Works of Henry James from 1866 to 1916*, 1944, 151).

3  *Scribner's Magazine*, XXI (March 1897), 351–67; and (April 1897), 425–47.

4  Among these were Harper's Half-Hour Series (which included 'The Diary of a Man of Fifty', 'Daisy Miller' and 'An International Episode') and the Tauchnitz 'Collection of British Authors' (Leipzig) with twenty-one volumes by James.

5  Cf. Edward Godfrey Cox, *A Reference Guide to the Literature of Travel*, *University of Washington Publications in Language and Literature*, IX (November 1935), X (May 1938) and XII (May 1949); also *Literary History of the United States*, edited by Robert E. Spiller, Willard Thorp, Thomas H. Johnson, Henry Seidel Canby, *et al.* (1953), 24–39, 827–42.

6  James commented that Ruskin's 'little books' would not 'bear the test of being read in . . . rich old Italy'; but he thought them 'extremely amusing' and worth reading 'on account of the great charm and felicity of much of their incidental criticism' (*Portraits of Places*, 1883, 67).

7  James reviewed Howells's *Italian Journeys* in 1868, and by the end of 1875 he had reviewed twenty-one travel books. A few of these have been included by Albert Mordell in *Literary Reviews and Essays by Henry James* (1957).

8  *English Hours*, 42. In *The Ambassadors* James calls them 'the wicked old Rows' (New York Edition, Volume XXI, 41).

9  *Transatlantic Sketches*, 42; revised in *English Hours*, 63.

10 Although James did not describe Shakespeare's birthplace in his travel essays, he did have much to say on the subject in the short story 'The Birthplace'. See also: William T. Stafford, 'James Examines Shakespeare: Notes on the Nature of Genius', *PMLA*, LXXIII (March 1958), 123–8.

11 Leon Edel, *The Complete Plays of Henry James* (1949), 43.

12 James not only conjured up literary ghosts from his reading, but later he conjured them up for his own novels and tales. His interest in ghosts has been fully explored by Mr Edel in his introduction to *The Ghostly Tales of Henry James* (1948). Even Lamb House had its own 'special ghost'.

13 James might have been describing his own work when he said of Tintoret (whom he considered 'the greatest artist of them all'; later he was to change his mind): 'You get from Tintoret's work the impression that he *felt*, pictorially, the great, beautiful, terrible spectacle of human life very much as Shakespeare felt it poetically – with a heart that never ceased to beat a passionate accompaniment to every stroke of his brush' (*Italian Hours*, 81).

14 *English Hours*, 63.

15 *Ibid.*, 69.

PART IV

1 These *New York Tribune* (now the *Herald Tribune*) articles have been collected and edited with an introduction and notes by Leon Edel and Ilse Dusoir Lind in *Henry James: Parisian Sketches* (1957).

2 *The Notebooks of Henry James*, edited by F. O. Matthiessen and Kenneth B. Murdock (1947), 27–8 passim.

3 Repeated by James in his review of Gautier's 'Winter in Russia' (*The Nation*, XIX, 12 November 1874, 322; reprinted in Mordell, *op. cit.*, 91).

4 James explained to his mother the reason for the British attitude toward the story: 'It is an entirely new sensation for them (the people here) to be (at all delicately) *ironised* or satirised, from the American point of view, and they don't at all relish it' (*Letters*, I, 68).

5 Cf. E. L. Volpe, 'The Reception of *Daisy Miller*', *Boston Public Library Quarterly*, X (January 1958), 55–9.
   *The Bostonians* was not included in the 24 volumes of the New York edition of James's novels and tales (1907–09). In 1908 James wrote to Howells that he wanted to reintroduce *The Bostonians* ('with a good deal of titivation and cancellation') because he felt the novel was 'tolerably full and good' but that it had not 'received any sort of justice' (*Letters*, II, 103).

6 Ford Madox Hueffer summarised James's depiction of this group by saying: 'He gives you an immense – and an increasingly tragic – picture of a leisured society that is fairly unavailing, materialist, emasculated – and doomed' (*The Question of Henry James*, edited by Frederick W. Dupee, 1945, 52). Newton Arvin contends that James saw the 'corruption' and 'philistinism' of his time 'as few of his contemporaries saw them' and that he 'became in his old age the chronicler of a festering society'. In his later works 'one sniffs, on the breeze, rancid odors wafted prophetically from the world of Cabell and Hergesheimer, of Lawrence and Eliot, even of Hemingway and Faulkner' ('Henry James and the Almighty Dollar', *Hound & Horn*, VII, April–June 1934, 436–8).

7 'Notes for the Ivory Tower' in *The Ivory Tower* (1917), 287. Graham Greene believes that James was as imbued with 'the sense of evil' as with 'the sense of the past' and that he had a 'passionate distrust' of human nature (*The Lost Childhood and Other Essays*, 1952, 25).

8 'In Scotland – II', *The Nation*, XXVII (24 October 1878), 255.

9 Robert Cantwell points out that James's plots often 'revolved around the relationship of representatives of the upper and lower classes, a wealthy painter and a fisherman's daughter, a wealthy woman who tries to induce

a poor young man to propose to her' ('A Little Reality', *op. cit.*, 498). Edna Kenton's discussion of these two stories is particularly sound (*Eight Uncollected Tales of Henry James*, 1950, 7–9).

10   Louise Bogan was one of the first critics to point out that James's 'knowledge of the relentless mechanisms of poverty – poverty's minutiae' stretched back to his childhood. 'The Younger James had, no doubt, seen Muniment's counter-part' among his father's friends ('Henry James on a Revolutionary Theme', *The Nation*, CXLVI 23 April 1938, 471–4; reprinted in *Literary Opinion in America*, edited by Morton Dauwen Zabel, rev. ed., 1951, 351–6).

11   *English Hours*, 171.

12   *Letters*, I, 70.

13   James did talk of Italy, particularly Venice, 'as a lover talks of his mistress'. His love of Venice increased with the passing years, and in 1909 he felt that the city itself had 'become human and sentient and conscious of your affection. You desire to embrace it, to caress it, to possess it; and finally a soft sense of possession grows up and your visit becomes a perpetual love-affair' (*Italian Hours*, 10). Indeed Italy was a 'beautiful dishevelled nymph' compared with England which was 'a good married matron'.

14   *English Hours*, 86.

15   Mr Trilling is right in saying that *The Princess Casamassima* 'is a brilliantly precise representation of social actuality' and that within the novel 'there is not a political event . . . not a detail of oath or mystery or danger, which is not confirmed by multitudinous records' (*The Liberal Imagination*, 1957, 71, 64). Surely the novel is more soundly based than Irving Howe indicates in *Politics and the Novel* (1957), 139–56.

16   *Letters*, I, 115.
     Christof Wegelin sees *The American* as a contrast between two social and political systems (*The Image of Europe in Henry James*, 1958, 38–9).

17   *Letters*, I, 122.

18   James did not approve of the British army's occupation of Ireland. He visited Ireland during the 'castle season' only to discover that the Irish boycotted the beautiful balls that were given every night. In spite of the fact that all the ladies looked like Joshuas, Gainsboroughs or Romneys, James concluded that there was 'too much pomp and state – for nothing and nobody' (*Letters*, I, 245–6).

19   But in *The Tragic Muse*, as well as in most of his stories of artists and writers, he dramatised the conflicting ideals of the world of art and that of politics. Cf. Lyall H. Powers, 'James's *The Tragic Muse* – Ave Atque Vale',

*PMLA*, LXXIII (June 1958), 270–4.

20 When Howells inquired whether James had translated one of Turgenev's poems, the reply came back: 'Yes . . . though I don't share the Russian eagerness for war' (Henry James to William Dean Howells, 29 October 1876, unpublished letter in the Houghton Library; quoted in *A Bibliography of Henry James*, 308).

21 Sometimes James put his sentiments directly into the mouths of his characters. Asked whether she approved of her sister marrying an American, Lady Beauchemin replied: 'I should like it very much. I think English and American society ought to be but one – I mean the best of each – a great whole.' Lord Canterville thought 'it a capital thing that the two countries should become more united. . . . They were all one race, after all; and why shouldn't they make one society . . .' 'Lady Barbarina', in *Tales of Three Cities*, 1884, 31, 55.

22 *Letters*, I, 58.

23 As a 'critic of life' nothing appealed more to James than 'the multiplied symptoms among educated people, from wherever drawn, of a common intelligence and a social fusion tending to abridge old rigours of separation'. The 'eventual sublime consensus of the educated' would constitute the drama of the future (Preface to 'Lady Barbarina' in *The Art of the Novel*, 202–3). R. W. B. Lewis says that James was 'essentially prophetic' in describing 'a different society altogether from the one visibly declining in Europe and the one struggling to be born in America' ('The Vision of Grace: James's "The Wings of the Dove"', *Modern Fiction Studies*, III, Spring, 1957, 34).

24 *Portraits of Places*, (1948), 117.

25 *Transatlantic Sketches*, 247.

26 Henry James, 'The Question of the Opportunities', *Literature*, II (26 March 1898), 356–8; reprinted in *Literary Opinion in America*, *op. cit.*, 51–5; and in *The American Essays of Henry James*, edited with an introduction by Leon Edel (1956), 202.

27 *The Notebooks of Henry James*, 24

28 *The American Essays of Henry James*, 187.

29 Disagreeing with Thomas Gray's idea of heaven ('to lie all day on a sofa and read novels'), James thought of a better heaven: 'to sit all night in a fauteuil . . . listening to Delaunay, watching Got, or falling in love with Mademoiselle Desclée' (*Transatlantic Sketches*, 98–9).

30 'The London Theatres', *The Galaxy*, XXIII (May 1877), 661–70; reprinted

in *Henry James: The Scenic Art*, edited with an introduction by Allan Wade, (1948), 93.

31 'The London Exhibitions – The Royal Academy', *The Nation*, XXVI (6 June 1878), 371–2; reprinted in *The Painter's Eye*, 167.

32 'The Bethnal Green Museum', *The Atlantic Monthly*, XXXI(January 1873), 69–75; reprinted in *The Painter's Eye* as 'The Wallace Collection in Bethnal Green', 69.

33 *The Middle Years*, 53.

Although James often referred to his physical discomforts, Mr Edel says that James was not in reality an invalid: 'He rode horseback, fenced, lifted weights (to fight off over-weight), took long daily walks and was an inveterate traveller . . . he spent hours daily at his desk; he combined literary labour with a crowded and intricate social life' (*The Untried Years*, 183).

34 *A Small Boy and Others*, 352.

35 In Mr Edel's words: 'In those galleries and streets, cathedrals and cafés, along the well-beaten American-travelled nineteenth century paths in Europe, he met face to face the host of Americans, rich and poor, the struggling artists, the wandering dispatriates, the innocent young girls who were henceforward to walk across the pages of his fiction' (*The Untried Years*, 305).

36 *A Small Boy and Others*, 411.

37 Wright Morris says that the word 'impressionism' has for James 'the same value precisely, as the impressionism of Cézanne . . . Cézanne's effort to "realise" his sensations is parallel to the effort of James – an act of possession, one for which he would go to the stake' ('Henry James's *The American Scene*', *The Texas Quarterly*, I, Summer-Autumn 1958, 29).

38 *Partial Portraits* (1888), 342.

Mervyn Jones-Evans says that James derived 'a sense of analysis' from his year in France, and that 'This essentially French faculty, which played such an important role throughout his work, enabled him to lead the novel into a channel hitherto completely unknown and to produce those fascinating prefaces to the collected edition of his works which are something unique in Anglo-Saxon literature' ('Henry James's Year in France', *op. cit.*, 60).

39 *Notes of a Son and Brother*, 97.

40 *A Small Boy and Others*, 263–4.

Although James deserted the brush for the pen, he continued to compose with 'the painter's eye'; and throughout his life the plastic arts were to mean almost as much to him as the literary arts. His knowledge of the vocabulary and technique of painting was to play an important role in all his works. Cf. Edwin T. Bowden, *The Themes of Henry James: A System of Observation Through the Visual Arts* (1956); and Robert L. Gale, 'Art Imagery in Henry James's Fiction', *American Literature*, XXIX (March 1957), 47–63.

Ralph Barton Perry also points out that although William put down his brush in favour of science, he remained essentially a painter: 'His descriptions of people were, like his father's, *portraits*. . . . He saw the landscape with a painter's eye and the artist's sense of plastic form' (Perry, *op. cit.*, I, 201).

41 *English Hours*, 128.

## Part V

1 A Continental edition of *Transatlantic Sketches* was published by Bernhard Tauchnitz in 1883 as *Foreign Parts*. Four essays and portions of a fifth were omitted ('The Parisian Stage', 'The After-Season in Rome', 'The Autumn in Florence', 'The Splugen', and Parts II, VI, VII, and VIII of 'Florentine Notes') and the sketches were revised.

2 Theodora Bosanquet says that 'it was the demonstration of values implicit in his early work, the retrieval of countless lost opportunities for adequately "rendering"' that prompted James to revise his work ('The Revised Version', *The Little Review*, V, August 1918, 58).

3 The 'picturesque' tradition which had held sway since the eighteenth century was on the wane. James had fallen under the spell of the tradition in the '70's and '80's during his numerous visits to Italy; but when he revised his novels and tales for the collected edition, he realised that he had overworked the tradition. Cf. F. O. Matthiessen, 'The Painter's Sponge and Varnish Bottle', in *Henry James: The Major Phase* (1944), 152–86.

4 Cf. R. Short, 'The Sentence Structure of Henry James', *American Literature*, XVIII (May 1946), 71–88.

5 Cf. *Notebooks*, 325; and *Letters*, II, 38. Joseph Pennell was also to illustrate *London Town*.

6 James's change in style parallels his change of opinion regarding Impressionist painters. In 1876 he thought the doctrines of these painters 'incompatible . . . with the existence of first-rate talent'; but in 1905, while visiting in America, he had nothing but praise for the 'wondrous examples' of impressionistic paintings which he saw 'in a great new house on a hilltop'. The power of 'that particular art . . . made everything else shrivel and fade: it was like the sudden trill of a nightingale, lord of the hushed evening' (*Parisian Sketches*, *op. cit.*, 132; and *The American Scene*, 1946, 45–6).

7   Mr Alvarez says of James's travel writings: 'They serve as a kind of dark side of the moon to the rest of his work; the harmony and incandescence of it all depends upon them' ('Intelligence on Tour', *The Kenyon Review*, XXI, Winter 1959, 23).

8   George Alvin Finch says that 'in fastidiousness of style and careful elaboration of his observations' James's travel writings 'are akin to his fiction' (Introduction to *Portraits of Places*, 1948, 18).

9   James wrote Howells in 1908 that he was 'beginning to re-do . . . certain little old Italian papers . . . in form to match with a volume of "English Hours" ' (which had sold 'quite vulgarly' for his 'wares'), not because he had 'retitivation on the brain' but because of his 'flat pocket-book' (*Letters*, II, 104). But no critic takes this statement at its face value; James had said the same thing about his reason for writing plays. James's interest was no doubt three-fold as Alfred R. Ferguson suggests ('The Triple Quest of Henry James: Fame, Art and Fortune', *American Literature*, XXVII, January 1956, 475–98).

## PART VI

1   Quentin Anderson points out that James's Americans face Europe with 'mingled fear and delight'. They delight in 'Europe's cultural achievement' but they fear 'its terrible cost in wickedness and suffering' (*The American Henry James*, 1957, 164).

2   Mr Zabel explains that travel in the works of James 'is a cognate of the moral and historical drama to which he addressed himself; of the conflict of culture he saw as basic to his century; of the "complex fate" which he discovered "being an American", but being no less a man of full modern sensibility and responsible intelligence, imposed on him' (*The Art of Travel*, 13).

3   *Notebooks*, 24.

4   *A Small Boy and Others*, 352.

5   *Letters*, I, 143.

6   As early as 1867 James predicted that Americans would eventually have 'a national *cachet*'. He explained to Thomas Sergeant Perry: 'We must of course have something of our own – something distinctive and homogeneous – and I take it that we shall find it in our moral consciousness, our unprecedented spiritual lightness and vigour.' And these qualities he bequeathed to his American characters (*Selected Letters of Henry James*, 52).

7   Although products of 'the age of innocence' James's Americans are not all as naïve as Daisy Miller and Christopher Newman; the protagonists of his later works may have the experience of Julia Bride or the wisdom of Maggie Verver. On this point see: Peter Buitenhuis, 'From *Daisy Miller* to *Julia Bride:* "a Whole Passage of Intellectual History" ', *American Quarterly*, XI (Summer 1959), 136–46; Robert P. Falk, 'Henry James and the "Age of Innocence" ', *Nineteenth Century Fiction*, VII (1952), 171–88; Annette Kar, 'Archetypes of American Innocence: Lydia Blood and Daisy Miller', *American Quarterly*, V (Spring 1953), 31–8.

In contrasting the innocents of James's day with the more informed traveller of today, D. W. Brogan has concluded that in mid-century there are 'No Innocents Abroad' (*Harper's Bazaar*, July 1958, 86–7, 98).

8   *Note, of a Son and Brother*, 366; 326–7.

9   T. S. Eliot was one of the first critics to defend James's action. The 'flavour' of James's origin was 'improved and given its chance, not worked off, by transplantation', he commented ('The Hawthorne Aspect', *The Little Review*, V, August 1918, 48). Ford Madox Hueffer also pointed out that James was 'the most American product that New England ever turned out' (*Henry James, A Critical Study*, 1918, 52). In spite of the controversy which Van Wyck Brooks sparked with *The Pilgrimage of Henry James* (1925), and to which Edna Kenton replied so ably ('Henry James and Mr Van Wyck Brooks', *Bookman*, LXII, October 1925, 153–7), most critics now agree with Quentin Anderson that James's 'American faith is the vessel of his power' (*The American Henry James*, 182).

10   *Letters*, I, 60.

11   *Letters*, I, 119.

12   According to Frederick W. Dupee, Catharine Barber James (third wife of William James, the founder of the family) was not of 'English blood' as James thought. Her grandparents had emigrated from Ireland. (*Henry James: Autobiography*, 1956, 602). See also *The Untried Years*, 39, 86.

13   *French Poets and Novelists*, (1878), 309.

14   Robert L. Gale says that James's 'only religion . . . seems to have been the adoration of art . . . Henry James saw in art such a power for international good that to him it was little short of a religion' ('Religion Imagery in Henry James's Fiction', *Modern Fiction Studies*, III, Spring 1957, 72).

15   Oliver Wendell Holmes was sometimes as eloquent on the subject as James: 'I hope that more Englishmen like James Smithson will help to build up our scientific and literary institutions. I hope that more Americans like

George Peabody will call down the blessings of the English people by noble benefactions. . . . Such acts as these make us feel more and more the truth of the generous sentiment which closes the ode of Washington Allston, "America to Great Britain!" "We are one!" ' (*Our Hundred Days in Europe*, 205–6).

16 Only two other novelists had been admitted to the Order at that time: George Meredith and Thomas Hardy. James's qualifications for the honour were set forth eloquently by Edward Marsh in a letter to the Prime Minister. After summarising James's literary merits, Marsh added: 'There are two extraneous considerations. His recent naturalisation was a generous and impressive gesture of adherence to our national cause, and deserves some grace of recognition. And the compliment would no doubt be appreciated in America' (Christopher Hassall, *Edward Marsh, Patron of the Arts: A Biography*, 1959, 374–5).

17 In a letter to Mr Asquith, then Prime Minister, James stated his reasons for wishing to become a British subject: 'I find my wish to testify at this crisis to the force of my attachment and devotion to England, and to the cause for which she is fighting, finally and completely irresistible . . . I can only testify by laying at her feet my explicit, my material and spiritual allegiance, and throwing into the scale of her fortune my all but imponderable moral weight – "a poor thing but mine own" ' (*Selected Letters of Henry James*, 260).

18 The spirit of James's decision was appropriately immortalised in the following memorial tablet which was placed on the south wall of the More Chapel in Chelsea Old Church.

In memory of Henry James, O. M., Novelist: born in New York 1843: died in Chelsea 1916: lover and interpreter of the fine amenities, of brave decisions and generous loyalties: a resident of this parish who renounced a cherished citizenship to give his allegiance to England in the first year of the Great War.

(The More Chapel was the only part of the Church not completely distroyed by bombing in 1941. The Church has been rebuilt and its monuments restored.)

19 Here I use Newman and Strether only as symbols of the American and the Ambassador. I do not infer that James resembled either character, or that he projected himself in these characters. For interesting analyses of these protagonists see: John A. Clair, '*The American*: A Reinterpretation', *PMLA*, LXXIV (December 1959), 613–18; and Quentin Anderson, *The American Henry James*, Chapter VIII.

## LONDON

1 The 'earlier vision' was that of 1855 and the 'fresh beginning' his arrival in London about 1 March 1869. He was later to recall both occasions with great vividness (*A Small Boy and Others*, 1913; and *The Middle Years*, 1917).

2 American and Commonwealth visitors will be especially interested in going to St Paul's to see two recent gifts of the British people: (1) the new High Altar and Canopy given in memory of the men and women of the Commonwealth who died in the two world wars; and (2) the American Memorial Chapel, which was dedicated in 1958 in the presence of Her Majesty Queen Elizabeth II and the Vice-President of the United States, Mr Richard Nixon. Placed beside the altar is a Memorial Volume in which are inscribed the names of the 28,000 citizens who lost their lives during World War II while based in Britain.

3 This great baroque cathedral was designed by Sir Christopher Wren and completed in only thirty-five years (1675–1710). The earlier Norman church of 1090–1130, with its classical exterior by Inigo Jones, was almost completely destroyed by the Great Fire of 1666.

4 Here James is recording the abject homesickness about which he wrote his mother the next day after his arrival in London: 'Here I am beating with my pen at this poor blank paper as grimly as my wretched infantile heart is thumping against my breast. . . . At all events, sitting here in this dreary London, between my fire and my candles, I must begin a letter, or else I shall begin to howl and drive the poor landlord to send out for a policeman. Yes, I confess it without stint or shame, I am homesick – abjectly, fatally homesick' (MS. letter from Henry James, Jr. to Mrs Henry James, Sr., 2 March 1869, Houghton Library, Harvard University; quoted in Robert Charles Le Clair, *Young Henry James, 1843–1870*, 429).

5 Nathaniel Hawthorne called London the 'central spot of all the world'; he 'acquired a home-feeling there, as nowhere else in the world' (*Our Old Home*, 239–40).

6 James kept rooms at the Reform Club; he also was a member of the Athenaeum. It was he who seconded Kipling's application for membership of the latter.

7 Few travellers miss Paddington, not only because of its association with Agatha Christie, but primarily because this great structure of glass and steel with its vaulted roofs and its cathedral-like nave and transepts is a masterpiece of engineering. A monument to the great engineer, Isambard Kingdom Brunel, it was completed in 1854.

8 Joseph Pennell, Cf. 'In London with Henry James', *The Century Magazine*, CIII (February 1922), 543–8.

9 James writes more subjectively here than he does in his novels and tales. Compare this paragraph with a similar scene in *A London Life*, Chapter IX. Hawthorne also wrote sympathetically of these 'watchers' (*Our Old Home*, 340–1).

## BROWNING IN WESTMINSTER ABBEY

1 James had been an admirer of Browning since 1860 when John La Farge helped him to 'see' the merits of the great poet. Years later, on 7 May 1912, he was asked to deliver an address in commemoration of the centenary of Browning's birth ('The Novel in *The Ring and the Book*', *Transactions of the Royal Society of Literature*, 2nd Series: Vol. XXXI, Part IV, 1912, 269–98; reprinted in *Browning's Centenary*, 1912). The address was also revised and reprinted in the *Quarterly Review*, CCXVII (July 1912), 68–87; the *Living Age* (24 August 1912); and later included in *Notes on Novelists*, 1914.

2 One of these devotees was Mrs Arthur Bronson (Katharine de Kay), whose tribute to the poet, 'Browning in Venice', was published with a prefatory essay by Henry James (*Cornhill Magazine*, XII, February 1902, 145–9). After her death, James reprinted his preface as a separate article, 'The Late Mrs Arthur Bronson' (*The Critic*, XL, February 1902, 162–4). Later he changed the title to 'Casa Alvisi' (her home in Venice which was always open to Browning and James) for his last travel book, *Italian Hours* (1909).

3 James knew Browning well and was frequently in his company, especially when they were neighbours in Kensington (Leon Edel, *Selected Letters of Henry James*, 75, 101, 169, 211).

## CHESTER

1 James had first visited Chester in 1869.

2 In his travel essays James often used an actual or imaginary conversation in order to give both sides of a subject.

3 James's analysis of these 'wicked old Rows' is even more harsh in *The Ambassadors*.

4 Still the property of the Dukes of Westminster, Eaton Hall has until recently been leased to the War Office as an Officer Cadet School.

5 Throughout his travel sketches James frequently remarked that an English Balzac was needed to give a proper account of a place. He once thought that

Kipling 'contained the seeds of an English Balzac', but by 1897 he had quite given up that fond hope (*Letters*, I, 278).

6  Sir George Gilbert Scott (1811–78), English architect and leader of the Gothic revival in England; he also 'renovated' Lichfield and Ely Cathedrals and many other monuments, including Westminster Abbey. He also designed the Albert Memorial in Hyde Park, St Pancras Station, the Home, Foreign, Colonial and War Offices.

7  Tradition says that Chester Cathedral stands on the site of an ancient Druid shrine on which the Romans later built a Temple of Apollo. The date of the first Christian church is uncertain but a Benedictine abbey was founded by Hugh Lupus, Earl of Chester, in 1093. The present cathedral, which is the result of much rebuilding during the centuries, was given the rank of cathedral by Henry VIII in 1541.

8  These late fourteenth-century stalls represent some of the finest woodwork in England. The new roof of the refectory, designed by F. H. Crossley and completed in 1939, is an example of modern woodwork.

9  A great preacher and a distinguished bishop, Jeremy Taylor (1613–67) wrote numerous treatises which are still read today, among them the celebrated *The Rule of Conscience* (1660).

## LICHFIELD AND WARWICK

1  David Garrick became one of the most famous Shakespearean actors of his day, a noted playwright, and manager of the Drury Lane Theatre.

2  Johnson's birthplace is certainly in harmony with his fame now. It is a museum which houses over a thousand volumes of Johnsonian material, a collection of rare prints, and many personal relics of Johnson such as the desk on which he wrote *The Rambler* and the chair he occupied during his last illness.

3  Samuel Johnson's only novel, published in March or April 1759. Accompanied by Garrick, Johnson went up to London in 1737 with a tragedy and five pennies in his pocket.

4  See fn. 6 to 'Chester'.

5  The Cistercian Abbey of Herkenrode in Belgium.

6  These spires, the 'Lovely Ladies of the Vale', are a superb example of the impressive beauty of a medieval cathedral. James's lengthy description of the Cathedral indicates that he would no doubt have agreed with modern critics that Lichfield has been underrated.

7  James's interest in ghosts has been explored by Leon Edel in his introduction to *The Ghostly Tales of Henry James* (1948).

8  The story of Lord John Manners's elopement with Dorothy Vernon, heiress of Haddon Hall, was revived by Sir Arthur Sullivan in the opera *Haddon Hall* (1892).

9  Considered as the most complete and authentic example of a medieval and manorial home in England, Haddon Hall was the seat successively of the Avenells, the Vernons and the Rutherfords, before becoming the property of the Dukes of Rutland, heads of the Manners family.

10  The home of the Duke of Devonshire, Chatsworth is one of the most famous of all the mansions of Britain. Begun in the reign of Queen Mary by Sir William Cavendish, it contains paintings by Claude Lorrain, Holbein, Lawrence, Landseer, Rembrandt, Reynolds, Watteau, and many others. The formal gardens were laid out by Sir Joseph Paxton for the Sixth Duke.

11  Warwick Castle has been the seat of the Earls of Warwick since the Norman Conquest. Among its priceless art treasures is the beautifully carved Warwick Vase ($5\frac{1}{2}$ feet high), which is said to be the work of Lysippus and was found among the ruins of Hadrian's village at Tivoli. It was brought to England by Sir William Hamilton.

12  Lord Warwick recently announced his decision to sell 'the whole of the family estates in the Warwick area, amounting to about 5,100 acres, as well as a number of cottages and other property in the town of Warwick.... The sale ... does not affect Warwick Castle and its park of 690 acres, which will be kept in the family' (*The Times Weekly Review*, 11 June 1959, 6).

13  As he travelled, James spent a good deal of time examining works of art and writing critical articles for various magazines. These articles have been reprinted with an introduction by John L. Sweeney in *The Painter's Eye* (1956).

## NORTH DEVON

1  James remarked that the flowers 'which grow among English ruins deserve a chapter to themselves'. It is equally true that his knowledge of flowers and birds is worthy of a separate essay.

2  Exeter was one of the most richly decorated churches of the fourteenth century. Its sculptured screen in the West Front with its three tiers of kings, saints, and angels has happily been restored, but its mutilation due to Guy

Fawkes bonfires was still evident when James observed it at twilight on a June evening in 1872.

3　James added these last two lines in 1905 in an attempt to emphasize the changes that had taken place in England's social life since the first publication of his English essays.

4　French painter, illustrator, and sculptor (1833–83) whose picturesque landscapes James particularly admired. One of Doré's most successful pieces of sculpture is the colossal vase, *The Vintage*, in Golden Gate Park, San Francisco, California.

5　James's changing style is evident in this passage, which is less personal, less specific than the version in *Transatlantic Sketches* (1875), 42.

## WELLS AND SALISBURY

1　The West Front of Wells Cathedral with its sculptured kings, priests, bishops, saints, ladies, nobles, and legendary characters is even more remarkable than the West Front of Exeter. Unlike Exeter, which follows a Norman plan throughout, Wells is completely Gothic with a beauty and grace that are almost feminine.

2　Although not formally a member of any religious group, James often attended services in the churches and cathedrals of Europe.

3　James had observed at Chester that in England the cathedrals belonged to 'respectability' and that the Dissenters had only 'the dusky brick chapels in provincial by-streets, the names out of Dickens. . . .'

4　It was not only landscapes, castles, and ruins that interested James. He was equally interested in the human scene, and he always took time to exchange a few words with paupers, beggars, washerwomen, and all manner of people from 'the lower orders'.

5　James often treated the reader to vignettes of this sort, which attest to his sense of humour, as well as his interest in situations of every type. His first travel book, *Transatlantic Sketches*, is full of these amusing sketches.

6　The spire is 404 feet high, the tallest and most impressive in England. Because of its unity of design and its imposing position, Salisbury has often been painted and photographed as a 'typical' medieval cathedral in spite of its academic style.

7　In an earlier version, James had been more personal: 'There are people who become easily satiated with blond beauties, and Salisbury Cathedral belongs, if I may say so, to the order of blondes' (*Transatlantic Sketches*, 1875, 53).

8　The property was granted by Henry VIII to William, first Earl of Pembroke, in 1539. During the course of three centuries such famous architects as Inigo Jones and James Wyatt had a hand in designing Wilton. The third Earl became Shakespeare's patron.

## AN ENGLISH EASTER

1 James often recalled this play, which he saw first as a small boy at The Olympic Theatre.

2 Russia was attempting to extend her dominions to the Mediterranean, which resulted in the Russo-Turkish War of 1877-78.

3 Evidently the 'shocking atrocities' committed by the Turks in May 1876, in an attempt to suppress the rebellion in Bulgaria.

4 Sir Henry Irving (né John Henry Brodribb, 1838-1905), famous English actor. He became manager of the Lyceum Theatre (one of the most renowned in the world) and one of the most celebrated actors on both sides of the Atlantic. Knighted in 1895, he was the first actor to be so honoured. The divergent views in regard to Irving's merit as an actor are reflected in James's dramatic criticism (Cf. Allan Wade, *Henry James: The Scenic Art*, 1948).

5 The rest of this section, as well as in numerous other passages throughout the following essays, testifies to the validity of this statement.

6 Rochester Castle (built between 1123-36) has the distinction of being besieged many times but never falling to a direct assault.

7 Rochester Cathedral is as significant historically as Canterbury Cathedral. Founded by St Augustine in A.D. 604, it also served as a Benedictine Priory during the Middle Ages. In beauty and fame it is, of course, eclipsed by Canterbury.

8 Becket was murdered on 29 December 1170; canonised in 1173.

## LONDON AT MIDSUMMER

1 This plan has long since been abandoned, but the London of today would be no surprise to Henry James. His 'studies of low life' as he strolled around London enabled him to see that the structure was crumbling, and his observation of England's upper-classes reminded him of the fall of Rome (*Letters*, I ,125).

2 James gave a good deal of thought to the status of the soldier in society: 'The British Soldier', *Lippincott's Magazine*, XXII (August 1878), 214-21; *Portraits of Places* (1883), 110-11; *Letters*, II, 499-500; *Notes of a Son and Brother* (1914), 310-316; and *Within the Rim and Other Essays, 1914-1915* (1919).

3  James often referred to these intimations of England's decline, but he was convinced that if 'the greatest drama in history' did take place that it would be 'well worth watching' (*Letters*, I, 58, 114).

4  Here James is much less enthusiastic about Gladstone (head of the Liberal Party and four times Prime Minister of England between 1868–94) than when he first met 'the great political leader' in 1876 (*Letters*, I, 58).

## TWO EXCURSIONS

1  A dinner conversation often gave James an idea for a short story or novel as his Notebooks testify (*The Notebooks of Henry James*, edited by F. O. Matthiessen and Kenneth B. Murdock, 1947).

2  Even when James attended a bullfight in Spain, it was not the spectacle in the ring he preferred to remember but a 'more innocent' scene: 'the bright-coloured southern crowd, spreading itself over the grass, and the women, with mantillas and fans, and the Andalusian gait, strolling up and down before the mountains and the sea' (*Portraits of Places*, 1883, 182).

3  James had first visited Oxford in late May or early June, 1869.

4  It was with pride that James received a doctorate of letters (an honorary D. Litt., *fecundissimus et facundissimus scriptor*) from Oxford in 1912 in the company of the Poet Laureate.

## IN WARWICKSHIRE

1  The property of the Earls of Clarendon, who acquired it after the Restoration, Kenilworth was founded by Geoffrey de Clinton in the time of Henry I (c. 1120) and subsequently owned by such notables as Simon de Montfort and John of Gaunt. It is not history, however, but fiction which the traveller remembers as he looks at Kenilworth. He remembers Sir Walter Scott's vivid account of the tragedy of Robert Dudley, Earl of Leicester, and his wife Amy Robsart.

2  Gwendolen Harleth (*Daniel Deronda*, 1876).

3  Founded by the Earl of Leicester as a hospital for a master and twelve soldiers 'such as had been or should be maimed in the wars of the said Queen's service, her heirs and successors'. The soldiers wear on Sundays the colourful uniforms of the Tudor period.

4  James only mentions Shakespeare's home here, but he treated the subject adequately in the short story 'The Birthplace'. Equally important is his letter to Miss Violet Hunt regarding the Bacon-Shakespeare controversy (*Letters*, I, 432) and his introduction to *The Tempest* (Vol. XVI, *The Complete*

*Works of William Shakespeare*, edited by Sidney Lee, 1907). Cf. William
T. Stafford, 'James Examines Shakespeare: Notes on the Nature of Genius',
*Publication of the Modern Language Association*, LXXIII (March 1958), 123–8.

5 'About Warwick', *Our Old Home*, 77–103.
6 Charlecote Park was built by the Lucy family in Tudor times, extensively
  rebuilt in the early nineteenth century and is now a National Trust property.
7 *Adam Bede* (1859).
8 Built in 1306 the Castle is surrounded by a broad moat. Owned by William
  of Wykeham, it was passed to the second Lord Saye and Sele in 1451.
  Among its treasures is an interesting collection of Civil War relics.
9 Built in 1480–1520, this peaceful-looking home, the residence of the Mar-
  quess of Northampton, was once seized and held by the Roundheads during
  the Civil War.
10 Originally an Augustinian Priory, it was rebuilt as a residence and occupied
  by the Pope and North families for over 400 years.

## ABBEYS AND CASTLES

1 Stokesay Castle, dating from the twelfth century, is the oldest and best
  fortified castle in Britain. Its 'curious gatehouse' is Elizabethan; both are in
  an excellent state of preservation.
2 Built in 1086 by Roger de Lacy, Ludlow Castle rises high above the Teme
  River. Several additions were made up until the end of the sixteenth century,
  but the Norman Keep is still one of its most interesting sections. Near by
  is the famous Feathers Inn, built in 1603.
3 Mrs Sarah Kemble Siddons (1755–1831), one of England's greatest actresses.
  Beginning life as a maid at Guy's Cliff House near Warwick, she became
  the 'queen' of the English stage. She was painted by many famous artists
  including Lawrence, Gainsborough, and Reynolds. Her portrait, *The
  Tragic Muse*, by the latter is one of the masterpieces of British art. There are
  statues of her in Westminster Abbey and Paddington Churchyard where
  she is buried.
4 Jane Austen's heroines in *Mansfield Park* (1814) and *Emma* (1816).
5 Fanny Burney's heroines, Evelina Anville (*Evelina*, 1778) and Cecilia
  Beverley (*Cecilia*, 1782).

## ENGLISH VIGNETTES

1 Chichester also resembles Salisbury in being admirably placed on the flat
  countryside which makes it visible for miles around. Built between the

eleventh and fourteenth centuries, Chichester is especially interesting for its lateral chapels and its painted vaults.

2 First built by Bishop Rede (ca. 1380), the spire was repaired once by Sir Christopher Wren. After it collapsed in 1861, it was restored to its old design by Sir Gilbert Scott between 1861–66.

3 James's use of guidebooks would make an interesting study in itself.

4 Perhaps the most beautiful in the world. The Chapel is considered one of the architectural wonders of the world. Its magnificent fan-vaulted ceiling and its sixteenth-century painted windows have few rivals. King's College was founded by Henry VI in 1440.

5 One of the most significant features of its antiquity seemed to have escaped James. It was before the high altar of the old Abbey that a group of Barons met on 20 November 1214 and swore a solemn oath to compel King John to grant certain rights to the people. The battle may have been fought at Runnymede, but the Magna Carta (1215) had its birth at Bury St Edmunds.

6 King Edmund (841–69) was slain by the Danes (tied to a tree and riddled with arrows and then beheaded) as he was surrendering in order to save his people. Originally buried at Hoxne, his remains were transferred to Bury thirty-three years after his death. The motto of Bury is *Sacraium Regis* (Shrine of the King) and *Cunabula Legis* (Cradle of Law).

7 His rapture might have rested upon the fame of The Angel Hotel where Dickens stayed and gave a reading from his books. It was here also that Mr Pickwick learned that he was to be sued for breach of promise.

## AN ENGLISH WINTER WATERING-PLACE

1 Among these James might have mentioned that Hastings was one of the original 'Cinque Ports' and that it is the site of the first castle William the Conqueror built after the Battle of Hastings (fought at Battle, however) in 1066. The older part of the town has always been a favourite resort for literary figures. It was here that Dante Gabriel Rossetti married the beautiful Elizabeth Siddal.

2 Since James was writing his English essays for American readers, he attempted to explain the subtle gradations of English social life. He once contemplated writing a rather pointed satire on the subject (*Notebooks*, 220),

but his barbs were usually 'very delicate' or much too subtle to be termed pointed.

3 The celebrated beauty Lily Langtry (née Emily Le Bretton, 1852–1929), wife of Irish landowner, Edward Langtry (whom she divorced after he lost his money) and, later of Hugo de Bathe. She was also an intimate friend of the Prince of Wales, later Edward VII. While in Scotland, James met this 'divinely handsome' woman at a ball given by Lord Huntly (*Letters*, I, 63).

## WINCHELSEA, RYE, AND 'DENIS DUVAL'

1 During his youth, James was an avid reader of the *Cornhill*, and later he became a frequent contributor to the magazine (*Notes of a Son and Brother*, 18–22).

2 Frederick Walker (1840–75), English illustrator and painter, whose illustrations appeared in both the *Cornhill* and in *Once a Week*. After 1865 he devoted most of his time to painting. Two of his oils are in the Tate Gallery.

3 Of monumental size, Rye parish church dates from 1120. Its carved altar is considered one of the most beautiful in Europe.

4 John Fletcher (1579–1625) and Francis Beaumont (1584–1616), the 'great Twin Brethren' of Jacobean drama.

5 John Wesley (1703–91), founder of Methodism, who preached some 40,000 sermons, often in the open air, travelling (mostly on horseback) over 250,000 miles.

6 The clock within the tower has an eighteen-foot pendulum; installed in 1561, the clock is still operating with its original works.

7 Perhaps James chose Rye for his home because it combined within its 'classic' note the beauty of the three countries he loved most. Lamb House, his home from 1898 to 1916, was given to the National Trust by the widow of the novelist's nephew, Mrs Henry James, as 'an enduring symbol of the ties that unite the British and American peoples'. Severely damaged during the last war, the house has now been restored and the author's Library is open to the public on Tuesday afternoons.

## OLD SUFFOLK

1 It is fitting that *English Hours* should conclude with David Copperfield's province, for James had first come to know England through the eyes of Dickens.

2   James had always walked everywhere; only in later years did he resort to the bicycle and the motor car. It was Edith Wharton who introduced him to the pleasures of travelling in a 'chariot of fire', which he thoroughly enjoyed, especially in her company.

3   In a postscript to a letter written to his cousin Mrs George Hunter, James related the 'oddest trio of coincidences' which occurred while he was reading Fitzgerald's letters (*Letters*, I, 267–8).

4   Myles Birket Foster (1825–99), English illustrator, etcher, engraver and painter, who illustrated the works of many British and American poets. He also did woodcuts for the *Illustrated London News* and *Punch*.

# Bibliography

A Selected List of the Writings of Henry James
*Indicates edition used by the editor

## I. BOOKS

*The American Scene.* New York: Harper & Brothers, Publishers, 1907. London: Chapman and Hall, 1907.

*The American Scene.* Edited with an Introduction by W. H. Auden. *New York: Charles Scribner's Sons, 1946.

*The Art of the Novel: Critical Prefaces by Henry James.* Introduction by Richard P. Blackmur. New York and London: Charles Scribner's Sons, 1947 (1st ed. 1934).

*The Art of Travel: Scenes and Journeys in America, England, France and Italy from the Travel Writings of Henry James.* Edited with an Introduction by Morton Dauwen Zabel. Garden City, New York: Doubleday & Company, 1958.

*The Complete Plays of Henry James.* Edited with an Introduction by Leon Edel. *Philadelphia and New York: J. B. Lippincott, 1949. London: Rupert Hart-Davis, 1949.

*Daumier: Caricaturist.* London: Rodale Press, 1954. Miniature Books.

*Eight Uncollected Tales of Henry James.* Edited with an Introduction by Edna Kenton. New Brunswick, New Jersey: Rutgers University Press, 1950.

*English Hours.* With ninety-two illustrations by Joseph Pennell.* London: William Heinemann, 1905. Boston and New York: Houghton, Mifflin and Company, 1905.

*Essays in London and Elsewhere.* *London: James R. Osgood, McIlvaine & Co., 1893. New York: Harper & Brothers, Publishers, 1893.

*The Finer Grain.* New York: Charles Scribner's Sons, 1910. *London: Methuen & Co., 1910.

*Foreign Parts.* Leipzig: Bernhard Tauchnitz, 1883.

*French Poets and Novelists.* London: Macmillan and Co., 1878.

*Gabrielle De Bergerac.* New York: Boni and Liveright, 1918.

*The Ghostly Tales of Henry James.* Edited with an Introduction by Leon Edel. New Brunswick, New Jersey: Rutgers University Press, 1948.

*Hawthorne*. \*London: Macmillan and Co., 1879. English Men of Letters Series edited by John Morley. New York: Harper & Brothers, Publishers, 1880.

*Henry James: The American Essays*. Edited with an Introduction by Leon Edel. New York: Vintage Books, 1956.

*Henry James: Autobiography*. Edited with an Introduction and Notes by Frederick W. Dupee. New York: Criterion Books, 1956. London: W. H. Allen, 1956.

*Henry James: Letters to A. C. Benson and Auguste Monod*. Edited with an Introduction by E. F. Benson. London: Elkin Mathews and Marrot, 1930. New York: Charles Scribner's Sons, 1930.

*Henry James: Parisian Sketches. Letters to The New York Tribune, 1875–1876*. Edited with an Introduction and Notes by Leon Edel and Ilse Dusoir Lind. New York: New York University Press, 1957. London: Rupert Hart-Davis, 1958.

*Henry James: Representative Selections*. Edited with Introduction, Bibliography and Notes by Lyon N. Richardson. American Writers Series. New York: American Book Company, 1941.

*Henry James: The Scenic Art. Notes on Acting & the Drama: 1872–1901*. Edited with an Introduction and Notes by Allan Wade. \*New Brunswick: Rutgers University Press, 1948. London: Rupert Hart-Davis, 1949.

*Italian Hours*. With sixty-four illustrations (thirty-two in colour) by Joseph Pennell. London: William Heinemann, 1909. \*Boston and New York: Houghton Mifflin Company, 1909.

*The Ivory Tower*. \*London: W. Collins Sons & Co., 1917. New York: Charles Scribner's Sons, 1917.

*A Landscape Painter*. With a Preface by Albert Mordell. New York: Scott and Seltzer, 1919 (1920).

*The Letters of Henry James*. Selected and edited by Percy Lubbock. 2 Volumes. \*London: Macmillan and Co., 1920. New York: Charles Scribner's Sons, 1920.

*Letters of Henry James to Walter Berry*. Paris: The Black Sun Press, 1928.

*A Little Tour in France*. With ninety-four illustrations by Joseph Pennell. \*London: William Heinemann, 1900. Boston: James R. Osgood and Co., 1885. Leipzig: Bernhard Tauchnitz, 1884. New York: Houghton, Mifflin and Company, 1900.

*Literary Reviews and Essays by Henry James on American, English, and French Literature*. Edited with Introduction and Notes by Albert Mordell. \*New

York: Twayne Publishers, 1957. London: J. Calder, 1958.

*The Middle Years.* \*London: W. Collins Sons & Co., 1917. New York: Charles Scribner's Sons, 1917.

'*A Most Unholy Trade*' *Being Letters on the Drama by Henry James.* Cambridge, Massachusetts: The Scarab Press, 1923. Privately Printed.

*The Notebooks of Henry James.* Edited by F. O. Matthiessen and Kenneth B. Murdock.\* New York: Oxford University Press, 1947. London, 1948.

*Notes of a Son and Brother.* Illustrated. \*New York: Charles Scribner's Sons, 1914. London: Macmillan and Co., 1914.

*The Novels and Stories of Henry James: New and Complete Edition.* London: Macmillan and Co., 1921–23. 35 Volumes.

*The Novels and Tales of Henry James: New York Edition.* New York: Charles Scribner's Sons, 1907–09. 24 Volumes.

*The Other House.* \*London: William Heinemann, 1896. New York: The Macmillan Company, 1896.

*The Outcry.* London: Methuen & Co., 1911. \*New York: Charles Scribner's Sons, 1911.

*The Painter's Eye. Notes and Essays on the Pictorial Arts by Henry James.* Selected and edited with an Introduction by John L. Sweeney. \*Cambridge, Mass: Harvard University Press, 1956. London: Rupert Hart-Davis, 1956.

*Partial Portraits.* London and New York: Macmillan and Co., 1888.

*A Passionate Pilgrim and Other Tales.* Boston: James R. Osgood and Company, 1875.

*Picture and Text.* New York: Harper and Brothers, 1893.

*Pictures and Other Passages from Henry James.* Selected by Ruth Head. London: Chatto & Windus, 1916. \*New York: Frederick A. Stokes Company Publishers, 1917.

*The Portable Henry James.* Edited with an Introduction, Notes, and Bibliography by Morton Dauwen Zabel. New York: The Viking Press, 1951.

*Portraits of Places.* London: Macmillan and Co., 1883.
\*Boston and New York: Houghton, Mifflin and Company, 1883.

*Portraits of Places.* Edited with an essay on 'James as a Traveller' by George Alvin Finch. New York: Lear Publishers, 1948.

*Selected Letters of Henry James.* Edited with an Introduction by Leon Edel. New York: Farrar, Straus and Cudahy, 1955. \*London: Rupert Hart-Davis, 1956.

*The Sense of the Past.* \*London: W. Collins Sons & Co., 1917. New York: Charles Scribner's Sons, 1917.

*A Small Boy and Others.* \*New York: Charles Scribner's Sons, 1913. London: Macmillan and Co., 1913.

*The Soft Side.* London: Methuen & Co., 1900. \*New York: The Macmillan Company, 1900. London: Macmillan & Co., 1900.

*Tales of Three Cities.* Boston: James R. Osgood and Company, 1884. \*London: Macmillan and Co., 1884.

*Theatre and Friendship: Some Henry James Letters.* With a Commentary by Elizabeth Robins. London: Jonathan Cape, 1932. \*New York: G. P. Putnam's Sons, 1932.

*Transatlantic Sketches.* Boston: James R. Osgood and Company, 1875.

*Travelling Companions.* Foreword by Albert Mordell. New York: Boni and Liveright, 1919.

*William Wetmore Story and His Friends, from Letters, Diaries, and Recollections.* 2 Volumes. Edinburgh and London: William Blackwood and Sons, 1903. Boston: Houghton, Mifflin & Co., 1903.

*Within the Rim and Other Essays, 1914–1915.* London: W. Collins Sons & Co. 1919.


## II. PERIODICALS

'The Afghan Difficulty', *The Nation*, XXVII (14 November 1878), 298–9 (unsigned).

'Americans Abroad', *The Nation*, XXVII (3 October 1878), 208–9 (unsigned).

'The Early Meeting of Parliament', *The Nation*, XXVII (26 December 1878), 397–8 (unsigned).

'The British Soldier'. *Lippincott's Magazine*, XXII (August 1878), 214–21.

'Henry James's Letters to the La Farges', edited with replies from the La Farges by John La Farge, S.J., *New England Quarterly*, XXII (June 1949), 173–92.

'The Letters of Henry James to Mr Justice Holmes', edited by Mark A. De Wolfe Howe, *Yale Review*, XXXVIII (Spring 1949), 410–33.

'The Manners of American Women', *Harper's Bazar*, XLI (April–July 1907), 355–9, 453–8, 537–41, 646–51.

'The Oxford-Cambridge Boat Race', *The Nation*, XXIV (12 April 1877), 221–2 (unsigned).

'The Presentation at Court', *Vanity Fair* (December 1922), 53, 108, 110.

'The Reassembling of Parliament', *The Nation*, XXVIII (20 March 1879), 197–9 (unsigned).

'In Scotland – I', and 'In Scotland – II', *The Nation*, XXVII (10 October 1878), 224–5; and (24 October 1878), 254–6.

'The Speech of American Women', *Harper's Bazar*, XL (November–December 1906), 979–82, 1103–6; and XLI (January–February 1907), 17–21, 113–17.

'The Suburbs of London', *The Galaxy*, XXIV (December 1877), 778–87.

' "A Tragedy of Error": James's First Story', with a Prefatory Note by Leon Edel. *New England Quarterly*, XXIX (September 1956), 291–317. ('A Tragedy of Error' was first published in *The Continental Monthly*, V, February 1864, 204–16.

' "Very Modern Rome" – An Unpublished Essay of Henry James', with a Prefatory Essay by Richard C. Harrier, *Harvard Library Bulletin*, VIII (Spring 1954), 125–40.

## Selected Critical Studies

## I. BOOKS

Anderson, Quentin. *The American Henry James* *New Brunswick, New Jersey: Rutgers University Press, 1957. London: J. Calder, 1958.

Andreas, Osborn. *Henry James and the Expanding Horizon*. Seattle: University of Washington Press, 1948.

Beach, Joseph Warren. *The Method of Henry James*. *Philadelphia: Albert Saifer: Publisher, 1954 (1st ed. pub. New Haven and London, 1918).

Bewley, Marius. *The Complex Fate*. With an Introduction by F. R. Leavis. *London: Chatto & Windus, 1952. New York: The Grove Press, 1954.

*A Bibliography of Henry James*. Compiled with an Introduction by Leon Edel and Dan H. Laurence. London: Rupert Hart-Davis, 1957 (Essential Books).

*The Book of the Homeless*. Edited by Edith Wharton. *New York: Charles Scribner's Sons, 1916. London: Macmillan & Co., 1916 (contains James's essay 'The Long Wards'. The book was sold for the benefit of the American Hostels for Refugees).

Bosanquet, Theodora. *Henry James at Work*. London: The Hogarth Press, 1924.

Brooks, Van Wyck. *New England: Indian Summer, 1865–1915*. New York: E. P. Dutton & Co., Inc., 1940.

——. *The Pilgrimage of Henry James.* \*New York: E. P. Dutton & Company, 1925. London: Jonathan Cape, 1928.

Burr, Anna Robeson. *Alice James: Her Brothers, Her Journal.* \*New York: Dodd, Mead & Company, 1934. London: Macmillan and Co., 1934.

Canby, Henry Seidel. *Turn West, Turn East: Mark Twain and Henry James.* Boston: Houghton Mifflin Company, 1951.

Cary, Elisabeth Luther. *The Novels of Henry James: A Study.* With a Bibliography by Frederick A. King. New York and London: G. P. Putnam's Sons, 1905.

Conrad, Joseph. *Notes on Life and Letters.* \*London: J. M. Dent and Sons, 1921. Garden City, New York: Doubleday, Page & Company, 1921.

Cooper, James Fenimore. *Gleanings in Europe: England. By an American.* 2 Volumes. Philadelphia: Carey, Lea and Blanchard, 1837.

Cox, Edward Godfrey. *A Reference Guide to the Literature of Travel. University of Washington Publications in Language and Literature,* IX (November 1935), X (May 1938) and XII (May 1949).

Darley, Felix O. C. *Sketches Abroad With Pen and Pencil.* New York: Hurd and Houghton, 1868.

Dupee, Frederick W. *Henry James.* \*New York: William Sloane Associates, 1951. American Men of Letters Series. London: Methuen & Co., 1951.

——, editor. *The Question of Henry James: A Collection of Critical Essays.* \*New York: Henry Holt and Company, 1945. London: Wingate, 1947.

Edel, Leon. *Henry James: The Untried Years, 1843–1870.* \*Philadelphia and New York: J. B. Lippincott Company, 1953. London: Rupert Hart-Davis, 1953.

Edgar, Pelham. *Henry James: Man and Author.* \*Boston and New York: Houghton Mifflin Company, 1927. London: Grant Richards, 1927.

Emerson, Ralph Waldo. *English Traits.* Boston: Phillips, Sampson, and Company, 1856.

Foley, Richard Nicholas. *Criticism in American Periodicals of the Works of Henry James from 1866 to 1916.* A Dissertation. Washington, D.C.: The Catholic University of America Press, 1944.

Garland, Hamlin. *Roadside Meetings.* \*New York: The Macmillan Company, 1930. London: John Lane, 1931.

Grattan, C. Hartley. *The Three Jameses: A Family of Minds.* London and New York: Longmans, Green and Company, 1932.

Greene, Graham. *The Lost Childhood and Other Essays.* London: William Heinemann, 1951. \*New York: The Viking Press, 1952.

Harlow, Virginia. *Thomas Sergeant Perry: A Biography, and Letters to Perry from*

*William, Henry and Garth Wilkinson James.* Durham, N. C.: Duke University Press, 1950.

Hassall, Christopher. *Edward March, Patron of the Arts.* London and New York: Longmans, Green and Co. 1959.

Hawthorne, Julian. *Nathaniel Hawthorne and His Wife: A Biography.* 2 Volumes. *Boston and New York: Houghton, Mifflin and Company, 1884. London: Chatto and Windus, 1885.

Hawthorne, Nathaniel. *Our Old Home: A Series of English Sketches.* *Boston: Houghton, Mifflin and Company, 1886 (1st ed. Ticknor and Fields, 1863). London: Smith, Elder and Co., 1863.

Holmes, Oliver Wendell. *Our Hundred Days in Europe.* *Boston and New York: Houghton, Mifflin and Company, 1892 (1st ed. 1887). London: S. Low, Marston, Searle & Rivington, 1887.

Howe, Irving. *Politics and the Novel.* New York: Horizon Press, Inc., 1957.

Howells, William Dean. *Certain Delightful English Towns, with Glimpses of the Pleasant Country Between.* Illustrated. New York and London: Harper & Brothers, Publishers, 1906.

——. *Seven English Cities.* Illustrated. New York and London: Harper & Brothers, Publishers, 1909.

Hueffer (Ford), Ford Madox. *Henry James: A Critical Study.* *London: Martin Secker, 1913. New York: A and C Boni, 1915.

——. *Return to Yesterday: Reminiscences, 1894–1914.* *London: Victor Gollancz, 1931. New York: H. Liveright, Inc., 1932.

Hussey, Christopher. *The Picturesque: Studies in a Point of View.* London and New York: G. P. Putnam's Sons, 1927.

Irving, Washington. *The Sketch-Book.* New York: G. P. Putnam's Sons, 1848.

James, William. *The Letters of William James.* Edited by his son, Henry James. 2 Volumes. *Boston: The Atlantic Monthly Press, 1920. London: Longman's, Green & Co., 1920.

Jones, Howard Mumford. *America and French Culture, 1750–1848.* *Chapel Hill, N. C.: The University of North Carolina Press, 1927. London: Oxford University Press, 1927.

Kazin, Alfred. *On Native Grounds.* New York: Reynal & Hitchcock, 1942.

Kelley, Cornelia Pulsifer. *The Early Development of Henry James. University of Illinois Studies in Language and Literature,* XV, nos. 1–2. Urbana: 1930.

Leavis, F. R. *The Great Tradition: A Study of the English Novel: George Eliot, Henry James, Joseph Conrad.* *London: Chatto & Windus, 1948. New York: G. W. Stewart, 1948.

——. *The Common Pursuit*. London: Chatto & Windus, 1952.

Le Clair, Robert Charles. *Three American Travellers in England: James Russell Lowell, Henry Adams, Henry James*. Philadelphia: Privately Printed, 1945.

——. *Young Henry James, 1843–1870*. New York: Bookman Associates, 1955.

*Literary History of the United States*. Edited by Robert E. Spiller, Willard Thorp, Thomas H. Johnson, Henry Seidel Canby, *et al*. Revised edition in one volume. New York: The Macmillan Company, 1953 (1st ed. 1948).

Long, Orie William. *Literary Pioneers: Early American Explorers of European Culture*. Cambridge, Mass: Harvard University Press, 1935.

Lowell, James Russell. *My Study Window*. Boston: James R. Osgood and Company, 1872.

McCarthy, Harold T. *Henry James: The Creative Process*. New York: Thomas Yoseloff, 1958. *London: W. H. Allen, 1959.

Manwaring, Elizabeth Wheeler. *Italian Landscape in Eighteenth Century England: A Study Chiefly of the Influence of Claude Lorrain and Salvator Rosa on English Taste, 1700–1800*. New York and London: Oxford University Press, 1925.

Matthiessen, F. O. *Henry James: The Major Phase*. London and New York: Oxford University Press, 1944.

——. *The James Family*. New York: Alfred A. Knopf, 1947.

Morrison, Helen Barber. *The Golden Age of Travel: Literary Impressions of the Grand Tour*. New York: Twayne Publishers, 1951. (Contains excerpts of James's travel essays.)

Mowat, R. B. *Americans in England*. Boston: Houghton Mifflin Company, 1935.

Norval, A. J. *The Tourist Industry*. London: Sir Isaac Pitman & Sons, Ltd, 1936.

Nowell-Smith, Simon, compiler. *The Legend of the Master*. London: Longmans, Green, & Co., 1947. *New York: Charles Scribner's Sons, 1948.

Nuhn, Ferner. *The Wind Blew from the East*. New York and London: Harper & Brothers Publishers, 1942.

Paine, Albert Bigelow. *Mark Twain: A Biography*. 4 Volumes. New York and London: Harper & Brothers, 1912.

Pennell, Joseph. *The Adventures of an Illustrator*. *Boston: Little, Brown, and Company, 1925. London: Fisher Unwin, 1925.

Perry, Ralph Barton. *The Thought and Character of William James*. 2 Volumes. *Boston: Little, Brown, and Company, 1935. London: Oxford University Press, 1935.

*A Portrait of English Cathedrals*. A Selection of Photographs by Herbert Felton, with text by John Harvey. London: B. T. Batsford, Ltd, 1957.

Rahv, Philip. *Image and Idea: Fourteen Essays on Literary Themes*. New York: New Directions, 1949.

Roberts, Morris. *Henry James's Criticism*. *Cambridge: Harvard University Press, 1929. London: Oxford University Press, 1929.

Ruskin, John. *Mornings in Florence: Being Studies of Christian Art for English Travellers*. *New York: J. Wiley & Sons, 1876. Orpington: G. Allen, 1875.

Smalley, Evelyn Garnaut. *Henry James Yearbook*.* Boston: R. G. Badger, 1911. London, 1912.

Smith, Janet Adam. *Henry James and Robert Louis Stevenson*. *London: Rupert Hart-Davis, 1948. New York: The Macmillan Co., 1949.

Spender, Stephen. *The Destructive Element*. London: Jonathan Cape, 1935. *Philadelphia: Albert Saifer, 1953.

Spiller, Robert E. *The American in England*. New York: Henry Holt and Company, 1926.

Stevenson, Elizabeth. *The Crooked Corridor: A Study of Henry James*. *New York: The Macmillan Company, 1949. London: Macmillan and Co., 1950.

Stewart, Randall. *Nathaniel Hawthorne: A Biography*. New Haven: Yale University Press, 1949.

Swan, Michael. *Henry James*. London: Longmans, Green & Co., 1950. *New York: Roy Publishers, 1952.

Trilling, Lionel. *The Liberal Imagination*. *Garden City, New York: Doubleday & Company, Inc., 1957 (1st ed. 1950). London: Secker & Warburg, 1951.

Twain, Mark (Samuel Langhorne Clemens). *The Autobiography of Mark Twain*. Edited with an Introduction and Notes by Charles Neider. New York: Harper & Brothers, Publishers, 1959.

——. *The Innocents Abroad*. Hartford, Conn.: The American Publishing Co., 1869. *London: G. Routledge & Sons, 1872.

Wegelin, Christof. *The Image of Europe in Henry James*. Dallas: Southern Methodist University Press, 1958.

West, Rebecca. *Henry James*. *London: Nisbet & Co., 1916. New York: Henry Holt and Co., 1916.

Wharton, Edith. *A Backward Glance*. New York and London: D. Appleton-Century Company, 1934.

Willis, Nathaniel Parker. *Pencillings By the Way: Written During Some Years of Residence and Travel in Europe*. 3 Volumes. New York: Charles Scribner, 1852.

Wilson, Edmund. *The Triple Thinkers*. New York: Harcourt, Brace, 1938.

Woodress, James L., Jr. *Howells & Italy*. Durham, N. C.: Duke University Press, 1952.

Young, Frederic Harold. *The Philosophy of Henry James, Sr.* New York: Bookman Associates, 1951.

Zabel, Morton Dauwen, editor. *Literary Opinion in America*. New York and London: Harper & Brothers, 1951. Revised edition (1st ed. 1937).


## II.  PERIODICALS

Alvarez, A. 'Intelligence on Tour', *The Kenyon Review*, XXI (Winter 1959), 23–33.

Arvin, Newton. 'Henry James and the Almighty Dollar', *Hound & Horn*, VII (April-June 1934), 434–43.

Auden, W. H. 'Henry James and the Artist in America', *Harper's Magazine*, CXCVII (July 1948), 36–40.

Baxter, Annette K. 'Independence vs. Isolation: Hawthorne and James on the Problem of the Artist', *Nineteenth Century Fiction*, X (December 1955), 225–231.

Bogan, Louise. 'Henry James on a Revolutionary Theme', *The Nation*, CXLVI (23 April 1938), 471–4.

Booth, Bradford A. 'Henry James and the Economic Motif', *Nineteenth Century Fiction*, VIII (September 1953), 141–50.

Bosanquet, Theodora. 'The Revised Version', *The Little Review*, V (August 1918), 56–62.

Brogan, D. W. 'No Innocents Abroad', *Harper's Bazaar* (July 1958), 86–7, 98.

Buitenhuis, Peter. 'From Daisy Miller to Julia Bride: "A Whole Passage of Intellectual History" ', *American Quarterly*, XI (Summer 1959), 136–46.

Cantwell, Robert. 'A Little Reality', *Hound & Horn*, VII (April-June 1934), 494–505.

Cargill, Oscar. 'Henry James and the Political Vocation', *Western Review*, XVIII (Spring, 1954) 199–208.

——.' "The Portrait of a Lady": A Critical Reappraisal', *Modern Fiction Studies*, III (Spring 1957), 11–32.

Clair, John A. '*The American*: A Reinterpretation', *Publications of the Modern Language Association*, LXXIV (December 1959), 613–18.

Edel, Leon. 'The Exile of Henry James', *The University of Toronto Quarterly*, II (July 1933), 520–32.

——. 'Henry James: The War Chapter, 1914–1916', *The University of Toronto Quarterly*, X (January 1941), 125–38.

Eliot, T. S. 'In Memory', and 'The Hawthorne Aspect', *The Little Review*, V (August 1918), 44–53.

Falk, Robert P. 'Henry James and the "Age of Innocence"', *Nineteenth Century Fiction*, VII (December 1952), 171–88.

Ferguson, Alfred R. 'The Triple Quest of Henry James: Fame, Art and Fortune', *American Literature*, XXVII (January 1956), 475–98.

Fleet, Simon. 'The Nice American Gentleman', *Vogue* (1 October 1949), 136, 183–5, 187.

Gale, Robert L. 'Art Imagery in Henry James's Fiction', *American Literature* XXIX (March 1957), 47–63.

——. 'Religion Imagery in Henry James's Fiction', *Modern Fiction Studies*, III (Spring 1957), 64–72.

Goldberg, M. A. ' "Things" and Values in Henry James's Universe', *Western Humanities Review*, XI (Autumn 1957), 377–85.

Gordon, Caroline. 'Mr Verver, Our National Hero', *The Sewanee Review*, LXIII (Winter 1955), 29–47.

Hastings, Katharine. 'William James of Albany, New York, and His Descendants', *New York Genealogical and Biographical Record*, LV (April, July, October 1924), 101–19, 222–36, 301–13.

Iddings, Lewis Morris. 'The Art of Travel. By Land', and 'The Art of Travel. Ocean Crossings', *Scribner's Magazine*, XXI (March 1897), 351–367; (April 1897), 425–47.

Jones-Evans, Mervyn. 'Henry James's Year in France', *Horizon*, XIV (July 1946), 52–60.

Kar, Annette, 'Archetypes of American Innocence: Lydia Blood and Daisy Miller', *American Quarterly*, V (Spring 1953), 31–8.

Kenton, Edna. 'Henry James and Mr Van Wyck Brooks', *Bookman*, LXII (October 1925), 153–7.

——. 'Henry James in the World', *Hound & Horn*, VII (April-June 1934), 506–13.

Leavis, Q. D. 'Henry James's Heiress: The Importance of Edith Wharton', *Scrutiny*, VII (December 1938), 261–76.

Lewis, R. W. B. 'The Vision of Grace: James's "The Wings of the Dove"', *Modern Fiction Studies*, III (Spring 1957), 33–40.

McFarlane, I. D. 'A Literary Friendship: Henry James and Paul Bourget', *Cambridge Journal*, IV (1951), 144-61.

Moore, Marianne. 'Henry James as a Characteristic American', *Hound & Horn*, VII (April-June 1934), 363-72.

Morris, Wright. 'Henry James's *The American Scene*', *The Texas Quarterly*, I (Summer-Autumn 1958), 27-42.

Oliver, Clinton. 'Henry James as a Social Critic', *The Antioch Review*, VII (Summer 1947), 243-58.

Pacey, W. C. D. 'Henry James & His French Contemporaries', *American Literature*, XIII (November 1941), 240-56.

Pennell, Joseph, 'In London with Henry James', *The Century Magazine*, CIII (February 1922), 543-8.

Perry, Ralph Barton. 'Henry James in Italy', *Harvard Graduates' Magazine*, XLI (June 1933), 189-200.

Powers, Lyall H. 'James's The Tragic Muse - Ave Atque Vale', *Publications of the Modern Language Association*, LXXIII (June 1958), 270-4.

Pritchett, V. S. 'The Writer as Traveller', *The New Statesman and Nation*, LI (16 June 1956), 693-4.

Rosenbaum, S. P. 'Letters to the Pell-Clarkes from their "Old Cousin and Friend" Henry James', *American Literature*, XXXI (March 1959), 46-58.

Rosenzweig, Saul. 'The Ghost of Henry James: A Study in Thematic Apperception', *Partisan Review*, XI (Autumn 1944), 436-55; also *Character & Personality*, XII (December 1943), 79-100.

Short, R. W. 'Henry James's World of Images', *Publications of the Modern Language Association*, LXVIII (December 1953), 943-60.

——. 'The Sentence Structure of Henry James', *American Literature*, XVIII (May 1946), 71-88.

Slabey, Robert M. 'Henry James and "The Most Impressive Convention in all History" ', *American Literature*, XXX (March 1958), 89-102.

Spender, Stephen. 'The School of Experience in the Early Novels', *Hound & Horn*, VII (April-June 1934), 417-433.

Stafford, William T. 'The "Americanism" of Henry James: Quentin Anderson and Van Wyck Brooks', *Western Review*, XXII (Winter 1958), 155-60.

——. 'Henry James the American: Some Views of His Contemporaries', *Twentieth Century Literature*, I (July 1955), 69-76.

——. 'James Examines Shakespeare: Notes on the Nature of Genius', *Publications of the Modern Language Association*, LXXIII (March 1958), 123-8.

Stallman, R. W. 'The Houses that James Built – *The Portrait of a Lady*', *The Texas Quarterly*, I (Winter 1958), 176–96.

Stone, Edward. 'Henry James and Rome', *Boston Public Library Quarterly*, III (April 1951), 143–5.

Swan, Michael. 'Henry James and the Heroic Young Master', *Harper's Bazaar*, LXXXIX (September 1955), 226–7, 270, 272.

Sweeney, John L. 'The Demuth Pictures (with illustrations)', *The Kenyon Review*, V (Autumn 1943), 522–32.

*The Times Weekly Review*, 11 June 1959, 6.

Tintner, Adeline R. 'The Spoils of Henry James', *Publications of the Modern Language Association*, LXI (March 1946), 239–51.

Vivas, Eliseo. 'Henry and William (Two Notes)', *The Kenyon Review*, V (Autumn 1943), 580–94.

Volpe, E. L. 'The Reception of *Daisy Miller*', *Boston Public Library Quarterly*, X (January 1958), 55–9.

Walpole, Sir Hugh. 'Henry James, A Reminiscence', *Horizon*, I (February 1940), 74–80.

Ward, J. A. 'Social Criticism in James's London Fiction', *Arizona Quarterly*, XV (Spring 1959), 36–48.

Wharton, Edith. 'Henry James in His Letters', *Quarterly Review*, CCXXXIV (July 1920), 188–202.

White, J. William. 'Professor White's Interpretation of Henry James's Action', *Spectator*, CXV (14 August 1915), 204–5.

Wilson, Edmund. 'The Ambiguity of Henry James', *Hound & Horn*, VII (April-June 1934), 385–406; reprinted and extended in *The Triple Thinkers* (1938).

Zabel, Morton Dauwen. 'The Act of Life', *The New Republic*, CXXXIV (30 April 1956), 25–6.

# Index